LET US REASON TOGETHER
CHRISTIANS AND JEWS IN CONVERSATION

LET US REASON TOGETHER
CHRISTIANS AND JEWS IN CONVERSATION

Joseph D. Small and Gilbert S. Rosenthal, editors

Publisher
Joseph D. Small

Editors
Joseph D. Small
Gilbert S. Rosenthal

Editor for Witherspoon Press
Mark D. Hinds

Cover Design
DesignPoint, Inc.

Published by Witherspoon Press, a ministry of the General Assembly Mission Council, Presbyterian Church (U.S.A.), 100 Witherspoon St., Louisville, Kentucky.

Unless otherwise indicated, Scripture quotations in this publication are from the New Revised Standard Version (NRSV) of the Bible, copyright © 1989 by the Division of Christian Education of the National Council of the Churches of Christ in the U.S.A. Used by permission. Every effort has been made to trace copyrights on the materials included in this book. If any copyrighted material has nevertheless been included without permission and due acknowledgment, proper credit will be inserted in future printings after notice has been received.

© 2010 Witherspoon Press, Presbyterian Church (U.S.A.), Louisville, KY.
All rights reserved.
No part of this book may be reproduced without the publisher's permission.
PRINTED IN THE UNITED STATES OF AMERICA
pcusa.org/witherspoon

Library of Congress Control Number: 2010924862

LET US REASON TOGETHER
Christians and Jews in Conversation

CONTENTS

Setting the Stage

Introduction ix
   Gilbert S. Rosenthal and Joseph D. Small
A Theological Understanding of the Relationship between
   Christians and Jews 1
Assessing *A Theological Understanding of the Relationship
   between Christians and Jews* 15
   Stephen R. Haynes

Probing the Relationship

Judaism's Relationship to Christianity: Covenantal Partners 29
   Daniel F. Polish
Christians and Jews in Covenant Partnership:
   Response to Rabbi Daniel F. Polish..41
   Anna Case-Winters
Jews and Presbyterians: The Current Controversy
   and Some Underlying Issues 47
   Stephen R. Haynes
Jews and Presbyterians: Response to Stephen Haynes 63
   David F. Sandmel

The Land

Land as Divine Gift and Human Responsibility.......................................73
   W. Eugene March
Land as Divine Gift and Human Responsibility:
   Response to Eugene March 85
   Vernon Kurtz
The Historical, Theological, Liturgical Significance of *Eretz Yisrael*...........89
   Reuven Hammer
The Significance of *Eretz Yisrael:* Response to Reuven Hammer................97
   Rebecca Weaver

Evangelism

A Presbyterian Understanding of Evangelism 107
Robert J. Weingartner

Presbyterian Evangelism: Response to Robert Weingartner 125
Richard Hirsh

Reflections on Conversion and Proselytizing
   in Judaism and Christianity 131
David Berger

Reflections on Conversion and Proselytizing:
   Response to David Berger 141
Leanne Van Dyk

Identity

Changes in American Jewish Identities since 1948:
   From Norms to Aesthetics 147
Steven M. Cohen

Presbyterian Disestablishment 163
Joseph D. Small

Contributors 176

Setting the Stage

Introduction

Gilbert S. Rosenthal and Joseph D. Small

The earliest Christian communities developed from within second Temple Judaism. Recent scholarship has shown that it is impossible to understand Jesus or the early Church apart from an appreciative understanding of the faith and history of Israel. Yet the relationship between Christians and Jews was marked by tensions from the outset. While Jesus' disputes with Pharisees (only one of the groups within first-century c.e. Judaism) had the character of intra-Jewish rabbinic debates, mutual antagonism soon developed between "the Jesus movement" and "the Jews." Christianity's mission to the Gentiles, coupled with Rome's subjugation of Jerusalem and the catastrophic destruction of the Temple in 70 c.e., set Rabbinic Judaism and Christianity on separate paths.

In the twenty centuries that have passed, the relationship between Christians and Jews has been marked by disengagement, sometimes benign but more often harmful. Too often, separation led to Christian maltreatment of Jews, punctuated by intolerance, ghettos, and pogroms. Yet, within a history of demeaning characterizations, hostility, and violence, some Christians and Jews have understood and appreciated the indissoluble bond between the two peoples who confess that "the Lord is our God, the Lord alone (Deuteronomy 6:4).

At its best, the Reformed tradition of Protestant Christianity has given positive expression to the relationship between Christians and Jews. John

Calvin understood the theological differences between Christianity and Judaism from the perspective of their harmony: "The covenant made with all the patriarchs is so much like ours in substance that the two are actually one and the same. Yet they differ in the mode of dispensation."[1]

Reformed theologian Karl Barth affirmed, "where this separation between the [Christian] community and the Jewish nation has been made complete, it is the Christian community which has suffered. . . . For in the person of the Jew there stands a witness before our eyes, the witness of God's covenant with Abraham, Isaac, and Jacob, and in that way with us all."[2]

While it is certainly the case that "Jews are not dependent on their existence being justified by the Church and her theology,"[3] faithful Christian existence *is* dependent on truthful theological and ecclesial understandings of the relationship between the two People of God. In the 1980s, the Presbyterian Church (U.S.A.) developed *A Theological Understanding of the Relationship between Christians and Jews* that marked a significant advance in the Church's appreciation of the links between the two faiths and an enhancement of the bonds between the two communities. For years, the relationship was quite cordial. The two faith communities worked together harmoniously on social justice issues such as poverty, homelessness, civil rights, and a number of other vital challenges.

But positive relationships between Christian and Jewish communities are always fragile, especially when they are not accompanied by regular consultation and dialogue. A serious rupture in Presbyterian-Jewish relationships was precipitated by the establishment in 2003 of a new church development in the suburbs of Philadelphia. Avodat Yisrael was designed to serve Christians of Jewish background. Services were held on Friday nights (called *Oneg Shabbat*), *yarmulkes* (head coverings) were distributed, the Torah scroll was prominent, and Passover and other festival services were conducted. Moreover, Christian symbols such as cross, baptismal font, and communion table were absent.

The Philadelphia Board of Rabbis was outraged by what they considered a syncretistic form of Judaism/Christianity. Jews in Philadelphia and elsewhere saw Avodat Yisrael as an insidious attempt to deceive unsuspecting Jews, persons in mixed Jewish-Christian marriages, and Jews from no religious background such as recent immigrants from the former Soviet Union. Presenting Christianity in the guise of Judaism seemed to be nothing less than underhanded proselytism. For many Jews, the establishment of Avodat Yisrael confirmed the perception that the Presbyterian Church (U.S.A.) was increasingly hostile not only to the State of Israel and slanted in favor of the Palestinians in the painful, bloody, ongoing battle between Israelis and Arabs, but also toward Judaism and the Jewish people. Bitterness and contention threatened to spoil a mutually beneficial relationship; a powerful force was driving the two communities apart.

"From powerful emerged sweet" (Judges 14:14). That is the way Samson put a riddle to his listeners. Can something sweet come from the powerful? And is it possible in our times? Indeed, from the powerfully destructive circumstances of Avodat Yisrael and its aftermath, something sweet has emerged in relations between the Jewish community and the Presbyterian Church (U.S.A.).

It began with a request from the National Council of Synagogues for a meeting with national leaders and theologians of the Presbyterian Church in order to air these vexing matters. A meeting was convened in Bethesda, Maryland, hosted by the then Moderator of the General Assembly, the Rev. Susan Andrews. Leaders of the Presbyterian Church, along with representatives of the Philadelphia Board of Rabbis and the National Council of Synagogues, spent an entire day debating these issues, discussing ways of clearing the air, and searching for means of repairing the breach between the faith communities lest the gap widen irreparably. Because of that frank and forthcoming meeting, the Presbyterian Church decided to fund a series of conversations and consultations between the Church and the Jewish synagogue community with the goal of dispelling mistrust and opening proper channels of dialogue and enlightenment.

The immediate result of the Bethesda meeting was an invitation extended to Rabbi Gilbert S. Rosenthal, director of the National Council of Synagogues, and his wife, Ann, to attend the 2004 annual meeting of the General Assembly of the Presbyterian Church (U.S.A.) held in Richmond, Virginia. It was the first time in the 218-year history of the General Assembly that a rabbi was included as an invited guest. But the General Assembly turned out to be a perfect storm of controversy, worsening Jewish-Presbyterian relations.

The Assembly adopted several overtures from regional presbyteries that Jewish observers understood to be skewed against Israel. Assembly actions included urging Israel to end its occupation of Arab lands, insisting that Israel tear down the security wall between Israeli and Palestinian territories, and calling upon the Presbyterian Church to study the possibility of selective divestment from companies that in any way contributed to continuing violence or the occupation of Palestinian territory.

Additionally, after a sharp contest, the General Assembly refused to cut off funding for the Avodat Yisrael new church development. Although commissioners to the General Assembly voted with limited understanding of the interrelations of the four separate actions, the effect was destructive and depressing. Many felt that the damage to the cause of Christian-Jewish understanding and dialogue was irreparable.

But that is not the end of the story. The General Assembly also authorized discussions between representatives of the Church and the Jewish community. Following a top-level meeting at the offices of the Union for Reform Judaism in New York, a small committee was established to plan a series of Jewish-Presbyterian consultations. Presbyterian representatives were the Rev. Dr. Joseph Small, director of the Office of Theology and Worship, the Rev. Dr. Jay Rock, coordinator of the Office of Interfaith Relations, the Rev. Dr. Charles Wiley, associate for theology in the Office of Theology and Worship, and a succession of persons from the Office of Evangelism staff. Jewish representatives appointed by the National Council of Synagogues were Rabbi Gilbert S. Rosenthal, Rabbi Barry Cytron, and Rabbi Shira Lander. The committee met numerous times over the next several years, engaging in frank discussion of contentious issues that led to deepened mutual understanding.

The committee's work resulted in four consultations, each addressing a contentious matter that was at the center of the rift between Presbyterians and Jews. The consultations focused on understandings of the relationship between Christians and Jews, the Land, Christian evangelism, and Christian and Jewish self-understanding. Each consultation was composed of a select number of invited persons from each faith community, including pastors and rabbis, scholars, and theologians. Participants were chosen for their expertise and their ability to represent a spectrum of Jewish and Presbyterian life.

The consultations featured major presentations and responses, followed by extended small-group discussion, study of classical texts from the Tanach (the Old Testament), the New Testament (Christian writings), rabbinic literature, the writings of the Church Fathers, and both Jewish and Christian theologians. Reports from each group and concluding remarks were rendered at the conclusion of the sessions.

The first consultation was held in October 2005 at Princeton Theological Seminary in Princeton, New Jersey, on the theme "The Relationship between Judaism and Christianity." Presentations were made by Stephen Haynes, professor of religious studies at Rhodes College, and Rabbi Daniel Polish of Congregation Shir Chadash, with responses by David Sandmel, professor of Jewish studies at the Catholic Theological Union, and Anna Case-Winters, professor of systematic theology at McCormick Theological Seminary.

The second consultation was held at Columbia Theological Seminary in Atlanta, Georgia, in May 2006. The theme was "The Significance of the Land in Judaism and Christianity." Presenters were Eugene March, professor emeritus of Old Testament at Louisville Presbyterian Theological Seminary, and Professor Reuven Hammer, at the time interim rabbi at the New London Synagogue in the U.K. Responses were made by Vernon Kurtz, rabbi of North Suburban Synagogue Beth El in Illinois, and Rebecca Weaver, professor of church history at Union Presbyterian Seminary.

The third consultation was convened in Swarthmore, Pennsylvania, in October 2006. The topic was "Mission and Evangelism." Presenters were Robert Weingartner, executive director of the Presbyterian Outlook Foundation, and David Berger, professor of Jewish history and dean of the Bernard Revel Graduate School of Jewish Studies, Yeshiva University.

Respondents were Rabbi Richard Hirsh, executive director of the Reconstructionist Rabbinical Association, and Leanne Van Dyk, dean and professor of theology at Western Theological Seminary. This consultation featured one interesting change: a public session at a nearby Presbyterian church to which Jewish rabbis, Presbyterian ministers, and area congregants were invited. We wanted to publicize some of our activities through this event so that the public would know that we were not prepared to allow disagreements between the faith communities to linger and fester.

The fourth consultation was again held at Princeton Theological Seminary, in March 2009. The topic was "Thinking Together about Identity." Presenters were Steven Cohen, professor of sociology at Hebrew Union College, and Eileen Lindner, editor of the *Yearbook of American and Canadian Churches* and executive presbyter of Palisades Presbytery.[4] A Presbyterian and Jewish panel also made presentations. The most concrete result of these consultations, discussions, and learning sessions is the present volume. It contains the 1987 Presbyterian Church (U.S.A.) document *A Theological Understanding of the Relationship between Christians and Jews*, followed by presentations and responses from each of the consultations, given by outstanding persons from all over the world who came to share their wisdom, insights, and experiences and to help Jews and Christians understand one another better and discern more clearly the issues that unite us and those that cause tensions between us.

Presentations and responses were presented in the context of a conversation that engaged all consultation participants in serious, respectful interchanges. Honest questions and honest answers produced mutual understanding. While it is impossible for a book to capture the spirit of lively conversation, the papers are presented with few editorial changes in order to preserve something of their original oral character.

As important as the presentations, the sessions we shared together helped forge friendships, dispel mistrust, clarify misunderstandings, and establish a sense of trust—trust that had been shattered by recent events. We came to know what was painful to each group, what issues disturbed us so deeply, and what events and policies we found so objectionable and even obnoxious. We came from far and wide geographically and spiritually; we ended up close intellectually, emotionally, and spiritually. It was important to confront the issues that hurt one another. In all of these matters, we were remarkably successful. It is our hope that this small book will widen the circle of conversation and understanding between Jews and Presbyterians as well as other Christians.

The Hasidic tale of the Passover Rebbe is appropriate. The Rebbe once taught his disciples that he learned to fathom what hurts another human being from listening to two half-drunk peasants in an inn.

> One peasant asked the other: "Boris, do you love me?"
> "Of course," was his reply.
> "Then, Boris, tell me what hurts me."
> "How should I know what hurts you?" queried the other peasant.
> "If you really loved me," said the first, "you would know what hurts me."

Words from a letter of the apostle Paul to the Corinthians also seem appropriate: "I made up my mind not to make you another painful visit. For if I cause you pain, who is there to make me glad but the one whom I have pained?" (2 Corinthians 2:1–2). As we come to know the pain of the other, we can resolve never to make another painful visit.

We are committed to continue on this path, in the spirit of Isaiah 1:18, "Come, now, let us reason together." The Jewish-Presbyterian Planning Committee has continued to meet, believing that there is no alternative to consultation and dialogue if we are ever to experience interreligious peace in a world that has already witnessed far too much interreligious strife, hatred, and bloodshed. There will be bumps ahead in the road; we will have our disagreements; we may encounter moments of frustrations. But we will not turn back or swerve from the path of understanding and learning, of sharing and peaceful settlement of disputes. We believe with Isaiah, that "the crooked shall be made straight, and the rough places made plain" (40:4). As Abraham said to his nephew, Lot: "Let there not be strife between us. . . . After all, we are kinsmen" (Genesis 13:8).

---

1. John Calvin, *Institutes of the Christian Religion*, ed. John T. McNeill, trans. Ford Lewis Battles (Philadelphia: The Westminster Press, 1960), 2.10.2., p. 429.
2. Karl Barth, *Dogmatics in Outline*, trans. G.T. Thompson (London: SCM Press, 1949), p. 75.
3. Markus Barth, *The People of God* (Eugene, OR: Wipf & Stock, 1983), p. 53.
4. Unfortunately, Eileen Lindner's paper cannot be included in this volume. An essay by Joseph Small has been added.

A Theological Understanding of the Relationship between Christians and Jews

Approved by the 199th General Assembly (1987) as "a pastoral and teaching document to provide a basis for continuing discussion within the Presbyterian community in the United States and to offer guidance for the occasions in which Presbyterians and Jews converse, cooperate, and enter into dialogue."

Introduction
Purpose
Christians and Jews live side by side in our pluralistic American society. We engage one another not only in personal and social ways but also at deeper levels where ultimate values are expressed and where a theological understanding of our relationship is required. The confessional documents of the Reformed tradition are largely silent on this matter. Hence, this paper has been prepared by the Church as a pastoral and teaching document to provide a basis for continuing discussion within the Presbyterian community in the United States and to offer guidance for the occasions in which Presbyterians and Jews converse, cooperate, and enter into dialogue. What is the relationship that God intends between Christians and Jews, between Christianity and Judaism? A theological understanding of this relationship is the subject that this paper addresses.

Context
Theology is never done in a vacuum. It influences and is influenced by its context. We do our theological work today in an increasingly global and pluralistic context—one that is interpersonal and intercommunal as well. Moreover, as Presbyterians, we do our theological work based on Scripture, in the context of our faith in the living presence of Jesus Christ through the

Holy Spirit, and of the Church's theological tradition. A few words about each of these dimensions of our context may be helpful in understanding this paper.

The context in which the Church now witnesses is more and more global and pluralistic. Churches have been planted in every nation on earth, but in most places, Christians exist as a minority. The age of "Christendom" has passed, and the age of an interdependent global society is fast emerging. Things said by Christians in North American about the relationships of Christians and Jews will be heard by Christians in the Middle East, where there are painful conflicts affecting the entire region. Moreover, it is increasingly difficult to ignore the existence of other religious communities and nonreligious movements in the world, many of which challenge our truth claims. What we say on the subject before us will be considered by these as well. We must be sensitive as we speak of the truth we know, lest we add to the suffering of others or increase hostility and misunderstanding by what we say.

The context in which the Church now witnesses is also interpersonal and inter-communal. The reality of which we speak consists of individual persons and of entire peoples who carry within themselves real fears, pains, and hopes. Whatever the Presbyterian Church (U.S.A.) says about the relationship of Christian and Jews must be appropriate to our North American setting and yet sensitive to the deep longings and fears of those who struggle with this issue in different settings, especially in the Middle East. Recent General Assemblies of the Presbyterian Church (U.S.A.) have maintained a clear and consistent position concerning the struggle in the Middle East as a matter of the Church's social policy. The General Assembly regards the theological affirmations of the present study as consistent with the Church's prior policy statements concerning the Middle East, which speak of the right of statehood in Palestine for Palestinians (cf. *Minutes*, 1986, Part I, page 62) and the right of the State of Israel to exist within secure borders established by the United Nations General Assembly resolutions. Therefore, the attention of the Church is again called to the Church's policy enunciated in 1974, reaffirmed in 1984, which reads in part:

> The right and power of Palestinian people to self-determination by political expression, based upon full civil liberties for all should be recognized by the parties in the Middle East and by the international community. . . . The Palestinian people should be full participants in negotiations. . . through representatives of their own choosing. The right and power of Jewish people to self-determination by political expression in [the State of] Israel, based upon full civil liberties for all, should be recognized by the parties in the Middle East and by the international community.[1]

The context of the Church's witness includes also the fact that our Church is deeply bound to its own heritage of Scripture and theological tradition. In discussing the relationship of Christians and Jews, we cannot separate ourselves from the Word of God, given in a covenant to the Jewish people, made flesh in Jesus Christ, and ever renewed in the work of the Holy Spirit among us. Acknowledging the guidance of the Church's confessional tradition, we recognize our responsibility to interpret the Word for our situation today. What the Presbyterian Church (U.S.A.) says on this complex subject will ultimately be evaluated in terms of the theological contribution that it makes.

The context of the Church's witness includes, finally and most basically, the real presence of the risen Lord. We make our declarations within the love of Jesus Christ who calls us to witness, serve, and believe in his name. Since our life is a part of what we say, we seek to testify by our deeds and words to the all-encompassing love of Christ through whom we "who were far off have been brought near" to the covenants of promise.

Background

This theological study is not unprecedented. Since World War II, statements and study documents dealing with Jewish-Christian relations have been issued by a number of Churches and Christian bodies. Among these are the Vatican's Nostra Aetate (1965), the Report of the Faith and Order Commission of the World Council of Churches (1968), the statement of the Synod of the Reformed Church of Holland (1970), the statement of the French Bishop's Committee for Relations with the Jews (1973), the report of the Lutheran World Federation (1975), the statement of the Synod of Rhineland Church in West Germany (1980), the report of the Christian/Jewish Consultation Group of the Church of Scotland (1985), and the study of the World Alliance of Reformed Churches (1986).

The present study has been six years in preparation. It is the product of a project begun in 1981 within the former Presbyterian Church, U.S., then redeveloped and greatly expanded in scope and participation in 1983 upon the reunion that brought into being the Presbyterian Church (U.S.A.). The study has been developed under the direction of the Church's Council on Theology and Culture, through a process that involved many people reflecting diverse interests and backgrounds, both in the United States and the Middle East.

In the course of addressing this subject, our Church has come to see many things in a new light. The study has helped us to feel the pain of our Jewish neighbors who remember that the Holocaust was carried out in the heart of "Christian Europe" by persons many of whom were baptized Christians. We have come to understand in a new way that our witness to the gospel can be perceived by Jews as an attempt to erode and ultimately to destroy their own communities. Similarly, we have been made sensitive the difficult role of our Arab Christian brothers and sisters in the Middle East. We have listened to the anguish of the Palestinians, and we have heard their cry.

The paper that we here present to the Church does not attempt to address every problem nor to say more than we believe that we are able truly to say. It consists of seven theological affirmations, with a brief explication of each. Together they seek to lay the foundation for a new and better relationship under God between Christians and Jews. They are:

1. a reaffirmation that the God who addresses both Christians and Jews is the same—the living and true God;
2. a new understanding by the Church that its own identity is intimately related to the continuing identity of the Jewish people;
3. a willingness to ponder with Jews the mystery of God's election of both Jews and Christians to be a light to the nations;
4. an acknowledgment by Christians that Jews are in covenant relationship with God and the consideration of the implications of this reality for evangelism and witness;
5. a determination by Christians to put an end to "the teaching of contempt" for the Jews;
6. a willingness to investigate the continuing significance of the promise of "land," and its associated obligations and to explore the implications for Christian theology;
7. a readiness to act on the hope that we share with the Jews in God's promise of the peaceable kingdom.

These seven theological affirmations with their explications are offered to the Church not to end debate but to inform it and, thus, to serve as a basis for an ever deepening understanding of the mystery of God's saving work in the world.

Definitions and Language

The defining of terms on this subject is complex but unavoidable. We understand *Judaism* to be the religion of the Jews. It is practiced by many today and extends back into the period of the Hebrew Scriptures. Judaism of late antiquity gave rise to that form of Judaism that has been developing since the first century, known as "Rabbinic Judaism." It gave rise to early Christianity as well. Both Christianity and Judaism claim relationship with the ancient people Israel; the use of the term "Israel" in this study is restricted to its ancient reference. When referring to the contemporary State of Israel this document will use "State of Israel."

We understand *Jews* to include those persons whose self-understanding is that they are descended from Abraham, Isaac, and Jacob, and Sarah, Rebekah, Rachel, and Leah, and those converted into the Jewish community.

We recognize that Jews are varied in the observance of their religion, and that many Jews do not practice Judaism at all.

The language of this paper is conformable to General Assembly guidelines for inclusiveness within the Presbyterian Church (U.S.A.). It avoids gender-specific references either to God or to the people of God, except in reference to the Trinity and the Kingdom of God and in direct quotation from Scripture. The word "Lord" is used only with reference to Jesus Christ. The paper acknowledges the role of both women and men in the Church's tradition.

The following affirmations are offered to the Church for our common edification and growth in obedience and faith. To God alone be the glory.

Affirmations and Explications

1. *We affirm that the living God whom Christians worship is the same God who is worshiped and served by Jews. We bear witness that the God revealed in Jesus, a Jew, to be the Triune Lord of all, is the same one disclosed in the life and worship of Israel.*

Explication

Christianity began in the context of Jewish faith and life. Jesus was a Jew, as were his earliest followers. Paul, the apostle of the Gentiles, referred to himself as a "Hebrew of the Hebrews." The life and liturgy of the Jews provided the language and thought forms through which the revelation in Jesus was first received and expressed. Jewish liturgical forms were decisive for the worship of the early Church and are influential still, especially in Churches of the Reformed tradition.

Yet the relationship of Christians to Jews is more than one of common history and ideas. The relationship is significant for our faith because Christians confess that the God of Abraham and Sarah and their descendants is the very One whom the apostles addressed as "the God and Father of our Lord Jesus Christ." The one God elected and entered into a covenant with Israel to reveal the divine will and point to a future salvation in which all people will live in peace and righteousness. This expectation of the reign of God in a Messianic Age was described by the Hebrew prophets in different ways. The Scriptures speak of the expectation of a deliverer king anointed by God, of the appearing of a righteous teacher, of a suffering servant, or of a people enabled through God's grace to establish the Messianic Age. Early Christian preaching proclaimed that Jesus had become Messiah and Lord, God's anointed who has inaugurated the kingdom of peace and righteousness through his life, death, and resurrection. While some Jews accepted this message, the majority did not, choosing to adhere to the biblical revelation as interpreted by their teachers and continuing to await the fulfillment of the messianic promises given through the prophets, priests, and kings of Israel.

Thus the bond between the community of Jews and those who came to be called Christians was broken, and both have continued as vital but separate communities through the centuries. Nonetheless, there are ties that remain between Christians and Jews: the faith of both in the one God whose loving and just will is for the redemption of all humankind and the Jewishness of Jesus whom we confess to be the Christ of God.

In confessing Jesus as the Word of God incarnate, Christians are not rejecting the concrete existence of Jesus who lived by the faith of Israel. Rather, we are affirming the unique way in which Jesus, a Jew, is the being and power of God for the redemption of the world. In him, God is disclosed to be the Triune One who creates and reconciles all things. This is the way in which Christians affirm the reality of the one God who is sovereign over all.

2. We affirm that the Church, elected in Jesus Christ, has been engrafted into the people of God established by the covenant with Abraham, Isaac, and Jacob. Therefore, Christians have not replaced Jews.

Explication

The Church, especially in the Reformed tradition, understands itself to be in covenant with God through its election in Jesus Christ. Because the Church affirms this covenant as fundamental to its existence, it has generally not sought nor felt any need to offer any positive interpretation of God's relationship with the Jews, lineal descendants of Abraham, Isaac, and Jacob, and Sarah, Rebekah, Rachel, and Leah, with whom God covenanted long ago. The emphasis has fallen on the new covenant established in Christ and the creation of the Church. Sometime during the second century of the Common Era, a view called "supersessionism," based on the reading of some biblical texts and nurtured in controversy, began to take shape. By the beginning of the third century, this teaching that the Christian Church had superseded the Jews as God's chosen people became the orthodox understanding of God's relationship to the Church. Such a view influenced the Church's understanding of God's relationship with the Jews and allowed the Church to regard Jews in an inferior light.

Supersessionism maintains that because the Jews refused to receive Jesus as Messiah, they were cursed by God, are no longer in covenant with God, and that the Church alone is the "true Israel" or the "spiritual Israel." When Jews continue to assert, as they do, that they are the covenant people of God, they are looked upon by many Christians as impertinent intruders, claiming a right that is no longer theirs. The long and dolorous history of Christian imperialism, in which the Church often justified anti-Jewish acts and attitudes in the name of Jesus, finds its theological base in this teaching.

We believe and testify that this theory of supersessionism or replacement is harmful and in need of reconsideration as the Church seeks to proclaim God's saving activity with humankind. The scriptural and theological bases for this view are clear enough; but we are prompted to look again at our tradition by events in our own time and by an increasing number of theologians and biblical scholars who are calling for such a reappraisal. The pride and prejudice that have been justified by reference to this doctrine of replacement themselves seem reason enough for taking a hard look at this position.

For us, the teaching that the Church has been engrafted by God's grace into the people of God finds as much support in Scripture as the view of supersessionism and is much more consistent with our Reformed understanding of the work of God in Jesus Christ. The emphasis is on the continuity and trustworthiness of God's commitments and God's grace. The issue for the early Church concerned the inclusion of the Jews. Paul insists that God is God of both Jews and Gentiles and justifies God's redemption of both based on faith (Rom. 3:29–30). God's covenants are not broken. "God has not rejected his people whom he foreknew" (Rom. 11:2). The Church has not "replaced" the Jewish people. Quite the contrary! The Church, being made up primarily of those who were once aliens and strangers to the covenants of promise, has been engrafted into the people of God by the covenant with Abraham (Rom. 11:17–18).

The continued existence of the Jewish people and of the Church as communities elected by God is, as the apostle Paul expressed it, a "mystery" (Rom. 11:25). We do not claim to fathom this mystery but we cannot ignore it. At the same time, we can never forget that we stand in a covenant established by Jesus Christ (Heb. 8) and that faithfulness to that covenant requires us to call *all* women and men to faith in Jesus Christ. We ponder the work of God, including the wonder of Christ's atoning work for us.

3. *We affirm that both the Church and the Jewish people are elected by God for witness to the world and that the relationship of the Church to contemporary Jews is based on that gracious and irrevocable election of both.*

Explication
God chose a particular people, Israel, as a sign and foretaste of God's grace toward all people. It is for the sake of God's redemption of the world that Israel was elected. The promises of God, made to Abraham and Sarah and to their offspring after them, were given so that blessing might come upon "all families of the earth" (Gen. 12:1–3). God continues that purpose through Christians and Jews. The Church, like the Jews, is called to be a light to the nations (Acts 13:47). God's purpose embraces the whole creation.

In the electing of peoples, God takes the initiative. Election does not manifest human achievement but divine grace. Neither Jews nor Christians can claim to deserve this favor. Election is the way in which God creates freedom through the Holy Spirit for people to be for God and for others. God, who is ever faithful to the word that has been spoken, does not take back the divine election. Whenever either the Jews or the Churches have rejected God's ways, God has judged but not rejected them. This is a sign of God's redeeming faithfulness toward the world.

Both Christians and Jews are elected to service for the life of the world. Despite profound theological differences separating Christians and Jews, we believe that God has bound us together in a unique relationship for the sake of God's love for the world. We testify to this election, but we cannot explain it. It is part of the purpose of God for the whole creation. Thus, there is much common ground where Christians and Jews can and should act together.

4. We affirm that the reign of God is attested both by the continuing existence of the Jewish people and by the Church's proclamation of the gospel of Jesus Christ. Hence, when speaking with Jews about matters of faith, we must always acknowledge that Jews are already in a covenantal relationship with God.

Explication
God, who acts in human history by the Word and Spirit, is not left without visible witnesses on the earth. God's sovereign and saving reign in the world is signified both by the continuing existence of and faithfulness within the Jewish people who, by all human reckoning, might be expected to have long since passed from the stage of history and by the life and witness of the Church.

As the cross of Jesus has always been a stumbling block to Jews, so also the continued existence and faithfulness of the Jews are often a stumbling block to Christians. Our persuasion of the truth of God in Jesus Christ has sometimes led Christians to conclude that Judaism should no longer exist, now that Christ has come, and that all Jews ought properly to become baptized members of the Church. Over the centuries, many afflictions have been visited on the Jews by Christians holding this belief—not least in our own time. We believe that the time has come for Christians to stop and take a new look at the Jewish people and at the relationship that God wills between Christian and Jew.

Such reappraisal cannot avoid the issue of evangelism. For Jews, this is a very sensitive issue. Proselytism by Christians seeking to persuade, even convert, Jews often implies a negative judgment on Jewish faith. Jewish reluctance to accept Christian claims is all the more understandable when it is realized that conversion is often seen by them as a threat to Jewish survival. Many Jews who unite with the Church sever their bonds with their people. On the other hand, Christians are commissioned to witness to the whole world about the good news of Christ's atoning work for both Jew and Gentile. Difficulty arises when we acknowledge that the same Scripture which proclaims that atonement and which Christians claim as God's word clearly states that Jews are already in a covenant relationship with God who makes and keeps covenants.

For Christians, there is no easy answer to this matter. Faithful interpretation of the biblical record indicates that there are elements of God's covenant with Abraham that are unilateral and unconditional. However, there are also elements of the covenant that appear to predicate benefits upon faithfulness (see Gen. 17:1ff.). Christians, historically, have proclaimed that true obedience is impossible for a sinful humanity and thus have been impelled to witness to the atoning work of Jesus of Nazareth, the promised Messiah, as the way to a right relationship with God. However, to the present day, many Jews have been unwilling to accept the Christian claim and have continued in their covenant tradition. In light of Scripture, which testifies to God's repeated offer of forgiveness to Israel, we do not presume to judge in God's place. Our commission is to witness to the saving work of Jesus Christ; to preach good news among all the "nations" (*ethne*).

Dialogue is the appropriate form of faithful conversation between Christians and Jews. Dialogue is not a cover for proselytism. Rather, as trust is established, not only questions and concerns can be shared but faith and commitments as well. Christians have no reason to be reluctant in sharing the good news of their faith with anyone. However, a militancy that seeks to impose one's own point of view on another is not only inappropriate but also counterproductive. In dialogue, partners are able to define their faith in their own terms, avoiding caricatures of one another, and are thus better able to obey the commandment, "Thou shalt not bear false witness against thy neighbor." Dialogue, especially in light of our shared history, should be entered into with a spirit of humility and a commitment to reconciliation. Such dialogue can be a witness that seeks also to heal that which has been broken. It is out of a mutual willingness to listen and to learn that faith deepens and a new and better relationship between Christians and Jews is enabled to grow.

5. *We acknowledge in repentance the Church's long and deep complicity in the proliferation of anti-Jewish attitudes and actions through its "teaching of contempt" for the Jews. Such teaching we now repudiate, together with the acts and attitudes which it generates.*

Explication

Anti-Jewish sentiment and action by Christians began in New Testament times. The struggle between Christians and Jews in the first century of the Christian movement was often bitter and marked by mutual violence. The depth of hostility left its mark on early Christian and Jewish literature, including portions of the New Testament.

In subsequent centuries, after the occasions for the original hostility had long since passed, the Church misused portions of the New Testament as proof texts to justify a heightened animosity toward Jews. For many centuries, it was the Church's teaching to label Jews as "Christ-killers" and a "deicide race." This is known as the "teaching of contempt." Persecution of Jews was at times officially sanctioned and at other times indirectly encouraged or at least tolerated. Holy Week became a time of terror for Jews.

To this day, the Church's worship, preaching, and teaching often lend themselves, at times unwittingly, to a perpetuation of the "teaching of contempt." For example, the public reading of Scripture without explicating potentially misleading passages concerning "the Jews," preaching which uses Judaism as a negative example in order to commend Christianity, public prayer which assumes that only the prayers of Christians are pleasing to God, teaching in the Church school which reiterates stereotypes and non-historical ideas about the Pharisees and Jewish leadership—all of these contribute, however subtly, to a continuation of the Church's "teaching of contempt."

It is painful to realize how the teaching of the Church has led individuals and groups to behavior that has tragic consequences. It is agonizing to discover that the Church's "teaching of contempt" was a major ingredient that made possible the monstrous policy of annihilation of Jews by Nazi Germany. It is disturbing to have to admit that the Churches of the West did little to challenge the policies of their governments, even in the face of the growing certainty that the Holocaust was taking place. Though many Christians in Europe acted heroically to shelter Jews, the record reveals that most Churches as well as governments the world over largely ignored the pleas for sanctuary for Jews.

As the embodiment of anti-Jewish attitudes and actions, the Holocaust is a sober reminder that such horrors are possible in this world and that they begin with apparently small acts of disdain or expedience. Hence, we pledge to be alert for all such acts of denigration from now on, so that they may be resisted. We also pledge resistance to any such actions perpetrated by anyone, anywhere.

The Church's attitudes must be reviewed and changed as necessary, so that they never again fuel the fires of hatred. We must be willing to admit our Church's complicity in wrongdoing in the past, even as we try to establish a new basis of trust and communication with Jews. We pledge, God helping us, never again to participate in, to contribute to, or (insofar as we are able) to allow the persecution or denigration of Jews or the belittling of Judaism.

6. We affirm the continuity of God's promise of land along with the obligations of that promise to the people Israel.

Explication
As the Church of Scotland's (1985) report says:

We are aware that in dealing with this matter, we are entering a minefield of complexities across which is strung a barbed-wire entanglement of issues, theological, political and humanitarian.[2]

However, a faithful explication of biblical material relating to the covenant with Abraham cannot avoid the reality of the promise of land. The question with which we must wrestle is how this promise is to be understood in the light of the existence of the modern political State of Israel that has taken its place among the nations of the world.

The Genesis record indicates that "the land of your sojournings" was promised to Abraham, and his and Sarah's descendants. This promise, however, included the demand that "You shall keep my covenant. . . ." (Gen. 17:7–8). The implication is that the blessings of the promise were dependent upon fulfillment of covenant relationships. Disobedience could bring the loss of land, even while God's promise was not revoked. God's promises are always kept, but in *God's* own way and time.

The establishment of the State of Israel in our day has been seen by many devout Jews as the fulfillment of God's divine promise. Other Jews are equally sure that it is not and regard the State of Israel as an unauthorized attempt to flee divinely imposed exile. Still, other Jews interpret the State of Israel in purely secular terms. Christian opinion is equally diverse. As Reformed Christians, however, we believe that no government at any time can ever be the full expression of God's will. All, including the State of Israel, stand accountable to God. The State of Israel is a geopolitical entity and is not to be validated theologically.

God's promise of land bears with it obligation. Land is to be used as the focus of mission, the place where people can live and be a light to the nations. Further, because land is God's to be given, it can never be fully possessed. The living out of God's covenant in the land brings with it not only opportunity but also temptation. The history of the people of Israel reveals the continual tension between sovereignty and stewardship, blessing and curse.

The Hebrew prophets made clear that those in possession of "land" have a responsibility and obligation to the disadvantaged, the oppressed, and the "strangers in their gates." God's justice, unlike ours, is consistently in favor of the powerless (Ps. 103:6). Therefore we, whether Christian or Jew, who affirm the divine promise of land, however land is to be understood, dare not fail to uphold the divine right of the dispossessed. We have been agents of the dispossession of others. In particular, we confess our complicity in the loss of land by Palestinians, and we join with those of our Jewish sisters and brothers who stand in solidarity with Palestinians as they cry for justice as the dispossessed.

We disavow any teaching that says that peace can be secured without justice through the exercise of violence and retribution. God's justice upholds those who cry out against the strong. God's peace comes to those who do justice and mercy on the earth. Hence, we look with dismay at the violence and injustice occurring in the Middle East.

For 3,000 years, the covenant promise of the land has been an essential element of the self-understanding of Jewish people. Through centuries of dispersion and exile, Jews have continued to understand themselves as people in relation to the God they have known through the promise of land. However, to understand that promise solely in terms of a specific geographical entity on the eastern shore of the Mediterranean is, in our view, inadequate.

"Land" is understood as more than place or property; "land" is a biblical metaphor for sustainable life, prosperity, peace, and security. We affirm the rights to these essentials for the Jewish people. At the same time, as bearers of the good news of the gospel of Jesus Christ, we affirm those same rights in the name of justice to all peoples. We are aware that those rights are not realized by all persons in our day. Thus, we affirm our solidarity with all people to whom those rights of "land" are currently denied.

We disavow those views held by some dispensationalists and some Christian Zionists that see the formation of the State of Israel as a signal of the end time, which will bring the Last Judgment, a conflagration that only Christians will survive. These views ignore the word of Jesus against seeking to set the time or place of the consummation of world history.

We therefore call on all people of faith to engage in the work of reconciliation and peacemaking. We pray for and encourage those who would break the cycles of vengeance and violence, whether it is the violence of states or of resistance movements, of terror or of retaliation. We stand with those who work toward nonviolent solutions, including those who choose nonviolent resistance. We also urge nation states and other political institutions to seek negotiated settlements of conflicting claims. The seeking of justice is a sign of our faith in the reign of God.

7. We affirm that Jews and Christians are partners in waiting. Christians see in Christ the redemption not yet fully visible in the world, and Jews await the messianic redemption. Christians and Jews together await the final manifestation of God's promise of the peaceable kingdom.

Explication
Christian hope is continuous with Israel's hope and is unintelligible apart from it. New Testament teaching concerning the Kingdom of God was shaped by the messianic and apocalyptic vision of Judaism. That prophetic vision was proclaimed by John the Baptist, and the preaching of Jesus contained the same vision. Both Jews and Christians affirm that God reigns over all human destiny and has not abandoned the world to chaos and that,

despite many appearances to the contrary, God is acting within history to establish righteousness and peace.

Jews still await the kingdom that the prophets foretold. Some look for a Messianic Age in which God's heavenly reign will be ushered in upon the earth. Christians proclaim the good news that in Christ, "the Kingdom of God is at hand," yet, we, too, wait in hope for the consummation of the redemption of all things in God. Though the waiting of Jews and Christians is significantly different on account of our differing perception of Jesus, nonetheless, we both wait with eager longing for the fulfillment of God's gracious reign upon the earth—the kingdom of righteousness and peace foretold by the prophets. We are in this sense partners in waiting. Both Christians and Jews are called to wait and to hope in God. While we wait, Jews and Christians are called to the service of God in the world. However that service may differ, the vocation of each shares at least these elements: a striving to realize the word of the prophets, an attempt to remain sensitive to the dimension of the holy, an effort to encourage the life of the mind, and a ceaseless activity in the cause of justice and peace. These are far more than the ordinary requirements of our common humanity; they are elements of our common election by the God of Abraham, Isaac, and Jacob, and Sarah, Rebekah, Rachel, and Leah. Precisely because our election is not to privilege but to service, Christians and Jews are obligated to act together in these things. By so acting, we faithfully live out our partnership in waiting. By so doing, we believe that God is glorified.

1. *Minutes,* UPCUSA 1974, Part I, page 584; cf. *Minutes,* 1984, Part I, page 338; see also pages 82, 335–339, "Resolution on the Middle East."
2. Church of Scotland's (1985) report.

Assessing *A Theological Understanding of the Relationship between Christians and Jews*

Stephen R. Haynes

In the short time I have, I want to offer a preliminary assessment of *A Theological Understanding of the Relationship between Christians and Jews* (*TURCJ*), the study paper produced by the Presbyterian Church (U.S.A.) in 1987. The paper was adopted by the PCUSA General Assembly as a pastoral and teaching document intended as a basis for discussion within the Church and as guidance in Jewish-Christian relationships. Can it—and should it—continue to serve this function nearly twenty years later?

I want to pursue this general question by addressing three specific questions to each of the paper's seven affirmations: First, is the affirmation implied by, or at least compatible with, the Church's theological/confessional tradition? Second, is the affirmation supported by, or at least not contradicted by, the beliefs of Presbyterians? And third, does the affirmation provide a promising basis for future Presbyterian-Jewish understanding and cooperation? I am hopeful that this exercise can provide a starting point for discussing *TURCJ*'s role in helping Presbyterians and Jews move forward from this difficult stage in their relationship.

Affirmation 1: We affirm that the living God whom Christians worship is the same God who is worshiped and served by Jews. We bear witness that the God revealed in Jesus, a Jew, to be the Triune Lord of all, is the same one disclosed in the life and worship of Israel.

1. Is the affirmation implied by, or at least compatible with, the Church's theological/confessional tradition?

In my view, yes. This affirmation is not only compatible with the Christian tradition but expresses a particular emphasis of the Reformed tradition—that the Father of Jesus Christ is the God of Abraham, Isaac, and Jacob. But while it may be uncontroversial, this affirmation is not self-evident. In fact, the affirmation's reference to the Christian doctrine of the Trinity reminds us that it is merely a starting point for discussion between Christians and Jews. It would have been easy, perhaps, to avoid Trinitarian language in this opening affirmation. That *TURCJ* does not avoid it indicates the authors' conviction that the quest for understanding not compromise theological integrity.

2. Is the affirmation supported by, or at least not contradicted by, the beliefs of Presbyterians?

I think most Presbyterians are likely to find this affirmation unobjectionable, particularly since it does not cost anything christologically. What I mean is that the affirmation that Christians and Jews worship and serve the same God is not incompatible with a supersessionist view of Judaism. However, don't ask Presbyterians to explain how the Holy One of Israel is also the Triune Lord of all. Most, I think, recognize that the doctrine of the Trinity is not to be found in the Christian Old Testament. But they are not likely to appreciate the barrier Trinitarian faith can create for conversations with Jews.

3. Does the affirmation provide a promising basis for future Presbyterian-Jewish understanding and cooperation?

Absolutely. The affirmation is a necessary, if not a sufficient, condition for Jewish-Christian understanding. It provides a basis for recognizing connections between the two faiths, including "the Jewishness of Jesus whom we confess to be the Christ of God."[1]

Affirmation 2: We affirm that the Church, elected in Jesus Christ, has been engrafted into the people of God established by the covenant with Abraham, Isaac, and Jacob. Therefore, Christians have not replaced Jews.

1. Is the affirmation implied by, or at least compatible with, the Church's theological/confessional tradition?

It can be argued that the substance of this affirmation draws directly on the Christian tradition, since it is based in Paul's metaphor of the olive tree in Romans. But honesty compels us to admit that this image of the Christian-Jewish relationship was rediscovered by Christians only in the wake of the Holocaust. Made aware of fateful connections between the Nazi Final Solution and the replacement motif so prominent in Christian thought for nearly two millennia, Christians have retrieved this new-old image of engraftment from Romans. However, while the affirmation of the Church's engraftment is "biblical," there is much in the Christian tradition with which it is in tension. With particular reference to Reformed theology, one is hard-pressed to find such a positive view of the relationship between the Church and Israel in the *Book of Confessions*.

TURCJ's explication of this affirmation presents the view that supersessionism is not a biblical concept, but arose "sometime during the second century of the Common Era . . . based on the reading of some biblical texts and nurtured in controversy" (*TURCJ*, 8). If this is an attempt to deny that supersessionism is found in the New Testament, I would respond: What about the book of Hebrews? Nevertheless, *TURCJ* is accurate in identifying supersessionism as a theological basis for "the long and dolorous history of Christian imperialism" and all manner of anti-Jewish acts and attitudes.[2]

2. Is the affirmation supported by, or at least not contradicted by, the beliefs of Presbyterians?

I concur with Joseph Small's assessment that "supersessionism remains commonplace in Christian piety, and shapes the reading of Scripture by many, if not most, Church members."[3]

I also believe the theological imaginations of most Presbyterians stock several images of the relationship between Judaism and Christianity. My guess is the dominant image is supersession, followed by the motif of promise and fulfillment (implied in terms such as "new covenant," "new people of God," and "New Testament") and the contrast between law and gospel (not a Reformed concept). Perhaps engraftment is among the images that populate the Presbyterian imagination. But the Church needs to do more in educating believers about engraftment's uniquely positive implications for our relationship with living Judaism.

3. Does the affirmation provide a promising basis for future Presbyterian-Jewish understanding and cooperation?

Yes. But this is precisely why Presbyterians must be educated to understand why a denial of supersessionism is a necessary condition for Presbyterian-Jewish understanding. If it is true that supersessionism is "harmful and in need of reconsideration" and that engraftment "finds as much support in Scripture . . . and is much more consistent with our Reformed understanding of the work of God in Jesus Christ,"[4] these facts ought to find their way into Presbyterian catechesis, officer training, and seminary education.

Affirmation 3: We affirm that both the Church and the Jewish people are elected by God for witness to the world and that the relationship of the Church to contemporary Jews is based on gracious and irrevocable election of both.

1. Is the affirmation implied by, or at least compatible with, the Church's theological/confessional tradition?

Without question, election is at the heart of the Reformed tradition, so speaking of mutual election is a way of holding Jews close to the heart of Reformed faith. The problem is that the tradition does not speak as if election were the only thing determining Jews' relationship to God. Reformed faith has never doubted God's election of Israel, for it is the basis of our election in Jesus Christ. But it has tended to affirm that Jesus Christ represents the normative relationship between the God of Israel and the world. What, then, is the status of Israel's election after the arrival of Jesus the Messiah and his rejection by the majority of Jews? I think it is fair to say that the tradition is ambiguous on this point—whether we look at Scripture, the Reformed confessions, John Calvin, or Karl Barth.

Is this affirmation *incompatible* with the Reformed tradition? Some who know Calvin's theology better than I do argue that to a remarkable degree he maintained respect for Israel's covenant relationship with God apart from Christ. But Barth, who also knew Calvin well, was able to affirm only the traditional view that *post Christum* Israel's is an ironic election that witnesses to divine wrath and judgment.

2. Is the affirmation supported by, or at least not contradicted by, current Presbyterian beliefs?

Probably, particularly if the affirmation is not interpreted to mean that Jewish election implies Jewish salvation apart from Jesus. To explain this point, let me quote Small's commentary on this affirmation:

> The doctrine of election, once a Presbyterian distinctive, is now little understood and widely ignored. Many, if not most, Presbyterians now hold to a generic Protestant notion of "faith [in Christ as Lord and Savior]" as the necessary element in God's gracious forgiveness and communion.[5]

I concur that among Presbyterians election is no longer a necessary tenet of Reformed faith and for many has been effectively replaced by an emphasis on a "personal relationship" with Christ. Thus, while there are few Presbyterians who would deny Israel's election or *TURCJ*'s claim that "the promises of God, made to Abraham and Sarah and to their offspring after them, were given so that blessing might come upon 'all families of the earth' (Gen. 12:1–3)," many Presbyterians would understand these promises as fulfilled in Christ. For these persons, it is not clear what advantage election confers apart from a relationship with Christ, the fulfiller of God's promises to Israel.

3. Does the affirmation provide a promising basis for future Presbyterian-Jewish understanding and cooperation?

The strength of this section of *TURCJ* is the explication's claim that God "does not take back the divine election. Whenever either the Jews or the Church have rejected God's ways, God has judged but not rejected them." This is a reminder for contemporary Presbyterians of an important theological truth—that election is about what God does, not about how we respond. Thus, this affirmation of *TURCJ* provides not only a promising basis for Presbyterian-Jewish understanding, but also a way to reeducate Presbyterians about the distinctive character of their own theological tradition and how it differs from American culture-protestantism.

Affirmation 4: We affirm that the reign of God is attested both by the continuing existence of the Jewish people and by the Church's proclamation of the gospel of Jesus Christ. Hence, when speaking with Jews about matters of faith, we must always acknowledge that Jews are already in covenantal relationship with God.

1. Is the affirmation implied by, or at least compatible with, the Church's theological/confessional tradition?

This is a bold affirmation, perhaps the boldest of the seven. While some of the others leave room for ambiguity concerning the salvific status of contemporary Judaism, this one does not. With regard to Israel at least, the Christian tradition does not regard election as synonymous with salvation. Karl Barth's theology of Israel makes this fact dreadfully clear, as does the common hope among American Protestants that Jews will "realize" or "fulfill" their election by coming to faith in Christ. But to state that Jews, apart from real, implicit, or future faith in Christ, "are [currently] in a covenantal relationship with God" is to say in effect that Jews don't need Jesus. I don't see any other way to interpret this affirmation.

Given this interpretation, we must also say that this affirmation approaches the tradition with an entirely new interpretive lens. The position of *TURCJ's* authors seems to be that the tradition *needs* to be reinterpreted in light of what the Holocaust has revealed about the effects of the Christian assumption that the only good Jew is one who has accepted or will accept Jesus. Thus, while there is little if any precedent in the tradition for viewing contemporary Jews as in a salvific relationship with God apart from Christ, we do find some precedent for such an affirmation in the statements of churches and intra-Church bodies over the past forty years. The document's claim that "Scripture . . . clearly states that Jews are already in a covenant relationship with God"[6] indicates that the authors are following these post-Holocaust documents in their focus on Romans 9—11.

2. Is the affirmation supported by, or at least not contradicted by, current Presbyterian beliefs?

As *TURCJ's* explication of this affirmation notes, "our persuasion of the truth of God in Jesus Christ has sometimes led Christians to conclude that Judaism should no longer exist, now that Christ has come, and that all Jews ought properly to become baptized members of the Church."[7] I believe this remains the case, even among Presbyterians. Less clear is what role Presbyterians believe *they* should have in bringing the dream of Jewish salvation to reality. It is my conviction that many of those who would not be personally involved in Jewish evangelism—and would agree that "a militancy that seeks to impose one's own point of view on another is not only inappropriate but also counterproductive"[8]—nevertheless have an interest in cultivating Jewish-Christianity. For them, it represents both a dimension of Christianity that is missing from most churches and a living embodiment of the organic bond between the Church and Israel.

Also leading to confusion on this issue is the denomination's recent affirmations that the gospel should be preached to "all people." In documents on evangelism from the PCUSA, the claim that "Jesus Christ is the only Savior and Lord, and all people everywhere are called to place their faith, hope, and love in him" is attended by the absence of any references to the unique relationship between Christians and Jews.[9]

Given that even *TURCJ* concedes "Christians are commissioned to witness to the whole world about the good news of Christ's atoning work for both Jew and Gentile,"[10] there is bound to be confusion among Presbyterians on this matter.

3. Does the affirmation provide a promising basis for future Presbyterian-Jewish understanding and cooperation?

Absolutely. While the affirmation invites us to consider the "forms of faithful conversation," it puts to rest the question of whether Jews *need* Jesus in order to be in right relationship with God. Even if it continues to make some Presbyterians uneasy, this affirmation can create the comfort among Jews that is required for genuine dialogue.

Affirmation 5: We acknowledge in repentance the Church's long and deep complicity in the proliferation of anti-Jewish attitudes and actions through its "teaching of contempt" for the Jews. Such teaching we now repudiate, together with the acts and attitudes which it generates.

1. Is the affirmation implied by, or at least compatible with, the Church's theological/confessional tradition?

Traditionally, Christians have been best at confessing the sins of others. So it is difficult to say that this act of repentance and repudiation is in keeping with Church tradition. Recently, however, many churches have been forced by their implication in phenomena such as slavery and the Holocaust to humbly apologize for the results of bad theology and biblical interpretation. This affirmation falls into this, rather recent and still narrow, stream of Church tradition.

While the affirmation may not represent the tradition, it engages the tradition at its very roots. Hostility between Christians and Jews left its mark on "portions of the New Testament," the explication notes; in subsequent centuries "persecution of Jews was at times officially sanctioned, at other times indirectly encouraged or at least tolerated" (12–13). The charges reach closer to the present day with the document's discussion of the Nazi era. Although phrases like "the Churches of the west" leave much to be desired with respect to specificity, the document is extraordinarily clear in its claim that "the Church's 'teaching of contempt' was a major ingredient that made possible the monstrous policy of annihilation of Jews by Nazi Germany." Furthermore, while nodding in the direction of Christian rescue, *TURCJ* acknowledges that "most Churches . . . largely ignored the pleas for sanctuary for Jews."[11]

If there is a flaw in the document's explication of this affirmation, it is that while blame is squarely faced it is not clear which charges leveled at "the Church" apply to those in the Presbyterian family. Since many Presbyterians do not identify with the Church as it existed before the Reformation, perhaps a stronger statement of responsibility for the evils enumerated here is needed. This is not the case when the document considers the present day, however. *TURCJ* is quite explicit about the kinds of activities and speech that can contribute to anti-Judaism. Among those mentioned are the public reading of Scripture, preaching, public prayer, and teaching, all of which may "contribute, however subtly to a continuation of the Church's 'teaching of contempt.' "

2. Is the affirmation supported by, or at least not contradicted by, current Presbyterian beliefs?

Most Christians know little about the history of Christian anti-Judaism before the twentieth century, yet I haven't encountered any Presbyterians who would completely deny Christian complicity in the Holocaust. However, signs of resistance are not uncommon. One strategy for deflecting responsibility for the Holocaust away from Christians is placing emphasis on the "paganism" or "anti-Christianity" of Hitler and other top Nazis. Another is to emphasize the brave deeds of Christian heroes like Corrie ten Boom or Dietrich Bonhoeffer. Among those who admit that there was Christian support for Nazi anti-Semitism, many blame this support on "conservatives" (if they are liberals) or "liberals" (if they are conservatives).

For all these reasons I have to say that, among Presbyterians, "acknowledg[ing] in repentance the Church's long and deep complicity in the proliferation of anti-Jewish attitudes and actions through its 'teaching of contempt' for the Jews" is a work in progress. As a well-educated denomination, we are no doubt ahead of some churches, but there is much work to be done in our sanctuaries, Sunday school classrooms, and seminary curricula.

3. Does the affirmation provide a promising basis for future Presbyterian-Jewish understanding and cooperation?

Without doubt. Impressively, the sort of defensiveness and ambivalence that permeate many Christian "apologies" for anti-Semitism are conspicuously absent from this affirmation. Such resistance is detectable in Catholic documents like *We Remember: A Reflection on the Shoah*, where the desire to protect the integrity and reputation of the institutional Church makes the authors reluctant to place blame where it belongs. There is no such reticence here. As Joe Small puts it in his own explication of this affirmation, "the Church's anti-Jewish history has its roots in flawed biblical interpretation and bad theology."[12]

Equally impressive is the document's pledge to be alert for acts of denigration and to resist those "perpetrated by anyone, anywhere." This pledge and the promise "never to participate in, to contribute to, or (insofar as we are able) to allow the persecution or denigration or the belittling of Judaism" are sobering and unequivocal statements of commitment to Jewish security and survival. Whether the Church has or can live up to these pledges is a matter for discussion.

Finally, it should be noted that identifying the "teaching of contempt" with the deicide charge, as *TURCJ* does, is problematic. The phrase was coined by Jules Isaac in the 1960s to refer to a three-pronged Christian ideology that included the ideas of Jewish dispersion as punishment for the crucifixion and the corrupt state of Judaism at the time of Jesus. While there is no reason to adhere to Isaac's specific usage, Presbyterians who are encouraged to interpret the "teaching of contempt" in terms of guilt in Jesus' death are likely to miss the complexity of Christian anti-Judaism.

Affirmation 6: We affirm the continuity of God's promise of land along with the obligations of that promise to the people Israel.

1. Is the affirmation implied by, or at least compatible with, the Church's theological/confessional tradition?

This is a difficult question. In most of Christian history the promise of land was understood to be forfeited with the rejection of Jesus the Messiah. In fact, beginning in the Gospels and continuing with the Church fathers, loss of land and dispersion were seen as divine punishments inflicted on God's original people for their role in Jesus' death. While many Christians have maintained an eschatological hope that Jews would be restored to the land in the last days, this hope has usually been tied to a scenario of conversion en masse upon Jesus' return.

2. Is the affirmation supported by, or at least not contradicted by, current Presbyterian beliefs?

This is a difficult question to answer. I believe many Presbyterians would find the affirmation congenial theologically, but this may suggest the influence of "Christian Zionism" the Church rejects. Other Presbyterians will reject the affirmation because they see it as giving carte blanche to the Israeli government. Between these two groups, many Presbyterians could be convinced that this affirmation is important for ensuring good interfaith relations with Jews.

3. Does the affirmation provide a promising basis for future Presbyterian-Jewish understanding and cooperation?

I am conflicted on this question. The authors' explication of Affirmation 6 contends that as a geopolitical entity the State of Israel "is not to be validated theologically," and subsequent interpretation has stressed that the "contemporary fulfillment of God's promise of land is not identical with the State of Israel."[13] Yet theological validation seems to be precisely what the affirmation gives the promise of land, and this theological validation is the germ from which Christian Zionism has sprouted. I suppose it is true that *TURCJ* says nothing about any particular piece of land. But once a theological-biblical claim on the land, however vague, is established, it becomes difficult to resist claims on specific locations that carry historical or religious significance.

Without doubt, Presbyterians need to understand the land's theological significance for Jews, and they need to affirm Jews' need for the security for which "land" is a metaphor in *TURCJ*. But I wonder if there is anything in our tradition, our interpretation of the Old Testament, or our relationships with contemporary Jews that *requires* us to affirm land as a divine promise.

One part of the explication of this affirmation ought to be considered in light of my critique of the way liberation theology has influenced Presbyterian views of Israel-Palestine. It is the claim that "God's justice, unlike ours, is consistently in favor of the powerless (Ps. 103:6)"; according to the document, the powerless and "dispossessed" are Palestinians.[14] If this identification becomes the basis for the application of a liberation perspective to the conflict, its implications for Presbyterian-Jewish relations ought to be carefully considered.

Finally, there is a tension, if not a contradiction, between this affirmation and Affirmation 4. If in the Presbyterian reading of the Old Testament "the blessings of the promise were dependent upon fulfillment of covenant relationships [and] disobedience could bring the loss of land,"[15] then the question arises whether the disobedience of a covenant partner can cancel the covenant's blessings.

Affirmation 7: We affirm that Jews and Christians are partners in waiting. Christians see in Christ the redemption not yet fully visible in the world, and Jews await the messianic redemption. Christians and Jews together await the final manifestation of God's promise of the peaceable kingdom.

1. Is the affirmation implied by, or at least compatible with, the Church's theological/confessional tradition?

Not really. There is nothing novel about Christian images of Jews in waiting. Most Christian theologies of Israel from Augustine to Barth might be described in terms of Jews awaiting final redemption. But the image of Jews as partners in waiting with Christians—both waiting for something that neither possesses—is quite new.

2. Is the affirmation supported by, or at least not contradicted by, current Presbyterian beliefs?

Yes. I think that even in the absence of a solid theological basis for doing so, Presbyterians and Jews have made common cause in many places and will continue to do so.

3. Does the affirmation provide a promising basis for future Presbyterian-Jewish understanding and cooperation?

Very promising, indeed. With the claim that "Christian hope is continuous with Israel's hope and is unintelligible apart from it"[16] we have a compelling rationale for working side by side with Jews as we await the "fulfillment of God's gracious reign upon the earth." The affirmation reminds us Presbyterians of another important fact: We, too, await redemption, though we believe our reconciliation with God has been accomplished in Christ.

One complaint: The spiritual service to which Jews and Christians are called might be described more robustly than "an attempt to remain sensitive to the dimension of the holy." If we worship and serve the same God, surely we can do a better job of describing our common spiritual inheritance.

1. *TURCJ*, 8.
2. It is significant that in explicating Affirmation 5 the document concedes that the hostility between Christians and Jews left its mark on "portions of the New Testament" (*TURCJ*, 12).
3. Joseph D. Small, "A Preliminary Reading of *A Theological Understanding of the Relationship between Christians and Jews*," p. 2 (unpublished paper).
4. *TURCJ*, 9.
5. Ibid.
6. *TURCJ*, 11.
7. Ibid.
8. *TURCJ*, 12.
9. Cited in *Christians and Jews: People of God*, pp. 44, 47.
10. *TURCJ*, 11.
11. *TURCJ*, 13.
12. Small, p. 4.
13. Ibid.
14. *TURCJ*, 14, 15.
15. *TURCJ*, 14.
16. *TURCJ*, 16.

Probing the Relationship

Judaism's Relationship to Christianity: Covenantal Partners

Daniel F. Polish

The subject at hand is a complicated one—the very title makes presuppositions that might well be rejected by members of either faith community. So let us enter the discussion incrementally, beginning with the most obvious and readily acceptable subjects and proceeding into more controversial areas.

That Judaism and Christianity interact is not a controversial issue. Much of the history of that interaction has now achieved the status of conventional wisdom. Christianity has its roots in Judaism. Indeed it was shaped within the crucible of Jewish religious and cultural values. The primary forms of Christian religious tradition reflect the Jewish religious milieu out of which it emerged. Many foundational elements of Christian belief constitute a particular refraction of ideas and concerns then current within the Jewish intellectual universe. The recent scholarly work of James Kugel demonstrates how, during the formative period of Christianity, both Judaism and Christianity were involved in the same sort of midrashic extrapolation of the Hebrew Bible. The earliest disputes within the nascent Christian community—between faith and works, James and Paul, Rome and Jerusalem—were about the extent to which the new community did or did not consider itself to be contained within the larger Jewish community. Did a Gentile have to become a Jew in order to be a Christian? In some cases, elements of Christian tradition are best understood as conscious and intentional reactions against the Jewish background from which the early Christian community ultimately sought to separate itself.

Through some accident of history, after the fall of the Second Temple masses of Jews found themselves on the continent of Europe, which was in the process of becoming predominantly Christian. Those who speak of the Christian heritage of Europe are largely historically correct. All of Europe rapidly became Christian. And although Christianity had its roots in the Middle East, it was Europe that became the center of Christian life. So it was in a Christian Europe that much of world Jewry found its home. For two millennia Judaism and Christianity interacted on the soil of Europe.

The nature of that interaction was multifaceted and complex. We are accustomed to what Salo Baron, a preeminent Jewish historian, characterized as "the lachrymose school of Jewish history," which identifies the interaction primarily in terms of disputations, Inquisitions, Crusades, expulsions, and the like. To such a reading, the interaction was primarily antagonistic and destructive. And, of course, this dimension was very much a part of the encounter of these two religious traditions. And it is neither inappropriate nor unrealistic to identify this tragic component of the interaction as establishing the precedent and context for the Shoah, which virtually ended Jewish life on the European continent.

But for a full understanding of the two thousand years of shared history we must take note of the fact that there were other aspects of the interaction as well. No less significant were the manifold ways in which the two traditions exerted influence upon one another—in both directions. Scholars in each of the groups were aware of the intellectual developments in the other and incorporated such developments in their own work. Disputational literature and apologetics written in both camps give evidence of deep familiarity with the teaching of the other group. David Qimhi's *Teshuvot LaNotzrim*, for instance, reflects a close reading of Christian exegesis of the book of Psalms. Jewish thinkers such as Maimonides had profound influence on Christian thinkers such as Aquinas. Christian forms of argument, if not the content of that argument, found their way into Jewish works. One wonders if such works as Judah Halevi's *Kuzari* could have been created without Christian precedent.

On the level of religious practice, too, we can find significant examples of borrowing back and forth. Liturgists and historians of theology, music, and the graphic arts have filled shelves of volumes with incidents of such mutual influence. To cite but one example, the late medieval phenomenon of Christian Kabbalism betrays profound cultural exchange. Reciprocally, Gershom Scholem traced the origins of Jewish Kabbalah, itself, to the influence of the Christian Catharist heresy. And still later, some have argued, the development of Hasidism in Eastern Europe was profoundly influenced by ideas and practices derived from the Orthodox Church. So to make full account of the history of two thousand years of interaction, we must take note of the many instances and forms of cultural exchange as well as the tragic and destructive realities.

This constellation of historical interactions has formed the basis of Jewish-Christian dialogue during the earliest phase of those conversations. As the dialogue deepens and matures, the discussion must appropriately turn to more theological considerations. Primary among these may well involve the issue of what *religious* sense Jews and Christians have made and can make about one another's existence.

For most of the two thousand years of interaction it largely sufficed for both Jews and Christians to regard one another as, at best, in error. Each group believed that the other's faith system was wrong. "They" simply believed the wrong thing. Jews maintained that faith in Jesus of any nature, and adherence to a triune vision of God, was in error. Christians affirmed that the Jewish denial of the messiahship or the divinity of Jesus was misguided.

Of course, this is the mildest way of expressing these reciprocal perceptions. A darker formulation would have each regard the other as deluded or, even worse, perversely indifferent, perhaps even hostile, to the truth. Of course, the notion of Jews as willfully rejecting the truth or hostile to what was demonstrably good and worthy was responsible for so much of the demonization of the Jews that was experienced during those two thousand years. On the Jewish side, it accounts for a subtler contempt and derision of the faith of Christians that persisted as an undertone in some Jewish literature and in the popular consciousness. In both cases, this mindset would necessitate a belief that the existence of the other group served no *religious* purpose. At best, they played no role in God's design. At worst, their obdurate embrace of error retarded the realization of God's ultimate goals for humankind. The relationship described in these terms must be characterized as negative. It entails, on both sides, no small degree of contempt for the teachings, and perhaps the adherents, of the other religious perspective. It can hardly be understood to either lead to any form of cooperation or lay the groundwork for any sort of collaboration. This is essentially the situation that has predominated for the past two millennia.

At the same time, there were thinkers within each of the groups who posited a more benign evaluation of the other. To such thinkers in the Jewish camp, Christianity was not simply dismissed as erroneous. Authorities as diverse as Maimonides and, much later, Jacob Emden argue against regarding Christianity as a form of idolatry, and insist, instead, that it be understood as a genuine expression of monotheism. In the Christian camp, thinkers such as the later Johannes Reuchlin and the younger Martin Luther argued that Judaism was not simply to be dismissed, but was of worth and did contain meritorious elements. Such thinkers opened the possibility of a relationship other than contempt and derision.

At the very least, such a new relationship would not require either tradition to view the other as wholly erroneous or as an obstacle to the fulfillment of the divine will. If the earlier relationship can be identified as negative, this one can be characterized as, at worst, neutral. In such a relationship neither tradition finds a great deal positive about the other, but neither is it wholly contemptuous. While this posture does not require the two communities of faith to collaborate with one another, it does not prohibit some degree of respect and even admiration. And it does not render some degree of collaboration impossible. Though decidedly a minority opinion within both camps, it has characterized some elements of thinking in both.

It is only in more recent times that the dialogue between the two faith communities has risen to a level that opened the possibility of discussing their relationship in terms of the category of covenant. That context will be explored here. At the most rudimentary level, even those Jews least congenial to interfaith dialogue are prepared to discuss the covenantal status of Christianity in terms of the traditional Jewish understanding of the covenant of the children of Noah. As will be remembered, at the end of the flood story in Genesis, God is depicted as establishing a "covenant forever" between God and all of the descendants of Noah's sons. Thus, Christians would be understood aboriginally (or, as we would say today, genetically) to be included in this covenant, which also applies to the Jewish descendants of Noah. From this perspective, Jews and Christians are regarded to be equally included in a covenant established by God (ten) generations before Abraham even appeared on the scene. For some, this is the first and last (thus ultimate) word about covenants that bind Jews and Christians.

What is finally unsatisfactory about this formulation is that its conception of covenant extends to Christians as people, but in no way addresses the validity or worth of Christianity as a religious profession. To that extent it paradoxically mirrors the famous Napoleonic formulation addressed to the newly emancipated Jews of France: "To Jews as individuals, everything; to the Jews as a people, nothing." Here we would say in terms of covenant: "To Christians as flesh-and-blood descendants of Noah, everything; to Christianity as a creed or a tradition, nothing." While this formulation accords Christians some status in the divine order of things, it is tantamount to no more than acknowledging the fundamental humanity of people who happen to hold Christian belief. What it does not do is make sense of the Christian affirmation per se of those people. It avoids the issue of how to assess the *religious* significance of their Christianity. For Jews, the challenge is what to make of the faith claims of Christians and what significance to accord that faith tradition in our view of this world or of God's design—that is, within the framework of our own covenant-based theology.

When Jews essay an evaluation of Christian tradition, it must be understood that they will be unable to accept whole dimensions of Christian teaching. Conventional Jewish ideology and elements of conventional Christian teaching are incompatible. (As an aside, it is this essential incompatibility of fundamental teaching that makes the concept of "Jewish Christians" an oxymoron.) I would suggest some elements of Christian teaching that are incompatible with normative Judaism. As might be expected, foremost among these—but not exclusively—is the Christology at the heart of the Christian tradition. But this does not exhaust the theological divergences of these two traditions. Whole parts of normative Christian eschatology are contrary to Jewish teaching. It is my own belief, perhaps idiosyncratic, that the aspect of Christian doctrine that is most at odds with conventional Jewish teaching is its "religious anthropology." The Christian view of the human condition as defined by original sin seems to be antithetical to the Jewish understanding of humanity as endowed with two conflicting "inclinations." From one perspective—not unknown among liberal Protestant theologians—it can even be conjectured that it is this "anthropology" that drives the Christology of the daughter tradition. In any event, it serves as the foundation for a worldview diametrically at odds with that of the mother tradition.

Yet having noted the logical impossibility of a Jew as a Jew accepting elements of Christian doctrine does not exhaust the issue of what to make of Christianity as a monotheism and Jewish understanding of it in the context of covenant. One may safely assert that, at this point in history, most normative Jewish teaching has rejected the position—whether it was a sincerely held belief or an assumed posture—that Christianity was a form of polytheism or idolatry. Today, Jews and Jewish teaching can comfortably acknowledge Christianity as a monotheistic faith like Islam and some of the Bhaktic traditions of India. For Jews, Christian monotheism (along with that of Islam) must be recognized as uniquely close to our own theological perspective for historical reasons. But to move from the vantage of history to that of theology, we must inevitably confront the question of *why* it is that Christians have an understanding of God so akin to our own. From the perspective of God, as it were, why do Christians have a perception of the Holy One so proximate to that held by Jews? This question must invariably lead us to consideration of the issue of covenant and the relationship in which Jews and Christians alike stand with God.

For monotheism is not the only theological perspective that Judaism and Christianity share. The fuller truth is that these two traditions are not only both monotheistic. Each might be characterized as a covenantal monotheism. Both Jewish and Christian teachings claim a covenantal relationship with God on behalf of their respective traditions and their adherents. At one point, each tradition asserted that its covenant was unique and exclusive. And each explicitly rejected the notion that the other stood in any kind of covenantal relationship with God whatever. Jewish teaching asserted that Jews alone enjoyed such a relationship. Christians, it claimed, by virtue of adhering to a tradition of religious teaching independent of Judaism had removed themselves from the covenant. Christian teaching, on the other hand, maintained that the Church possessed a dispensation and covenant that superseded the earlier one of the Jews. Jews, it maintained, by rejecting Jesus, had forsaken the covenantal relationship that had been theirs in the past. Needless to add, Christians and Jews alike rejected the characterization of their covenantal status in the teaching of the other tradition.

In the past century both Christian and Jewish teaching have been moving in the direction of a doctrine of what might be termed nonexclusive covenant—a position whose existence is implied by the title assigned this presentation. Of course, such a position raises profound and fundamental issues for both Judaism and Christianity. From a Christian perspective, is it to be asserted that Jews continue to enjoy a covenantal relationship with God after all? And in this case, "after all" means after the explicit rejection of Jesus in any capacity and certainly in a salvific one. From a Jewish perspective, are Jews content to admit that one can be a non-Jew—not bound by the commandments—and still enjoy the special relationship claimed by Jews who bear a special set of obligations because of their covenant? More pointedly, is there room in Jewish teaching to accord Christians some covenantal status not despite, but because of, what they believe?

On the Jewish side, one of the most frequently cited attempts to address the issue of nonexclusive covenants is the putative formulation by the towering twentieth-century German-Jewish thinker Franz Rosenzweig of a dual-covenant theory. This construct supposedly posits that each of the communities has its own specific covenant. Judaism is covenanted to testify to the pure vision of monotheism unsullied by the flux of history and other material and mundane factors. Christianity, this theory is supposed to maintain, is covenanted to carry the monotheistic idea into the world—to express it in terms more readily apprehended by finite mortal minds.

This "theory" presents us with certain problems. First is the fact that however attractive the idea may be, no such formulation is to be found in any of Rosenzweig's work. Second, and from my perspective more compelling, is the fact that the idea in itself, whatever its origins, does injustice to both traditions it purports to describe. In enunciating its neat symmetry, it distorts the reality of each. Even as it denies the more worldly historical dimensions of Judaism, it seems to depict Christianity as tarnished, compromised in the purity of its monotheism through its engagement with the world. There are many who have, with equal inaccuracy, proposed the exact opposite representation of the two traditions. In these renderings, such as the one proposed by Rabbi Leo Baeck in his *Judaism and Christianity,* Christianity is depicted as the more ethereal, romantic tradition, and Judaism as the more earthly, historical expression of the monotheistic idea. Still, this conceptualization, whatever its source and however flawed in articulation, testifies to a Jewish assertion of a covenantal role for Christianity qua Christianity alongside Judaism.

From the Christian side, it is becoming increasingly commonplace to find Paul's depiction of Christianity as a shoot grafted onto the living stock of Judaism (Romans 11) taken as a starting point. This image is now commonly interpreted to mean that the Jewish covenantal relationship with God persists and is of enduring worth. In the wake of Vatican II, documents of the Catholic Church routinely assert that the Jewish covenant has not been invalidated and has continuing worth. This is a dramatically different position than has been expounded in the past.

In more recent years, the Protestant theologian Paul Van Buren has articulated a version of this position in his depiction of Christianity as the way in which the Gentile world can participate in the Jewish covenant. This rendition of Christianity as a Judaism for Gentiles raises several problems. In a subtle way it is a reversion to a single-covenant perspective. Rather than positing two covenants, it argues for a single covenant in which two religious communities participate. Independent of this, Van Buren's position may be troubling for many Christians, as it is likely to be for many Jews. Jews may be discomforted to find Christianity depicted as a form of Judaism, equally as valid as their own. Christians may be troubled by the fact that it deprives their tradition of autonomous validity. By defining Christianity as a form of Judaism, it may depict Christian truth as being of a derivative—and thus perhaps even inferior—quality.

Despite these concerns, what is notable about Van Buren's formulation is that it represents a struggle, from a Christian perspective, to come to theological terms with the relationship of these two communities of faith. Van Buren's model strives to articulate a relationship of the two traditions that respects the autonomy of each while acknowledging their interconnectedness. Without using the specific formulation of Rosenzweig's idea, he echoes its underlying vision of a dual—though not joint—covenant.

To this point, no one has formulated a fully persuasive or wholly satisfactory articulation of a two-covenant theory. What we are left with may be vague or imprecise. Without the details, we have the outlines of a way to understand the two traditions and their relationship with God—and with each other. At this point in the dialogue, many of us on both sides of the conversation come at the project from the position of an impressionistic sense of the two traditions as bearing witness to the same God in terms that have significant elements of commonality—but also real, and no less important, differences in articulation and symbol system. Each tradition can, and does, have a relationship with that God to whom they both testify. That relationship involves commitment and responsibility on the human side, and a perception of reciprocal commitment and responsibility from the Divine. Such a relationship can properly be represented by the term *covenant*. That this term is descriptive of both the Jewish and the Christian relationship with God impels us to opt for some kind of two-covenant model.

And yet, accepting some formulation of the two-covenant model does not conclude the conversation. In many ways it gets us to a new starting point. If we conceive of these two traditions as each being in a covenantal relationship with God, we must ask what that says about, or demands of, their relationship with one another. It is inconceivable that the two traditions be in covenant with the same God and remain wholly alienated from each other. Implicitly, the two-covenant concept demands that Judaism and Christianity regard themselves as in covenant not only with God but also with each other. And if we are to accept the notion of a covenant joining them to one another, we might begin by asking what the parameters of their reciprocal covenant might be. For covenant (even from what we learn from the historical origins of the concept) implies obligations beyond oneself. Let us ask, what are the obligations of mutual covenant?

Two religious communities in covenant would each be obligated to abandon any claims to exclusive truth. Each would have to acknowledge that the other possessed some measure of truth as well, even if articulated in different fashion and even if conjoined with elements not part of their own set of beliefs. Each would have to affirm that the other possessed some measure of truth even while embracing ideas antithetical to their own belief system. Can Christians affirm that the Jews have the truth even as they reject any claims for Jesus? Can Jews affirm that Christians possess the truth even while accepting Jesus as Messiah, Savior, or Lord? Mutual covenant requires that neither assert that they have the complete or only truth.

Eager as politeness or goodwill might make us to embrace such a position, it is a remarkably fraught one. Indeed, it enters us into the charged issue at the heart of Pope Benedict's critique of religious relativism. Can there be such a thing as a religion that does not make absolute truth claims? And does the positing of truth claims not logically involve the denial of the "untruth" of competing truth claims?

And there are other problems for Jews in embracing such a position. Jews of today would have to reenter the two-thousand-year-old struggle between James and Paul, albeit from a different perspective: Can a person be in covenant with God without observing the *mitzvot* and without entering into the body of the Jewish people? Can Jews truly accept Christianity as covenanted with the same God whose covenant with Israel comes freighted with obligations and responsibilities and is regarded as a "family possession" of the children of Israel in the flesh and not merely in faith?

None of these are easy questions to answer. And all of them must be engaged before we can celebrate the mutual acceptance of such a concept.

If a dual-covenant theory were to be accepted, such mutual affirmation would require that the two communities, in effect, recognize, acknowledge, and celebrate those elements of both that they hold in common. But it would require, as well, that they accept the differences of belief and practice that give each its unique character. Such differences cannot merely be tolerated, but must be accepted—and celebrated—as part of the intrinsic identity of the other.

This implies that each community would be obligated to accept the self-understanding of the other as complete and sufficient. Neither could indulge in the luxury of defining the other in terms suitable or congenial to itself. Neither community could interpret the other in its own terms. Rather, each would have to accept the other in the other's own terms and affirm that that other community, despite those differences, was in covenant with God and with itself.

For two faith communities to be in covenant with one another implies that neither can even assert themselves to be superior or possess a "truer" truth than the other. Covenant in this sense requires a fundamental sense of equality and mutuality.

From this would flow the operational requirement that neither community could, under the terms of the mutual covenant, engage in activities to proselytize members of the other community. If each regards the other as possessing truth and if each regards the other as its equal, then missionizing would be incompatible with those commitments. At most, each might engage in what the Catholic scholar Tomasso Federici characterized as witness as opposed to mission. By the way that one conducted one's life one bore witness to the unique truths of one's own tradition. This is distinguished from the active task of proselytizing or missionizing members of the other community. More normatively, it would require a mutually supportive relationship and the functional disinterest in attracting members from the other community.

The notion of being in covenant with one another and with God might be seen as imposing one additional expectation on the two communities of faith. The covenant can be understood as being more than an end in itself. It might also be conceived as having a goal. Both traditions include aspects that point to salvation as the end of faith—its purpose, conclusion, and ultimate consequence. Covenant can be regarded as the pact into which one enters to facilitate the achievement of that goal. Partners with God in covenant might be understood as those who work to bring salvation closer. The concept of two communities in covenant with one another might include the commitment to work together to eliminate the human conditions that stand in the way of the redemptive moment: alienation, injustice, human suffering. To be in covenant with one another might carry the responsibility to serve together as God's partners in making the world a more fit place for human habitation and thus a more proper arena for human redemption.

Thus, the implications of covenantal partnership for the two covenant communities, communities covenanted to God—and to one another. Partnership implies mutual acceptance. It also implies mutual responsibility each toward the other. And it involves responsibility in discharging a task, for there cannot be covenant without obligation. To truly be partners in covenant must imply the obligation to share the work of repairing the world.

The notion of two communities being partners in covenant has become commonplace in theological conversation, all the more so among those engaged in dialogue. But an analysis of the implications of the concept and its obligations may reveal that it is too heavy a burden. Making that assessment is the beginning of the task for the next stage of the conversation.

Fuller exploration of a dual-covenant theory would inevitably open the door to the question of Islam. Granted that the tensions of this moment make such a discussion impracticable, it would ultimately become the inescapable subject of conversation. Can Jews and Christians regard themselves as equally covenanted without acknowledging some similar covenant made with the children of Ishmael? Does not Islam, too, qualify as Abrahamic? And, as such, is it not itself covenanted? Certainly Islam is no less monotheistic than the two predecessor traditions: Muslims may well argue that it is more so. And does not Muslim ideology include the notion that Muslims are, no less than Jews and Christians, called to a special relationship with God? Although now the undertone of Muslim spiritual triumphalism and the fundamentally religious tensions that have caused civilizations to clash make the dispassionate analysis or discussion of such issues immensely complicated, no honest discussion of a dual-covenant theory can help but evolve into a discussion of a tripartite covenant.

And then, if we venture down this path, we become confronted with a still more complicated question of a multiplicity of covenants. At one point in his career, Ramon Panikkar spoke of the "hidden Christ of Hinduism." Such a proposition came to be dismissed as its own kind of spiritual imperialism. But the underlying question it raises continues to be valid: Can we as readily dismiss the image of a self-disclosing God who discloses Godhood in the forms and images appropriate to each people and each civilization? Such a self-disclosure of the same God must perforce carry with it the implication of covenants with each group, thus confronting us with the issue of a multiple-covenant theory.

This is precisely the theology made explicit in Islam and implicit in certain schools of Hindu thought. Could we give a new gloss to the assertion in John 14:2, "in my Father's house are many rooms"? One rabbinic midrash comes suggestively close to asserting the idea of a multivocal revelation. In discussing Sinai, the moment of revelation par excellence, the rabbis suggest that the moment was not univocal, but given in a multiplicity of voices, each attuned to the various human conditions:

> How did the voice [of G-d at Sinai] reveal itself? To each and every Israelite according to their own capacity: to the elderly in terms appropriate to their capacity; to the young in terms appropriate to their capacity; to children in terms appropriate to their capacity; to babes in terms appropriate to their capacity; to women in terms appropriate to their capacity. Even to Moses in terms appropriate to his capacity . . .

In a voice each of them was able to endure . . . To each and every one according to their capacity (Exodus Rabbah 5:9).

Another midrash in this collection carries this line of thought even further. Midrash Exodus Rabbah 18:2 tells us that God, rather than delivering the revelation exclusively in Hebrew, "divided His voice" into all the seventy languages of humankind and addressed each of the nations of the world in its own tongue.

As is well known, various verses of the Qur'an teach the idea of multiple revelations. Each people receives its own messenger bringing a teaching to it in its own language. Here, perhaps we can take language to mean its own symbol system and its own cultural referents in terms appropriate to it:

We sent to every nation a messenger (16.3).
Every nation has been summoned to its [own] book (45.27).
To every one of you we have appointed a right way and an
  open road (5.53).
We have appointed for every nation a holy rite that they
  should perform (23.65).

Numerous strands of religious teaching in India address the concept of the "real" God who is behind all the various gods that are worshiped. The apparent gods become manifestations of the ultimate reality, which in some schools can, and in other schools cannot, be named.

Much more can be said on this subject. Reference can be made to Paul Tillich's "God above God." Such more extended discussion may well be fruitful. Suffice it to note here that the ultimate outcome of those conversations will lead beyond a dual- or even triple-covenant theory to a multiple-covenant theory. And such a theory will inevitably involve people of various faiths finding themselves in covenantal relationship with people whom they hardly regard as monotheists (or even as religious) at all.

In this paper we have examined the possibility of a partnership between Judaism and Christianity that defines itself in terms of covenant. We have explored some of the implications of such a theory—its benefits and its challenges (especially its challenges to elements of our respective current theological understanding). And we have noted some "unanticipated consequences" of defining ourselves in such terms. We are far from the end of a most significant conversation. We have barely dragged ourselves to the starting point. Still, in the words of *Pirkei Avot (Sayings of the Fathers),* "The task is much, the rewards . . . [can be] great—and the Master is urgent." Come, let us reason together.

Christians and Jews in Covenant Partnership: Response to Rabbi Daniel F. Polish

Anna Case-Winters

I want to begin by thanking Rabbi Polish for this wonderful paper, generous and thought provoking. It provides an excellent frame for our continuing discussion and fruitful suggestions regarding how all that might go.

The brief review of the mixed character of the interactions between Jews and Christians in these two millennia names honestly the negativities: the history of disputations, inquisitions, crusades, and expulsions, and all that led up to the tragedy of the Shoah. Generously, the paper acknowledges that this is not the whole story. There were, in fact, important instances of real cultural exchange and mutually appreciative influence. Perhaps this is a history on which we may begin to build a new reality in our relationship.

Rabbi Polish centers on the prospect of our covenant relation. I find many points of resonance. I concur that a claim for our sharing in God's covenant with Noah really does not go very far since, theoretically, all are children of Noah and no one is excluded from this covenant—Christian or whatever. The question, as he so rightly suggests, is a more pointed one: What is the *religious* significance we have to one another?

To assess this, we will need to adopt a *theological* angle of vision and inquire more deeply into places of difference and places of connection if we mean to make real progress. The differences turn out not to be what or where they were claimed to be in occasions of our mutual anathematizing: that Christians are polytheists and idolaters or that Jews have forsaken the covenant in not accepting Jesus as the Messiah. This is not to say that monotheism and Christology are not key to the discussion, but we stand in need of a less contentious, more nuanced, and considerably broadened analysis of where the differences lie and why they are there.

Rabbi Polish does just this sort of work when he takes theological anthropology as a hinge point of differentiation. (I know this was a "just for example" moment in the paper, but I want to unpack it a bit to show how productive such observations that are off the beaten path may be.) Both traditions seek to understand the ambiguities of human existence and the struggle of good and evil in our lives. We grapple with this reality differently. The Jewish understanding makes sense of it all with a view of the human being as endowed with two conflicting "inclinations." For Christians, God creates the human being completely good—no dual aspect here—but in the exercise of God-given freedom a radical disorientation from that created goodness has occurred, such that we are not what God created us to be. We stand in need of a reorientation, restoration, *redemption,* if you will. And Polish is right on target, I think, in seeing this assessment of the human predicament as driving the Christology of Christian tradition. This analysis really helps in our understanding of one of the central differences, while, at the same time, it also helps us see ourselves *connected* in a shared challenge of how to make sense of the human experience of the paradox of good and evil in our lives. Both traditions also seek to place condition under the all-sheltering horizon of our relationship with God.

How compatible are these views? In one sense, they may be incompatible. I think this sort of difference should be allowed to stand as an irreducible difference. We may conclude that an individual cannot "have it both ways" in a coherent life of faith. There may be many such incompatible perspectives; I am agreeing that Jewish-Christian is an oxymoron. But I do think it is possible to be in *covenant relation* with persons who hold a somewhat different assessment of the human predicament—and in *that* sense there may still be compatibility.

Next, I want to turn fully to the matter of covenant relation. Both traditions claim a covenant relation with God and each has, as Polish notes, claimed that its covenant is unique and exclusive. I want to raise a question internal to both traditions as to whether the claim of exclusivity was ever *theologically* sound. Perhaps we do not disagree in this; we can discuss the matter further. Covenant has been variously interpreted in both traditions. There has always been "the scandal of particularity"— God choosing a particular people in the people of Israel, or a particular person in the person of Jesus of Nazareth. Nevertheless, it seems to me that the sounder theological interpretations have always seen in God's gracious and particular election a *universal* trajectory. Israel is blessed to be a blessing: "by you *all the families of the earth* shall bless themselves" (Genesis 12:1–3, emphasis added), "I have given you as . . . a light *to the nations*" (Isaiah 42:6, emphasis added). In Christian tradition, what God has done in Jesus Christ is taken to be for *all the world,* a world that "God so loves." There is a particularity, but it always opens out into the universality of God's larger purposes. I am arguing that the exclusivist claims in either tradition have always been a misreading, and that people in covenant with such a God always have their exclusivist claims severely chastened and an openness to others implied. Exclusivism is excluded, if you will.

As to the two-covenant approach, I agree that the dual-covenant theory has never made a good case for itself—neither the alleged one from Rosenzweig nor the one from Van Buren. Christianity as "Judaism for Gentiles" seems as odd to me as the notion of "Jewish Christians." These approaches feel contrived, too eager to gloss over differences. This is a habit in interreligious dialogue that is hard to break. Hoping to find commonalities, we are quick to read the other in *our* terms—calling faithful people of other religious traditions "anonymous Christians," for example, seems a form of religious imperialism. When people claim that "it all boils down to the same thing if we just talk long enough," I am not convinced. It seems rather that if we just *listen* long enough we will hear the others in their own terms and find some real differences. We do better to articulate the differences rather than to gloss over them, which is to disrespect difference. We need to do difference, differently—embracing rather than obliterating difference.

What are the shared ingredients in covenant life for us? What are the differences? Covenant is a mutually binding relationship with God. It includes dimensions of promise and obligation. That much I think we share. As to differences, the further elaborations might reveal some. From a Christian perspective, there has been an emphasis on how the covenant is divinely initiated and reveals the graciousness and faithfulness of God even in the face of our undeserving and our frequent failings. One of the elements I picked up from the paper is that from where you sit, it seems that the Christian reading of covenant differs from your reading in our "not being bound by the commandments." This difference bears further discussion.

Within Christian tradition there are rather different interpretations of the place of the law in relation to the gospel. Lutherans tend to contrast law and gospel and see law as that which accuses us and drives us to grace, and the gospel as that which sets us free from the law. Calvin's reading is a bit different. For Calvin, law is always God's gracious provision to us; its primary use is as a guide for living. We are not *bound* by it, but by grace are set free to live life toward God. The law lights the way for our covenant life.

A last comment on covenant and then I will wrap up. I think we are much helped by the Pauline analogy in Romans 11 where Christianity is pictured as a shoot grafted into the living tree that is Judaism. Judaism is not just another branch. While I agree that the analogy cannot do all the theological work for us, I think it helps on several fronts. It presents an organic and mutually life-giving relation. Differentiation with connection is better, I think, than a two-covenant notion. It is certainly better for showing our vital connectedness to one another—that we even need one another. The analogy is also potentially a help in discouraging supersessionist thinking. Supersessionism has always struck me as an odd sort of move. Calvin, who was no supersessionist, kept coming back to Romans 11, emphasizing, "It is not you that support the root, but the root that supports you" (cf. Rom. 11:18). To cut ourselves off is self-destructive. Another point Calvin makes is that it would be an odd thing to say that the covenant with the people of Israel is somehow lapsed; it is as if to say that God is not faithful to the promises God makes, in which case all our covenant relations are rather tenuous! This covenant theme is all about God's gracious faithfulness. This is part of why our statements go the way they do in affirming, as in Affirmation 4, "Jews are already in a covenant relationship with God, who makes and *keeps* covenants."

There are certain implications of how Christians should proceed that grow out of central convictions of our faith:

1. We should maintain a spirit of humility and not claim to know the mind of God or how God is at work among other people. This humility is grounded in our being frail and fallible, but also in our being "not God." God alone is God. There is a reformed reserve that is fitting for us.
2. We should treat others with respect as persons in the image of God, honoring them *in their difference*—not in spite of difference and not only if we can overcome or ignore the difference.
3. We should not proselytize, but rather we should practice our faith and bear witness to the good news we have received in Jesus Christ—news that God loves *the world*. A companion to this is that we should be open to learning from others in the practice and witness of their faith in awareness of the limitless presence, power, and grace of God.
4. We should work with others for justice, freedom, and peace, assuming goodwill and common cause with all others, working together to bring salvation closer.

In conclusion, a rallying cry: Interreligious dialogue has never been more urgent than it is today—not only for the challenging and deepening of our own faith as we engage in mutual witness, but for the work of justice, freedom, and peace the world over. The press is not good on religion in general today. I received a revelation recently, from a representative who was speaking on behalf of the World Bank. Perhaps you are thinking this is an unlikely source, but God speaks when and where God will, right? Well, she was trying to convince her colleagues to include religious leaders in the World Bank Dialogue on Values and Ethics. We say, "Of course!" but her colleagues said this would certainly *not* be helpful because (and this is all in my own shorthand) religion is defunct—this is a fully secular society. Not only that, but also where religion still has influence, its influence is divisive, even dangerous. Unfortunately, such charges are not without foundation; religious discord has been the source of much conflict and violence. Jonathan Swift's acid observation is to the point when he says that we have "just enough religion to make us hate one another—but not yet enough to make us love one another."[1]

Can we do better? Can we as religious leaders find our way to come together to be convincingly and actually helpful in the wider world? Our coming to a better understanding of one another in gatherings like this is an essential step. More than theoretical things are at stake here. I am glad for this opportunity to come together.

Resources:

Campbell, Cynthia. *A Multitude of Blessings*. Louisville: Westminster John Knox Press, forthcoming.

Heim, Mark. *Salvations: Truth and Difference in Religion*. Maryknoll: Orbis, 1995.

Sacks, Jonathan. *The Dignity of Difference: How to Avoid the Clash of Civilizations*. London: Continuum, 2002.

Available at pcusa.org: *A Theological Understanding of the Relationship Between Christians and Jews; Hope in the Lord Jesus Christ; The Crucified One Is Lord; Guidelines for Interfaith Dialogue; Witness and Evangelism Among People of Other Faiths; Israel in the Theology of Calvin: Towards a New Approach to the Old Testament and Judaism*

---

1. Jonathan Sacks, *The Dignity of Difference: How to Avoid the Clash of Civilizations* (London: Continuum, 2002), p. 4.

Jews and Presbyterians: The Current Controversy and Some Underlying Issues

Stephen R. Haynes

In a telephone conversation inviting me to participate in this consultation, Joseph Small, director of the Presbyterian Church (U.S.A.)'s Office of Theology and Worship, described the influence of resolutions adopted by the denomination's 2004 General Assembly as a "perfect storm." I think most of us would agree with Joe's assessment. Before the assembly was over in early July, this storm's ferocious winds were beginning to batter the comfortable shore of Presbyterian-Jewish relations. Many of us can remember where we were and what we were doing when the storm hit our particular locale. I was sitting at home in Memphis when I received a call from a good Jewish friend. Paul is originally from Chattanooga, one of those southern Jews who is southern not only in origin but in inflection and temperament, as well. But on this day Paul's voice was lacking all southern civility. "Steve," he said, "what in the world is going on with you Presbyterians?"

Paul's question—and its bluntness—caught me by surprise. Like most Presbyterians, I was focused on what the General Assembly might say on issues of sexuality. What interest could my Jewish friend have in the latest battle in the Presbyterian sex wars? I wondered. But as Paul made painfully clear in the conversation that followed, his concern was over statements the Church had made regarding the State of Israel and Presbyterian evangelism of Jews. I don't remember exactly what he said, but I do recall the pain in his voice, which intimated a feeling of deep betrayal. The words behind his words were these: "I'm confused. I've known you a long time. You had me believing that Jews could trust Presbyterians, that you people had learned something from the Holocaust, that you understood the importance of Israel. Now the Church's highest body passes a series of resolutions that undermines the integrity of Jewish faith and gives aid and comfort to Palestinian terrorists. I guess Christians are all alike."

I suspect that many of us who are identified with the Presbyterian Church (U.S.A.) had similar conversations during the summer of 2004. And Jews weren't the only ones asking us to defend the actions of our General Assembly. Conservative Presbyterians were outraged at positions that did not represent their own views of things. I encountered this outrage while visiting my parents in the mountains of North Carolina in August. As news of the General Assembly resolutions percolated through the American Jewish community, my parents' Jewish friends started sending them articles expressing varying levels of outrage at the GA. One, I recall, compared the PCUSA resolution regarding divestment to the work of Islamic terrorists.

To understand why my parents turned to me, you need to know something about the political fault lines within the Presbyterian Church. My parents are lifelong Presbyterians who over time have gravitated toward the evangelical wing of the Church and in the process have grown increasingly uncomfortable with the denomination's social and theological positions. They are alienated from most of what takes place in the denomination at the national level and rarely feel that it speaks for them. They are poised to leave the PCUSA entirely if it alters its stance on homosexual ordination and are active in organizations dedicated to making sure that does not happen. Since I am a theological moderate and a denominational loyalist, one of my roles in the family system is to defend the positions of the national Church. As my parents related their Jewish friends' outrage at the PCUSA, they added their own. In asking my opinion of the controversy, they were presenting a challenge: "Let's see you defend the denomination this time."

What I told them is the substance of what I will say today. While I cannot defend statements I had no role in formulating, I can try to offer some insight into Presbyterian-Jewish relations and the way Presbyterians understand and interpret some of the thorniest issues in that relationship.

The Presbyterian-Jewish Relationship as Viewed by Presbyterians

Let me begin by describing how the relationship with Jews is viewed by most mainline Presbyterians. To do so I will use four words—*affiliation, pride, ambivalence,* and *fear.*

Presbyterians' sense of natural *affiliation* with Jews is expressed in many ways. In most cities there are examples of Presbyterian-Jewish cooperation, including dialogue groups, pulpit exchanges, interfaith prayer services, cooperative relief efforts, and participation in ministerial associations. Where these cooperative endeavors exist, the alliances are real and the affection is genuine. Truth is, mainline Presbyterians often have more in common with non-Orthodox Jews than with more conservative Protestants, including Presbyterians. My church in Memphis, for example, enjoys closer ties with Temple Israel than with the other large Presbyterian congregation in our area, even though—or perhaps because—many of our members formerly belonged to that church.

These experiences of cooperation and the sense of affiliation they foster have become the source of justifiable *pride* among Presbyterians. This pride stems not only from our bonds with Jews and Jewish congregations, but from the knowledge that we are trustworthy interfaith partners whose history and theology contain relatively little for Jews to be worried about. Jewish-Christian relations are burdened by various Christian impediments: Roman Catholics have the Crusades and the Inquisition; Southern Baptists have outspoken leaders like Jerry Falwell and their frightening social agendas; evangelicals have their penchant for proselytizing and their instrumentalist view of Israel; Lutherans have—well, Luther. Comparatively speaking, Presbyterians approach the encounter with Jews with a clear conscience.

Even when we look at the Holocaust—that darkest of chapters in the history of Christian apostasy—there is more light to be found among the descendants of Calvin than among the representatives of other mainline Christian groups. We have the Huguenots of Le Chambon-sur-Lignon, France, a village of five thousand that managed to rescue about five thousand Jews from the Nazi Final Solution. We have the Dutch Reformed in Holland, whose characteristic philosemitism is evident in the disproportionate number of Righteous Gentiles that hail from that country. And when the classic texts of Christianity are interrogated with an eye to exposing latent anti-Judaisms, the children of John Calvin have less to account for than those who claim Augustine or Luther as their theological father.

However, these undoubtedly positive aspects of the Presbyterian relationship with Jews are tempered by two that are less positive. The first is *ambivalence*. Presbyterian ambivalence toward Jews is rooted in two sources—theological anti-Judaism and cultural anti-Semitism. Presbyterianism may contain fewer theological resources for anti-Judaism than many Christian traditions, but the anti-Judaism that does find a home in our tradition can be insidious in its subtlety. Furthermore, because Presbyterians stress the revelatory quality of Scripture, it is difficult for them to dismiss anti-Judaism in the New Testament as a reflection of first-century sectarian hostility. Nor is it easy to displace from the psyche of this biblical people the various images of the relationship with Judaism found in the New Testament with a single normative image, as was attempted in 1987 in *A Theological Understanding of the Relationship between Christians and Jews (TURCJ)*.

Presbyterian ambivalence toward Jews is also a reflection of American cultural anti-Semitism. I do not want to belabor this point, but I know of no reason to suspect that cultural anti-Semitism is less prevalent among Presbyterians than among Christian groups with similar ethnic and socioeconomic features. Thus, though it is difficult to quantify such things, I think it fair to conclude that as a group Presbyterians share the ambivalence toward Jews that is characteristic of Christian groups that emphasize God's revelation through Scripture and lack a theological magisterium charged with authoritatively interpreting it. Furthermore, I think it is fair to say that Presbyterians share in whatever anti-Jewish prejudices are characteristic of white, upper-middle-class Americans.

Finally, Presbyterian self-understanding vis-à-vis Jews is characterized by *fear*: fear that something will happen to strain our relations with Jews; fear that our tradition will turn out to be less friendly to Judaism than we thought (my own fear is that Karl Barth's thoughts on "Israel" will become more widely known); fear that our commitment to interfaith understanding will be pitted against something we regard as being just as important; fear that our support for justice in the Middle East will be construed as anti-Israelism or anti-Semitism.

Nevertheless, Presbyterians justifiably regard themselves as unusually dependable interfaith partners for American Jews. We are not trying to repress the anti-Jewish tirades of a Martin Luther; we do not feel obligated to protect the reputation of a Pius XII; we do not have to disassociate ourselves from the embarrassing missteps of televangelists; and we do not have to convince Jews they have nothing to fear from the Rapture, the tribulation, or the battle of Armageddon. Given the alternatives, in other words, Jews are lucky to have us. This is what many Presbyterians felt in their heart of hearts prior to the summer of 2004.

The Perfect Storm and the Presbyterian-Jewish Relationship

This description of Presbyterian self-understanding will, I hope, provide my Jewish auditors with a sense of what was lost on the Presbyterian side when the perfect storm obliterated the assumptions that had firmly anchored Presbyterian-Jewish rapprochement. There has been much reflection on the damage caused by the storm and what it will take to repair Presbyterian-Jewish relations. My own assessment, one I believe is confirmed by the decision to call this consultation, is that the dialogue, cooperation, and personal goodwill that had accumulated between Jews and Presbyterians over the years obscured significant theological, social, and political differences.

Accentuating what we agree upon engendered feelings of trust and security, but it left us ill-prepared for dealing with conflict. Now that we know not all is well with the relationship, the time has come to analyze the Presbyterian decisions that caused so much Jewish consternation, as well as the fault lines that have persisted beneath a landscape of mutual concern and interfaith cooperation. To illuminate these fault lines I will focus on features of the landscape that have been epicenters of controversy since July 2004: Jewish evangelism and Israel-Palestine.

Christian Evangelism and Jews

Among the 2004 PCUSA General Assembly actions that provoked the ire of many Jews was the refusal to overturn presbytery and synod funding for Avodat Yisrael, a so-called messianic congregation planted by local Presbyterians in Philadelphia. When the decision became known, many associated with the denomination pointed out that what may have looked like advocacy of evangelism targeting Jews was in fact Presbyterian respect for local autonomy and a reluctance to engage in top-down governance.[1] This explanation, while technically accurate, obscured the complex feelings of many Presbyterians around the question of Jewish evangelism, a complexity evident in the close vote on the matter of funding for Avodat Yisrael.

On the right wing of the denomination are traditionalists for whom the Great Commission applies to "all nations," including Jews. They feel that while Christian anti-Semitism in general and the Holocaust in particular require that Christians exercise care in their interactions with Jews, to withhold the gospel from the Jewish people would be the supreme act of Jew-hatred. This perspective is represented by *The Willowbank Declaration on the Christian Gospel and the Jewish People* (1989), which calls evangelism "the supreme way of demonstrating love for Jews." The declaration speaks for these Presbyterians when it declares that "the growing number of Jewish Christians brings us great joy."[2]

On the other side of the Presbyterian spectrum are those whose interaction with Jews and familiarity with post-Holocaust theology has led them to conclude that Jewish evangelism is a theological impossibility. These Christians "recognize in the Jewish tradition," as the authors of *A Sacred Obligation: Rethinking Christian Faith in Relation to Judaism and the Jewish People* (2002) put it, "the redemptive power of God at work."[3] This conclusion is based in moral revulsion at Christianity's anti-Jewish past, as well as a conviction that religious tolerance precludes proselytizing adherents of other religions. But it may also be rooted in the belief that Jews' salvation is not in question because they are in covenant relationship with God. This belief is expressed in Affirmation 4 of *TURCJ*, which reminds Presbyterians that "when speaking with Jews about matters of faith, we must always acknowledge that Jews are already in a covenant relationship with God."[4]

Between these two theological poles lies a much larger group of Presbyterians who are unfamiliar with the denomination's statements on Christian-Jewish relations and with the ferment in Christian thinking following the Holocaust. If members of this group are uninterested in

Jewish evangelism, it is not because they are convinced of contemporary Jews' "gracious and irrevocable election," but because they are troubled by a vague sense that traditional evangelism is impolite. This group of "average" Presbyterians, though not likely to be personally involved in Jewish evangelism, cannot understand why the Church should not accommodate Jews who embrace the Christian faith. Like my parents, they may have friends or acquaintances who are "Jewish Christians," people whose stories of rejection by "their own people" can be quite poignant. In the view of these Presbyterians, "messianic Jews" bring a perspective on Christian faith that is missing from Gentile churches; in some mysterious way they embody the organic connection shared by Christians and Jews.

Thus, while the average Presbyterian may sense that active mission to the Jews is theologically suspect, his or her understanding of salvation does not rule it out. If I am right, this is one place where Presbyterian ambivalence toward Jews is apparent. On one hand, Presbyterians believe they ought to treat Jews with respect and conceal whatever exclusivist notions of religious truth they might have. On the other hand, the Bible seems to be clear that there is no salvation apart from Christ and that the Messiah was sent for no one if not for Jews. If someone has the courage to share the good news with these persons in this day and age of political correctness, more power to them.

In March 2005, many Presbyterians noted with relief that effective July 1 the Presbytery of Philadelphia would terminate its relationship with Avodat Yisrael, thus eliminating a cause of confusion within the denomination and disapproval among Jews. But the problem of Jewish evangelism is not synonymous with Avodat Yisrael. As the denomination acknowledged in responding to the crisis, "since at least the 1930s some Presbyterians have been part of a network to support the growth of 'Hebrew Christian' or 'Messianic' Churches" and "many Presbyterian congregations and individuals support such efforts."[5]

The Deeper Issue: Images of the Christian-Jewish Relationship

What Presbyterians on either end of the theological spectrum have in common is a clear and consistent image of Christianity's relationship to Judaism. For those on the right, the image is supersession: Jews were once God's chosen, but forfeited that privileged status with the rejection of their Messiah. With regard to salvation, they are in the same sinking boat inhabited by every non-Christian. Presbyterians on the theological left have an equally clear perception of the relationship. Christians, like Jews, are beneficiaries of an irrevocable election, participants through Christ in Israel's covenant. This position is clearly articulated in *TURCJ*, which describes the connection between these elect communities in terms of engraftment. This image is taken from chapter 11 of Romans, where Paul depicts Gentile Christianity as a wild olive shoot that has been grafted onto a living root in the place of unfruitful branches.

Most Presbyterians, however, remain ignorant of *TURCJ,* despite the document's circulation in the Church for nearly twenty years.[6] Lacking any clear picture of the special relationship between Judaism and Christianity, the average Presbyterian may alternate between the many images expressed in Scripture, preaching, or adult education. If they are particularly faithful Presbyterians, they might look to the *Book of Confessions* for guidance on this question. There, they will find a number of references to Israel and the biblical patriarchs and the Old Testament, but they will look in vain for a stable image of the relationship between Christianity and Judaism.

A few summary comments on the documents found in the *Book of Confessions* will indicate why even Presbyterians familiar with the Church's confessional tradition are likely to be confused about their relationship to the Jewish people. The most explicit references to the connection between Christians and Jews are found in the creeds of the sixteenth and seventeenth centuries that describe "two covenants." These covenants do not correspond to "law" and "grace" as one familiar with traditional Christian theology might expect. Rather, the "covenant of works" governed the relationship of God and humanity only until the Fall, after which a "covenant of grace" was instituted. While this second covenant was not fully realized until the coming of Christ, in the time of the law "it was administered by promises, prophecies, sacrifices, circumcision, the Paschal Lamb, and other types and ordinances delivered to the people of the Jews, all foresignifying Christ to come, which were for that time sufficient and efficacious, through the operation of the Spirit, to instruct and build up the elect in faith in the promised Messiah, by whom they had full remission of sins, and eternal salvation; and is called the Old Testament."[7]

Since those who were faithful under the law were saved by implicit faith in Christ, this two-covenant view is compatible with an understanding of Israelite religion as a vehicle of God's grace. But what of Jews who insist on living "under the law" *after* the appearance of Christ—that is, adherents of Judaism? The answer of the classic Reformed confessions seems to be that their religion has been superseded. Relative to other strands of the Christian tradition this may be a kinder, gentler form of supersessionism; but we should not lose sight of the fact that it foresees no possibility of salvation apart from Christ, at least not after Christ. As the *Second Helvetic Confession* puts it, "from all these people [Israelites and Gentiles] there was and is one fellowship, one salvation in the one Messiah."[8]

More recent creeds in the Presbyterian *Book of Confessions* bespeak more mutuality between Christians and contemporary Jews. Beginning with the *Confession of 1967,* Christianity is depicted as a new chapter in Israel's story. As with the older confessions, however, the focus is on the patriarchs, covenants, and Scriptures of the ancient Hebrews, making unclear the status of contemporary Jews. Ironically, the most explicit discussion of the connection between Christianity and Judaism appears in *A Declaration of Faith* (1977), a confession originating in the PCUS (the Southern Church before reunion in 1983) that is not included in the PCUSA *Book of Confessions*. *A Declaration of Faith* offers the closest thing one can find among Presbyterian confessions to a disavowal of supersessionism:

> We can never lay exclusive claim to being God's people,
> > As though we had replaced those
> > To whom the covenant, the law, and the promises belong.
> We affirm that God has not rejected his people the Jews.
> The Lord does not take back his promises.
> We Christians have often rejected Jews throughout our history
> > With shameful prejudice and cruelty.
> God calls us to dialogue and cooperation
> > That do not ignore our real disagreements,
> > Yet proceed in mutual respect and love.
> We are bound together with them in a single story
> Of those chosen to serve and proclaim the living God.[9]

But even this remarkable document does not offer clear guidance for comprehending the relationship between Church and synagogue. We are told that God has not rejected God's people, with whom we are somehow "bound together," and we are called to dialogue and cooperation. But how are we to think of Christ's relationship to Israel and our relationship to the Jews?

Thus, the Church's confessional resources for understanding the relationship between Presbyterians and contemporary Jews are equivocal and confusing. This makes *TURCJ* all the more important, for it does two things Presbyterians and other Christians desperately need: It presents a clear and biblically sound model of Christianity's relationship to Judaism, and it sets out the implications of this model for the Church's witness among Jews. In *TURCJ*, Presbyterians have a great gift; sadly, it remains unclaimed by too many.

Strangely, even the denomination's theological and catechetical literature reflects an uneven awareness of *TURCJ*. On one hand, the 1998 *Presbyterian Catechism* resonates with *TURCJ*'s affirmation of Jews' enduring election. In answer to the question "Was the covenant with Israel an everlasting covenant?" we read:

> Yes. With the coming of Jesus the covenant with Israel was expanded and confirmed. By faith in him Gentiles were welcomed in the covenant. This throwing open of the gates confirmed the promise that through Israel God's blessing would come to all peoples. Although for the most part Israel has not accepted Jesus as the Messiah, God has not rejected

Israel. God still loves Israel, and God is their hope, "for the gifts and the calling of God are irrevocable" (Rom. 11:29). The God who has reached out to unbelieving Gentiles will not fail to show mercy to Israel as the people of the everlasting covenant.[10]

This statement, which has no precedent in the Presbyterian confessions, is essentially a paraphrase of affirmations 2 and 3 in *TURCJ*.

On the other hand, one searches in vain through the Church's recent statements on evangelism for confirmation of the unique connection between Christians and Jews. In *Turn to the Living God: A Call to Evangelism in Jesus Christ's Way* (1991), we learn that Christians are "called to make joyful witness to persons of other faiths in a spirit of respect, openness, and honesty," without any suggestion that these other faiths might bear distinct relationships to Christianity.[11] Likewise, we find that *Hope in the Lord Jesus Christ* (2002) contends that "Jesus Christ is the only Savior and Lord, and all people everywhere are called to place their faith, hope, and love in him." While this statement is tempered by the observation that Presbyterians do not "restrict the grace of God to those who profess explicit faith in Christ," there is no suggestion that Jews as a people represent an exception to the original affirmation.[12]

Given such conflicting signals from the denomination, it is not surprising that Presbyterians are confused about their theological relationship with contemporary Jews. The 2004 General Assembly's decision to "reexamine the relationship between Christians and Jews and the implications of this relationship for our evangelism and new Church development" is welcome indeed. Yet the fact that this is to take place in the general context of the Church's "bearing witness to Christ in a pluralistic age" raises doubts about whether this reexamination will be conducted with specific reference to Jews and Judaism. If *TURCJ* is reaffirmed, steps must be taken to ensure that the document more fully informs the Presbyterian theological imagination.

Israel-Palestine

The issue of Presbyterian and Jewish perspectives on Israel-Palestine is much too complicated to be treated in a presentation such as this one. In fact, it is controversial enough to warrant avoiding it altogether. But if the aftermath of the perfect storm of 2004 clarified any aspect of the relationship between Presbyterians and Jews, it is that we view the Middle East through different lenses. There are several possible explanations for this.

For one, the nation of Israel is central to the identity of many Jews in a way that most Christians do not and cannot understand. This failure to appreciate the meaning of "land" for Jewish identity may be more acute for us than for other Christians, as Presbyterians are not known for their keen sense of sacred space. Further, post-Holocaust Jews in the Diaspora live with a sense of insecurity that most Gentiles do not and cannot understand.

f you have not been the victim of violence directed at your people or your family in a place where you live at the discretion of the majority, it is doubtful that you will ever appreciate what Jewish independence and Jewish power mean to Jews, whether or not they choose to live in the Jewish state.

There is also a genuine longing among Jews for peace in the region, a concern for justice and prosperity among Palestinians, and a hope that Israeli men and women will one day no longer be required to perform military duty in the West Bank.

Finally, American Jews can harbor a complex mixture of pride and guilt with regard to Israel. While the reasons for pride are obvious, the reasons for guilt may not be. Very simply, some American Jews feel in their heart of hearts that they should be in Israel experiencing the joys and hardships of life in the Jewish state, subjecting themselves to the deprivations and threats that attend daily life there. This feeling can be encouraged by Israelis. If you doubt the reality of the pressure put on non-Israeli Jews to participate in building the Jewish state, visit the country with a group of American Jews and listen to the subtle and not-so-subtle messages communicated by Israelis.

The perspective of American Presbyterians on Israel-Palestine is no less complex. Let me suggest some of the factors that influence Presbyterian perceptions of this knotty problem. First, there is the Holocaust. While I believe most Presbyterians have yet to come to terms with what the Shoah means for Jewish life, for Christian witness, or human life in general, I do think they understand that the Holocaust demonstrates the necessity of an independent and secure Jewish homeland. Second, most Presbyterians want peace and they would like to see our government constructively engaged in the Middle East peace process. The intractable struggle in this part of the world frustrates them; they would like to see it end, even if they do not grasp the conflict's underlying causes. The desire to see peace in Israel-Palestine has increased in recent years as Presbyterians have come to appreciate its role in motivating Arab antipathy toward the U.S. Third, most American Presbyterians, unlike most American Jews, have never been to the Middle East and will never go. Their understanding of the Israeli-Palestinian conflict is mediated primarily through news reports and vague memories of Sunday school lessons on Revelation.

Finally, American Presbyterians are genuinely sympathetic to the plight of Palestinian Christians. This is something I suspect Jews struggle to understand. This sympathy is rooted in a long-standing missionary presence in the Arab world, in the ecumenical partnerships[13] to which this presence has given rise, and in a sense of religious obligation toward this threatened community. The challenges facing this dwindling remnant of Palestinian Christians are poignantly described by PCUSA missionaries in the region[14] and by representatives of Arab Christianity who are invited to visit the U.S. The underlying message of these stories is simple but powerful, and has a way of working on the Christian conscience: "The support given to Israel by American Christians makes our lives very difficult; do not let your guilt for the suffering of one people prolong the suffering of another."

I do not know if there were Arab Christians present at the 2004 General Assembly. But it is significant that commissioners to the General Assembly voted to initiate a Palestine Mission Network that would create "currents of wider and deeper Presbyterian involvement with Palestinian partners, aimed at demonstrating solidarity and changing the conditions that erode the humanity of Palestinians living in Jerusalem, the West Bank, and Gaza."[15]

The Deeper Issue: Interpreting Political Conflict

Having discussed some of the factors that may contribute to differing perspectives of Jews and Presbyterians on Israel-Palestine, I want to illumine an underlying issue. In focusing on the PCUSA's interpretation of political conflict in the Middle East, I hope to help Presbyterians consider how they might communicate their concerns for peace and justice in the region without alienating Jews so quickly or so completely.

American Christian views on the Israeli-Palestinian conflict can be helpfully grouped into three broad categories. Many on the conservative side interpret the dispute in biblical-theological terms, understanding the establishment of Israel in 1948 as beginning a countdown to Jesus' return, viewing the Six-Day War as a symbol of God's intervention on Israel's behalf, and construing God's promise to Abraham in Genesis 15 as justification for a "greater Israel" between the Mediterranean and the Euphrates. These and related views were renounced by the PCUSA in the 2004 "Resolution on Confronting Christian Zionism."

A second group, one that includes conservative Presbyterians such as my parents, argues that the Church has no business making political judgments, especially on issues that are not amenable to clear biblical or theological solutions. The third group—and this is where *most* Presbyterians stand—is determined to speak out on pressing social issues in a way that is faithful to the Church's theological commitments and helpful in establishing peace and justice in the world. This is the prophetic option; it is predicated on the assumption that God cares for creation and that God's people should not hesitate to speak words of judgment and hope to that world.

Over the past thirty years or so, liberation theology has been the tool Presbyterians and other mainline Christians have used most often to determine the content of their prophetic statements. Developed by Third World theologians working among the poor and oppressed, liberation theology has enabled First World Christians to hear prophetic voices from the margins of society. Thus, it has provided First World theologians with resources for political critique unavailable in classical theology. The theology of liberation has found a home in the seminaries and graduate schools where Presbyterian clergy and teachers are trained and has been quite influential among those who shape denominational policy. It is not surprising, then, that a liberation perspective is reflected in the Church's statements on the Middle East. But it is fair to ask how well this theology has served the Church in its attempt to speak a prophetic word to a complex political situation while maintaining relationships with Jews on one side and Arabs on the other.

A symbol of liberation theology's function as the lens through which Israel-Palestine is viewed by the PCUSA may be found in the word *occupation*. According to a summary of General Assembly resolutions on the PCUSA Web site, the term *occupation* reaches back to 1988, when the General Assembly asked Israel to "end its occupation of the West Bank and Gaza as part of a larger peace process." The term appeared again in reference to the West Bank and Gaza in 1992, 1995, 2001, and 2002.[16] In 2003, the Assembly's "Resolution on Israel and Palestine: End the Occupation Now" traced "Israel's heavy-handed military occupation" to "the war of June 1967" and used the phrases "military occupation," "illegal occupation," "occupation of Palestinian territories," and "this occupation that violates United Nations resolutions." These same resolutions routinely refer to the "occupied territories."

The 2004 General Assembly "Resolution on Israel and Palestine" went further, claiming the occupation has "proven to be at the root of evil acts committed against innocent people on both sides of the conflict."[17] Even the explanatory literature disseminated by the Church in the wake of that summer's storm, while ostensibly conciliatory, continued to refer to occupation as the "principal cause of the conflict" and claim that the cycle of escalating violence in the region was "rooted in Israel's occupation of Palestinian territories."[18] Such statements seem to imply that all violence in the region—including terrorism against civilian targets—has its ultimate cause in Israel's illegal occupation of Palestinian lands.[19]

In light of the Church's consistent focus on Israeli occupation as the root of the region's problems—and the recent escalation in the intensity of this focus—that summer's call for divestment from companies viewed as aiding the occupation is not so surprising. Significantly, the resolution was titled *Initiating Divestment and Ending Occupation,* its focus "multinational corporations *that profit from Israel's occupation* of the West Bank, Gaza, and East Jerusalem" (emphasis added). Those who were offended by the resolution—Presbyterians and Jews alike—expressed surprise at the General Assembly's sudden consideration of such a drastic measure. But viewed in the context of previous PCUSA statements, the action can be seen as an incremental step in a steadily intensifying campaign to strike at the root of the region's troubles. As the Stated Clerk would later write in his explanation of the General Assembly's actions on Israel-Palestine, "where the issue is occupation, selective divestment has been a proven, responsible strategy to address injustice."[20]

Back to my question: Has liberation theology served the Church well in its attempt to speak a prophetic word to a complex political situation while maintaining relationships with all parties to the conflict? If it has not, it is because this powerful interpretive lens was fashioned for situations where the identities of oppressor and oppressed are horribly clear: situations in which dictatorial regimes deny basic freedoms while ruling through military force and administrative terror. When one approaches a political situation through the template of liberation theology, the first step is to identify the victims of oppression. Everything else develops from that distinction. For this reason, liberation theology is not well suited for interpreting conflicts where victims and victimizers reside on both sides, where a democratically elected government is charged to protect its populace from real external threats, and where groups associated with both sides make credible threats to destroy the other.

Defenders of the PCUSA's stance on Israel-Palestine note a careful balance in the Church's statements, which, they point out, call for a cessation of violence on both sides, decry terrorism as well as military action against civilians, and support the existence of Israel alongside a Palestinian state.[21] Yet, as long as the conflict is understood to be the result of an illegal military occupation, can those who seek justice maintain neutrality? One of the fundamental insights of liberation theology is that because God takes sides God's people are called to side with the victims of oppression against their oppressors. Neutrality, then, is in effect conspiring with the oppressor. Can a Christian who is convinced of his or her obligation to pursue justice remain balanced once he or she has defined one group of people as occupiers and the other as the victims of occupation?

The controversy over the 2004 General Assembly's statements on the security barrier/separation wall provides a useful example of how the liberationist lens colors what Presbyterians see in Israel-Palestine. The barrier's defensive role, paramount for Jews, was ignored by the General Assembly, which was determined to associate it with "land confiscation," "de facto annexation" of Palestinian territory, and "protect[ion of] illegal Israeli settlements."[22] For the General Assembly, the wall's security features were completely obscured by the way it purportedly "ghettoizes the Palestinians and forces them onto what can only be called reservations."[23] Why such a one-sided view? Because liberationists have taught us that "security" is the term oppressor states use to justify their violation of human rights in the court of world opinion. Israel's talk of security, the General Assembly seemed to be implying, should not be allowed to distract us from the fundamental issue, which remains occupation.

At another level, liberation theology may be responsible for the failure of General Assembly statements to fully acknowledge the terrorist threat facing Israel. For liberationists argue that traditionally Christians have tended to ignore the sorts of violence used by entrenched regimes to control their victims, while decrying the sorts of violence these victims rely upon to resist those regimes. Thus, the influence of liberation thought on Presbyterian policy may be seen in individual General Assembly statements (such as the reference in 2001 to "the occupation, which is itself a form of violence"), as well as a general conviction that "the occupation" represents a violence before which violent resistance is understandable, if not justified.

Conclusion

The perfect storm of 2004 had much in common with the controversy that accompanied the release of Mel Gibson's *The Passion of the Christ* in February 2004. Both surprised Christians and Jews who are committed to maintaining friendly interfaith relations; both reminded us that Jews and Christians can look at the same phenomenon and interpret what they see very differently; and both suggest that real differences lay beneath the calm surface of interfaith rapprochement.

Richard L. Rubenstein writes that *The Passion of the Christ* controversy exposed the fault line that historically has separated Christians and Jews—the conviction that a good Jew is one who believes in Jesus.[24] I have argued that the perfect storm of 2004 revealed a pair of fractures in the superstructure of Presbyterian-Jewish relations: the lack of a stable image of the relationship between Church and synagogue that communicates the unique bond between the two covenant peoples and demands respect for adherents of living Judaism; and the application to the Israeli-Palestinian conflict of a theological perspective that traffics in simple dichotomies and makes an often gray situation appear black and white. Perhaps in our time together we can make progress toward better identifying these fractures, if not healing them.

1. According to a *Statement of the Stated Clerk of the General Assembly of the Presbyterian Church (U.S.A.)* that sought to interpret the actions of the General Assembly, "here it is important to note that primary decisions regarding the funding of new Church developments are made at the presbytery (regional) level of our denomination; in nearly all cases, national funding for such work is made only to complement funds already committed by presbyteries and synods with the understanding that presbyteries take the lead in determining the appropriate projects." At pcusa.org, January 2005.
2. In *Christians and Jews: People of God* (Louisville: Presbyterian Church [U.S.A.] Office of Theology and Worship, n.d.), p. 62.
3. Ibid., p. 60.
4. Ibid., p. 14.
5. *Perspective on a Presbyterian "Messianic" New Church Development in Philadelphia*. At pcusa.org, October 2005.
6. In the adult education classes I have taught at Presbyterian churches in several states, I have yet to meet a layperson who had heard of *TURCJ* before I arrived.
7. *Westminster Confession of Faith*, 6.041.
8. *Book of Confessions*, 5.129.

9. From Chapter 3, "God and the People Israel," cited in *Christians and Jews: People of God,* p. 33.
10. Cited in *Christians and Jews: People of God,* p. 36.
11. Cited in *Christians and Jews: People of God,* p. 40.
12. Cited in *Christians and Jews: People of God,* pp. 44, 47.
13. A list of these partnerships may be found at pcusa.org/worldwide/israelpalestine/international.htm.
14. On the PCUSA Web site, for example, one can find a study guide developed by one of the Church's missionaries in Palestine that describes in detail the demographic collapse of Palestinian Christianity since 1940, stresses the importance of preserving a "living remnant of the Church of the first Pentecost," testifies to Palestinian Christians' role in maintaining Christian holy places, and notes that these churches administer and operate hospitals, clinics, schools, rehabilitation centers, and vocational training programs. See "Letter from Doug Dicks," preface to The Middle East Research and Information Project's *Palestine, Israel and the Arab-Israeli Conflict: A Primer.* At pcusa.org, January 2005. My own connection to Presbyterian missionaries in the Middle East is a personal one. Marthame Sanders was a member of my youth group at First Presbyterian Church in Atlanta in the mid-1980s. Between 2000 and 2004 Marthame and his wife, Elizabeth, lived and worked in Zababdeh, located in the northern West Bank between Jenin and Nablus. Reading their monthly reports from Palestine has given me a different sense of Palestinians than is available from the American news media.
15. "Resolution on a Palestine Mission Network" adopted by 2004 General Assembly. At pcusa.org, January 2005.
16. In 1992, the General Assembly "call[ed] upon the United States government to press for the end to the Israeli occupation of southern Lebanon, West Bank, and Gaza, and for the withdrawal of Syrian troops from Lebanon." In 1995, the General Assembly vowed to "continue to appeal to those in a position of authority to use their good offices to maintain the momentum of the peace process, to bring about an end to military occupation." In 2001, the General Assembly "call[ed] on Mr. Sharon's government to desist from its policy of excessive military force, and to signal its commitment to peace negotiation by ending the occupation, which is itself a form of violence, and a continuing hindrance to the resumption of a peace process." In 2002, the General Assembly referred to "Israel's occupation of East Jerusalem, the West Bank, and Gaza."
17. "Resolution on Israel and Palestine." At pcusa.org, October 2005.
18. *Ending the Occupation and Divestment.* At pcusa.org, January 2005.
19. This implication is even clearer in a preface to a study guide on Israel-Palestine by one of the Church's missionaries. The document is so steeped in the language of occupation that it uses the acronym OPT for "Occupied Palestinian Territories." It describes the Al Aqsa Intifada as a "reaction to the oppressive Israeli military occupation of the West Bank, Gaza Strip and East Jerusalem," calling it the "underlying cause for Palestinian anger and ultimately resistance to that occupation." The document also highlights the suffering of Palestinian children. See "Letter from Doug Dicks," preface to The Middle East Research and Information Project's *Palestine, Israel and the Arab-Israeli Conflict: A Primer.* At pcusa.org, January 2005.
20. *Ending the Occupation and Divestment.* At pcusa.org, January 2005.
21. According to *A History of the Presbyterian Church (USA)'s Steps Toward Peace in Israel and Palestine,* General Assemblies have consistently since 1948 "affirmed Israel's right to exist as a sovereign state within secure, internationally recognized borders; affirmed the Palestinians' right to self-determination, including the establishment of an independent, sovereign state; and condemned anti-Semitism, terrorism and all violence against innocent people." At pcusa.org, October 2005.
22. *The Separation Wall.* At pcusa.org, January 2005.
23. *Resolution on Calling for an End to the Construction of a Wall by the State of Israel.* At pcusa.org/worldwide/israelpalestine/wallresolution.htm#1.
24. "The Exposed Fault Line," in J. Shawn Landres and Michael Berenbaum, eds., *After the Passion Is Gone: American Religious Consequences* (Walnut Creek, CA: AltaMira Press, 2004), pp. 207–218.

Jews and Presbyterians: Response to Stephen Haynes

David F. Sandmel

I am pleased to have the opportunity to respond to the thoughtful words of Stephen Haynes and, more broadly, to participate in the dialogue that has opened up between the National Council of Synagogues and the Presbyterian Church (U.S.A.)—henceforth referred to as the PCUSA—in the aftermath of the actions taken at the PCUSA General Assembly in 2004. Given both the emotions involved and the complexity of the issues themselves (and which, on some fronts, continue to worsen),[1] I would like to think that these unfortunate circumstances have provided us—Jews[2] and Presbyterians— with an opportunity to revitalize our relationship and, perhaps, even move it forward. It is clear that there is a great deal we do not understand about each other both in terms of belief and theology and in terms of institutional structure and process.[3] I will address most of my comments to Dr. Haynes' paper, "Jews and Presbyterians: The Current Controversy and Some Underlying Issues," with only occasional reference to his analysis of *A Theological Understanding of the Relationship between Christians and Jews* (TURCJ), since many of the same issues appear in both papers.

I would like to begin, however, with a brief comment on the paper "Assessing *A Theological Understanding of the Relationship between Christians and Jews*." If one were to reduce Dr. Haynes' careful response to the three questions he asked about each affirmation to a simple "yes" or "no," then only one of the seven generates three "yeses." Only one is compatible with the Church's theological/confessional tradition, is supported by (or at least not contradicted by) the beliefs of Presbyterians, and provides a promising future for Presbyterian-Jewish understanding and cooperation. Six of the seven do provide a promising future for dialogue. There is only one other unqualified "yes," that Jews and Christians are partners in waiting. Affirmation 6, on the promise of land, not surprisingly, proved to be the most challenging. In answering the first two of his own questions on the issue of land, Dr. Haynes uses the word *difficult* twice and admits that he is conflicted about how to answer his third question.

This is, of course, an unfair oversimplification of Dr. Haynes' thoughtful examination of *A Theological Understanding of the Relationship between Christians and Jews,* but it is nonetheless useful in assessing the real life of that document within the PCUSA, regardless of its institutional authority. It would seem, as Dr. Haynes himself admits, that the document is not well-known within the PCUSA; while it may have a certain institutional status in theory, in practice it does not inform the thinking of the majority of Presbyterians. I agree with Dr. Haynes that this is an unfortunate situation and hope that the dialogue process on which we are embarking will help to remedy this situation.

At the beginning of "Jews and Presbyterians: The Current Controversy and Some Underlying Issues," Dr. Haynes cites the Rev. Dr. Joseph Small's use of the image of a perfect storm to describe the state of affairs in the PCUSA. I believe this metaphor may also be useful in understanding the reaction of the Jewish community, as well. The Jewish community as a whole is generally touchy about both Israel and missionary activity that targets Jews. It is my sense that over the past few years, a number of factors have combined to exacerbate the Jewish community's sensitivity to these and other issues that it finds threatening.[4]

The failure of the negotiations between Ehud Barak and Yasser Arafat was devastating for many in the Jewish community who were hoping against hope that finally a settlement of the Israeli-Palestinian conflict was going to be reached. Instead, those talks failed, and shortly thereafter the Second Intifada began, plunging them once again into violence. Only recently, with the withdrawal from Gaza and a few West Bank settlements, has a new glimmer of hope emerged.

Many Jews find that the political success of Christian right and the resulting assault on the separation of church and state is ominous. Jews consider the separation of church and state to be the cornerstone of American freedom and the key value that has made the United States so hospitable to Jews. We Jews have a long and unhappy history of life under religious-dominated political regimes, especially in Christian Europe. Challenges to the separation of church and state pose a serious threat to our sense of well-being and acceptance in this country.

The release of Mel Gibson's film *The Passion of the Christ* did not provoke the surge of anti-Semitic incidents that some had predicted. I think the Jewish community erred in not appreciating the significance of the religious message that many Christians found in the movie. Any number of observers have pointed out that Jews and Christians watched the same screen but saw two very different movies. Nonetheless, the Jewish community was, in my opinion, justifiably disappointed at the lack of willingness on the part of Christian leaders to address the anti-Semitic images and messages in the film.

Finally, over the past few years, there has been a sharp increase of anti-Semitism in Europe. While some of this upsurge is connected to the political situation in the Middle East, in many instances that situation serves as a cover (or justification) for classic Jew-hatred. It seems that the taboo against anti-Semitism that followed the Second World War is breaking down and that disapproval of Israel's policies provides license for prejudice.[5]

I believe that American Jews feel the immediacy of the Shoah (the Holocaust) much more than Christians, especially those born after World War II. For Jews, whose 3,500-year-old historical memory is, as a matter of theology, both immediate and personal, the Shoah is a fresh wound; it happened to our parents and grandparents. For the majority of Americans, to the extent that they know anything about the Holocaust, it is merely part of "history," something that happened a long time ago in a place far away, in black and white.

It may be a surprise to Presbyterians, and Americans in general, that their perception of American Jews and Israel is quite different from the way we American Jews see both ourselves and Israel. While many Americans see the American Jewish community as wealthy and politically powerful (in part because of the anti-Semitism to which Dr. Haynes refers), we Jews tend to see ourselves as a small and, according to all the demographic studies, shrinking community (around 2 percent of the population) that must be continually vigilant against anything that threatens our well-being. Similarly, most Americans tend to see Israel as a nation with powerful armed forces in conflict with the Palestinians, a poorly armed, oppressed people. American Jews and Israelis tend to see Israel as a small nation, both in terms of population and geography, surrounded by twenty-three hostile Arab nations who reject Israel's right to exist and are bent on its destruction. We recall that not too long ago, in 1967, this genocidal aspiration came close to fruition. On the eve of the Six-Day War, which ended in a decisive victory for Israel and resulted in the occupation of the West Bank and Gaza Strip, it appeared to many observers that Israel was on the brink of annihilation. The euphoria in Israel and among Jews around the world that followed that war was attributable not only to the speed of Israel's victory and the symbolic significance of the capture of the old city of Jerusalem (including the Western Wall), but to the fact that Israel had overcome what seemed to be overwhelming odds against it. Most Jews are sympathetic to both the plight and the rights of the Palestinians; recent polls show that the majority of Israeli Jews support a two-state solution in the Israeli-Palestinian conflict. At the same time, most Jews believe that Israel has every right to protect its citizens from Palestinian terrorists who attack public buses, pizzerias, nightclubs, and the like. Most Americans—and, I imagine, most Presbyterians—see both Jews and Israel as secure and powerful; in contrast, American Jews and Israelis see themselves as vulnerable and threatened. I believe this is what lies behind the comment of Prof. Haynes' friend, when he said, "I guess Christians are all alike." Presbyterians and Jews will have to address this difference in perception if we are to move toward greater understanding.

I now want to turn to the four words Dr. Haynes used to describe a Presbyterian view of Presbyterian-Jewish relations. When discussing affiliation, Dr. Haynes wrote that "mainline Presbyterians often have more in common with non-Orthodox Jews than with more conservative Protestants, including Presbyterians." This predicament is, on one level, applicable to the Jewish community, as well. Liberal Jews often have more of a political, social, and even lifestyle affinity with liberal Christians than with our more traditional co-religionists. However, regardless of the religious or theological differences between Jews, we see ourselves as part of one people, united by both culture and history. We often work together in coalition to represent ourselves to the broader community and to support Israel.

Dr. Haynes' statement that "Presbyterians approach the encounter with Jews with a clear conscience" is, from a Jewish perspective, surprising. Few Jews are aware of the differences between the many Protestant denominations, other than a vague idea that some are labeled "liberals" and others "conservatives" (usually understood in terms of biblical inerrancy and social conservatism, rather than Christology, works vs. faith, or other theological categories). I think few Jews reckon the actions of Huguenots or the Dutch Reformed to the credit of the Calvinists. For us, these were the rare exceptions among what we tend to see as the undifferentiated mass of Christian Europe. Dr. Haynes may be right that the descendants of Calvin "have less to account for," but Jews do not know this. And I cannot help but wonder whether the fact that Calvinism did not wield political power nearly as often or as long as Roman Catholicism or other Protestant denominations may not also be a factor in the relation between light and darkness.

At the same time, I must commend Dr. Haynes for his forthrightness in addressing the issue of both "theological" and "social" (my terms) anti-Semitism among Presbyterians. I am not in a position to comment on the extent of anti-Semitism among Presbyterians, but the willingness to be self-critical about these issues is essential to our dialogue: We Jews will need to be self-critical as well. We need to be more precise in how we speak and teach about Christianity in general and become more informed about the differences between various forms of Christianity. We need to examine our reactions and our defensiveness to ensure that our fear of the other, even if well-founded based on our historical experience, accurately reflects the world in which we now live.

I appreciate the way that Dr. Haynes elucidated the complexities of the issue of evangelism for Presbyterians; this is important for Jews to understand. I doubt that most Presbyterians are aware of the depth of Jewish aversion to Christian mission. On this issue, too, the Jewish awareness of history is much keener and undoubtedly longer than that of Presbyterians. In the Middle Ages, Jews were forced to listen to conversionary sermons, or, in some cases, simply forced to convert. Persecution and mission often went together. This history has shaped our reaction to conversionary efforts. In the wake of the Shoah, among a people who see their numbers dwindling, missionary activity is seen as a threat to Jewish survival and is considered to be tantamount to genocide. A Christian may believe that trying to bring a Jew to belief in Christ is an act of love; most Jews see it as just the opposite.

The gap between Jewish and Christian perceptions in the matter of mission is also apparent in attitudes toward "Jewish Christians" or "messianic Jews." It would be difficult to underestimate the Jewish aversion to mission in general and to "Jewish Christianity" in particular, something I doubt most Presbyterians consider. From the Jewish perspective, however, these groups are the worst kind of Christian missionaries. Even if some of them were born as Jews, the religion they profess is not Judaism, which by definition does not allow for belief in Jesus as the risen Christ. By "pretending" to be Jewish and cloaking their Christianity in Jewish packaging (using Hebrew and other Jewish cultural or liturgical trappings), their goal is to lure unsuspecting Jews to Christianity. I think Jews understand that, on a certain level, witness and mission are essential aspects of what it means to be Christian. To be blunt, targeting Jews for conversion, especially with what are viewed as deceptive and dishonest means, engenders revulsion. If Presbyterians want to have good relations with Jews, they will have to pay close attention to this dynamic.

The lack of clarity regarding images of the Christian-Jewish relationship that Dr. Haynes spells out in this paper is seen even more clearly in his analysis of *A Theological Understanding of the Relationship between Christians and Jews*. I am not in a position to affirm or challenge his perception of the state of Presbyterian doctrine or belief. I would point out that, on the Jewish side, there is no document that can be compared to it. No Jewish group has, to my knowledge, attempted to define the relationship of Judaism to Presbyterianism. There have been few attempts by Jews to define a theological relationship to Christianity. With the notable exception of "*Dabru Emet:* A Jewish Statement on Christians and Christianity" (September 2000), written by four Jewish scholars and endorsed by over two hundred rabbis and Jewish academics representing a broad range of the Jewish community, most other efforts in this regard have been undertaken by individuals and therefore cannot be said to reflect the view of the community or even some subset thereof. As stated in the preamble to *"Dabru Emet,"* the changes in Christian theology and doctrine represented by *A Theological Understanding of the Relationship between Christians and Jews, Nostra Aetate,* and numerous other Church documents deserve a considered Jewish response. Perhaps this dialogue that we have initiated will help lead in that direction.

Dr. Haynes is correct that the complexities of the Israel-Palestine situation defy brief description or facile delineation. While he is also correct in pointing to a different understanding of land, I would add that many Christians fail to appreciate the fact that we Jews do not view ourselves primarily as a religion, at least not in the same way that Christians do. Judaism is not only or even primarily a matter of belief; indeed, Jewish identity is not constrained by belief. As noted several times above, Jews are a people whose identity consists of—in addition to religious—national, ethnic, cultural, and linguistic components. Whereas faith is essential to Christian identity—one is a Christian because one has faith in Jesus as the risen Christ—many committed and involved Jews are not religious and do not define their Jewishness in religious terms.

For most Jews, peoplehood and land are inextricably linked. In this regard, then, the argument that the Shoah demonstrates the necessity of the land, while true, is in fact secondary to the belief that the Jewish nation, like every other nation on earth, has a right to national self-expression in its ancestral homeland. The invocation of the Holocaust as the justification for Israel is, on a certain level, unfortunate, since it suggests that the right to national self-expression is circumstantial rather than integral to what it means to be a Jew.

Here, I would like to address a question asked by Dr. Haynes in his analysis of *A Theological Understanding of the Relationship between Christians and Jews,* specifically: Is there anything in our tradition or in our relationships with contemporary Jews that *requires* us to affirm land as a divine promise? It is worth pointing out that, while that may be of importance to Presbyterians, my argument in the preceding paragraph for the Jewish perspective on land makes no mention of divine promise. For most Jews today, the existence of the State of Israel is justified in national terms, not religious terms. We Jews are a nation. The land of Israel is our ancestral homeland. We have the right to national self-determination in that land. While some Jews may trace the connection to the *land* of Israel to a divine promise, few if any, justify the existence of the *state* of Israel, not to mention its government or policies, as a result of a divine promise. There is no scriptural verse or rabbinic interpretation that can be mustered to justify the *state* of Israel. Though this is often a surprise to Christians, a vast majority of Jewish Israelis define themselves as secular rather than religious. And many of the religious Jews see the state not as fulfillment of a divine promise but as the result of human endeavor and therefore subject to the same weaknesses as every human endeavor. There are those in the Jewish religious community who view the creation of the state as problematic, since Jewish tradition teaches that after the destruction of the Second Temple in 70 c.e. the state would be reconstituted only by God in the end of days. Those Jews who consider the founding of the state to be a sign of the impending advent of the Messiah are a small, but vociferous and, since many of them are settlers, a politically significant minority.

I would respectfully disagree with Dr. Haynes that most Jews struggle to understand the plight of Palestinian Christians. It might be more accurate to say that they are ignorant of it, but they understand the Palestinian Christians' precarious situation when it is explained to them. I think the majority of Jews are also sympathetic to the plight of all Palestinians, Christian and Muslim, and to their desire for national self-expression, and hope for a just and equitable solution of the conflict. As Dr. Haynes rightly pointed out, however, much of the criticism of Israel, including that in the PCUSA overtures, puts all the blame on Israel. When described in these terms, Israel cannot help but be seen as the villains and the Palestinian as the victims. In this vision, every Israeli action, even self-defense, is suspect, and every Palestinian tactic, including terrorism, is at least "understandable," if not justified. At the heart of this view, I believe, is a rejection of the basic legitimacy of the Jewish state and, once again, a lack of knowledge of the history of the conflict. To give but one example, in September 1967, not even three months after the Six-Day War, eight Arab nations at Khartoum issued what have come to be known as the "three nos": no peace with Israel, no recognition of Israel, no negotiations with Israel. This absolutist position meant that there was nothing Israel could do to ameliorate the situation other than to commit national suicide. To place the blame solely on Israel, or to name the occupation as the root of evil in the Middle East, does not reflect historical reality and is at best naïve, at worst, anti-Semitic.

Many Jews, both in America and in Israel, recognize that Israel has made serious errors in its foreign policy. Many Jews regret or actively disapprove of some of the tactics Israel has used in its administration of the West Bank and Gaza. However, the lack of balance, the thinly veiled anti-Semitism, and the denial of Israel's basic right to exist that seem to underlie so much criticism of Israel make open, constructive discussion even between Jews and Presbyterians difficult if not impossible.

Dr. Haynes' discussion of liberation theology is welcome, but I would add another dimension to it. Much liberation theology, as pointed out by Amy-Jill Levine of Vanderbilt University at the convention of International Council of Christians and Jews in 2005 in Chicago, uses the language of traditional Christian anti-Semitism. Thus, the poor and oppressed, and their suffering, are identified with Jesus, while the oppressors are identified, not with Rome, but with Jews who plot against Jesus and eventually crucify him. While the continued promulgation of this kind of rhetoric of deicide is bad enough, when applied to the Middle East, Israel becomes the Jews crucifying Jesus again, just as they did two thousand years ago.[6]

Dr. Haynes argues, correctly I think, that the lack of stable images of the relationship between Church and synagogue and the application of a simplistic theology to the Israel-Palestine conflict are central issues in the current tension between Jews and Presbyterians. In responding to Dr. Haynes, I have tried to augment his analysis by identifying points in the relationship between Jews and Presbyterians where there is often lack of understanding among Christians of the beliefs or sensitivities of Jews. I have focused exclusively on Presbyterian views of Jews and Judaism and hardly at all on Jewish views of Presbyterians or Christians. As the dialogue continues, we Jews will have to examine our prejudices and misconceptions as well.

1. I refer specifically to the revelation that, on a recent trip to the Middle East, the Middle East Task Force of the Chicago Presbytery met with representatives of Hezbollah, an organization that takes pride in its acts of terror and is committed to the destruction of Israel.
2. The reader should keep in mind that the Jewish community is quite diverse and, therefore, references to "Jews" are, by necessity, generalizations.
3. For example, most Jews do not know what an "overture" is, nor do we understand the relationship between the PCUSA and the individual presbytery.
4. This is not based on any scientific studies of attitudes within the Jewish community, but is rather a personal observation based on my work both in interfaith relations and as a congregational rabbi.
5. For example, in 2002, Daniel Bernard, the French ambassador to Britain, called Israel a "shitty little country" and then asked, "Why should the world be in danger of World War III because of *those people?*" [emphasis added].
6. The PCUSA Web site lists several works that fall into this category as "resources for study and engagement on the Israel-Palestine situation."

The Land

Land as Divine Gift and Human Responsibility

W. Eugene March

To presume to present an essay on the Christian understanding of the significance of the land in the Bible requires an immediate set of disclaimers. First, as we all know full well, Christians are quite diverse. On a topic such as this, I know that there is no single understanding that all Christians would endorse. Nonetheless, though I clearly do not speak for all Christians, I do think that I fairly represent the position of many Presbyterians. Second, whether the topic is "the land" or "land" in the Bible is of considerable importance. From the standpoint of the Reformed tradition, I think, "the land" is subsumed, finally, by "land," but that is not always the way some would prefer. Finally, this is not a research paper. I did publish a book titled *Israel and the Politics of Land* (Westminster John Knox Press, 1994) from which I will draw, but this paper is in the style of a reflective essay. I will discuss the significance of "land," "the land," "the State of Israel," and the responsibilities that come with the gift of land, particularly as these topics affect or are informed by my theology and that of the Presbyterian Church (U.S.A.). With this brief introduction, then, let me turn to the assigned topic as I have interpreted it.

The Bible
The primary source for this essay is the Bible. This is, perhaps, to state the obvious, but a few comments are in order about how I understand my

assertion. For Presbyterians, the Bible is composed of the Old Testament (I prefer First Testament) and the New Testament (Second Testament). The First Testament contains the same biblical books, though in a different order, that are found in the Tanach. For Presbyterians, the Old Testament is equally authoritative with the New Testament, at least in policy if not always in practice. This is quite important in dealing with this topic. Presbyterians consider that the material in the First Testament addresses Christians as much as it addresses Jews. There are many other non-Presbyterian Christians, however, for whom the First Testament is not authoritative in any meaningful way even though it is a part of their Bible. It is also obvious that the inclusion of the Second Testament as part of the primary source does introduce material peculiar to the Christian movement.

The interpretation of the Bible is both a historical-literary and a theological exercise. The Bible is a collection of ancient writings that had a place in a real world with real, historically bound people as the audience. That has to be taken into consideration as we read the texts in new, quite different circumstances. But the Bible is also a book cherished and read for instruction and guidance by three different religious communities. Thus, considerable theological "translation" is required!

The reading of the Bible, then, is marked by several assumptions that should be noted. On the one hand, while "spiritualizing" (e.g., "land" doesn't really refer to "dirt" or "earthly territory" but rather to "heaven" or some other spiritual sphere) has had a long history among Christian interpreters, Presbyterians, following Reformation insights, have preferred to emphasize what we call the "plain sense" or the "literal" meaning of texts. Thus, the "land" promised to Abram and Sarai is not understood in the first instance as signifying some spiritual sphere called heaven. No, it refers to a real, historical, earthly part of the land of Canaan. On the other hand, simply identifying "the land of Canaan" as the "West Bank" and/or "Judea and Samaria" with Nablus designated as "Shechem" ignores a great deal of history and makes theological, as well as political, claims that must be considered. Presbyterians (at least in terms of policy) acknowledge that interpretation is always affected by theology and thus it is important to recognize our theological assumptions.

There is no attempt here to consider the extensive extrabiblical sources (especially the Talmud, the contribution of Jewish sages, and the writings of the early Church) now available to Jews and Christians that, in some places, have clear bearing on the topic. This is not a value judgment concerning that literature, but an honest acknowledgement of the limits of this writer. These remarks reflect primarily on the Bible as their primary source.

Land

At least one matter seems quite clear in the Bible, namely the conviction that "the earth is the Lord's and all that is in it, the world, and those who live in it" (Psalm 24:1). Genesis 1 and 2 attest to the creative power of God (see Psalm 33:6–9; 89:9–13; 104:1–35; Proverbs 8:22–31; John 1:1–5; Hebrews 11:3). This claim is not debated in the First or Second Testament. It is announced. Then it is reinforced by texts that suggest that "in the end" God may create a "new heaven" and a "new earth," solely the right of an owner, in order to accomplish divine intentions (see Isaiah 65:17; 66:22; Revelation 21:1–5). This is a theological assertion that many in the modern world do not accept.

No one but God has everlasting ownership of land in this earth. The jubilee year eloquently attests this conviction. Every fifty years the jubilee year was to be observed as a Sabbath for seven "weeks of years" (Leviticus 25:8). At that time, original property distributions made when Israel entered into the land of Canaan were to be restored (see v. 13). No Israelite family would be allowed to fall into perpetual servitude. Property rendered in payment of debt was to be returned, and any land or any individual Israelite sold into slavery in payment of debts was to be released (see vv. 28, 31, 41).

Whether the year of jubilee was ever observed is debated (see Jeremiah 34:1ff), but the ideal expressed is clear. Because God owns the land, the Israelites were *never more* than caretakers. They were not free to do whatever they wished with the land because it was only in their keeping. At the same time, they were *no less* than caretakers either, because the land was entrusted to them for safekeeping, a grave responsibility and an encouragement to deal justly with one another and care for land as the holy people they were chosen to be (see Exodus 19:6).

A brief aside is probably in order here. The term "Holy Land" is widely used by many Christians (and a few Jews) in reference to the territory currently occupied by modern Israel. When Christians use the term, they generally think of only a small portion of the land: namely Bethlehem, Nazareth, the area around the Sea of Galilee, and parts of Jerusalem. When Jews use the term, I think, they have in mind a much larger area that includes Hebron, Shechem, Jericho, Bethel, Beersheba, or, in other words, the whole territory through which, according to Genesis, Abraham and Sarah traveled. For many Christians, the term "the Holy Land" is, in their thinking, a religious way of talking about the land that enables them to ignore, or at least avoid dealing with, the reality of modern Israel as a geopolitical reality.

To my knowledge, in the Bible the term "holy land" is found only once in a vision reported by Zechariah: "The LORD will inherit Judah as his portion in the holy land, and will again choose Jerusalem" (Zechariah 2:12). Most other uses of the term *holy* in connection to places are in reference to particular sites in Jerusalem associated with Mount Zion and the Temple (see Isaiah 52:1; Nehemiah 11:1, 18; Psalm 2:6; 3:4; 15:1, Joel 3:17; 1 Kings 6:16; 8:6). "Land" or "ground" may become "holy" because of the divine presence (see Exodus 3:5). Otherwise, rather than "holy land," the term "holy people" is much more in order. Because of the divine holiness, Israel was enjoined to be a holy people by keeping the commandments entrusted to them (see Leviticus 19:2ff; cf. 1 Peter 1:15–16). In my opinion, the current use among many Christians of the term "Holy Land" is one more instance of our age-old tendency to "spiritualize" matters that were/are quite concrete and "earthy" and thereby often somewhat messy.

The Land

If our discussion were to stay centered on the divine ownership of the earth, general agreement might be more readily achieved, but, of course, that is not our primary concern. What is more to the point for us, I think, is the relationship between "land" and "the land"—or, more directly, what one is to make of *eretz Yisrael,* the land of Israel.

The decision by those who established modern Israel to name it *eretz Yisrael* clearly reflected traditional Jewish reference and served to claim the legacy of ancient Israel for the modern state. But the term *eretz Yisrael* occurs but infrequently in the Bible (see 1 Samuel 13:19; Ezekiel 40:2; 47:18; 1 Chronicles 22:2; 2 Chronicles 2:17; 34:7), and then somewhat vaguely in terms of exact reference. So what are we to make of it?

Outside of the Talmud and later Jewish writings where the term *eretz Yisrael* occurs regularly, two other terms have been more often employed in reference to the territory now occupied by the modern state of Israel: the "land of Canaan" and "Palestine." The first term is that most used in the First Testament (see Genesis 11:31; 12:5; 17:8; Exodus 6:4; Leviticus 25:38; Joshua 5:12; 14:1; and many more). Sometimes the "land of Canaan" was subdivided into specific peoples said to occupy it: "the Kenites, the Kenizzites, the Kadmonites, the Hittites, the Perizzites, the Rephaim, the Amorites, the Canaanites, the Girgashites, and the Jebusites" (Genesis 15:19–21; and with some variation in number and order in 10:16–18; Deuteronomy 7:1; Joshua 3:10; Nehemiah 9:8).

The second term, Palestine, is derived from the term "the land of the Philistines" (Genesis 21:32, 34; Exodus 13:17). Originally, the territory thus designated consisted of five city-states located on the coastal plain: Gaza, Ashdod, Ashkelon, Gath, and Ekron. In the first century of the common era, the Romans, expressing their exasperation with and contempt for the Judeans, resurrected the ancient name "Philistia" (the Greek rendering of *Philistine*) and with variants of it (Palaestina prima, Palaestina secunda, and Palaestina tertia) renamed the whole region that now encompasses the Gaza Strip, the West Bank, Israel, large parts of Jordan, Lebanon, and most of Syria. Then, after the First World War, Great Britain again reclaimed the term *Palestine* and applied it as a name to the land under their authority west of the Jordan River, as opposed to the emirate now known as Jordan, created in 1923, on the east side of the Jordan.

But neither of these two names, the land of Canaan and Palestine, helps us make the connection between the Bible and *eretz Yisrael*. What I mean is that there was an ancient people called "Israel" that had a deep association with both the land of Canaan and Philistia. The forebears of this people traveled through the territory and believed that God promised them and their progeny at least some (perhaps all) of the land formerly occupied by the Canaanites and later the Philistines and others (see Genesis 12:1–7; 13:14–17; 15:5, 7, 18–21; 17:4–8; 26:3–4; 28:3–4, 13–15; 35:9–12; 48:21; 50:24; Exodus 3:8, 15–17; 6:3–8; Joshua 24:1–13).

There is no question that this "promised land" was central in the self-understanding that God's people developed. Long after the actual entry and "fulfillment" of the promise to Abraham and Sarah accomplished at the time of Joshua, God's faithfulness was celebrated in part by reference to this land-promise (see Psalm 105:6–11; 37–45; Nehemiah 9:7; Luke 1:54–55, 73). In the traditions of "promised land," it is essential to acknowledge the this-world character of the divine commitment. While the actualization of the promises made to Abraham and Sarah lay in the future, the land they expected was real land, territory in this world, not just a metaphorical place. For many Jews, as with most Christians, the promise across the centuries was somewhat "spiritualized," becoming to a degree a symbol of hope but not an actual expectation. But with Jews, in contrast with most Christians, the subject of the promise was understood to include a real, this-world Jerusalem where people could live and work and worship. God's promises represented an intention that the people would have a place *in this world* where they could live out their lives fully as God's people.

Unfortunately, for many Christians the land-promise was understood as a reference to a spiritual reality, such as heaven, or it was ignored altogether. For many Western Christians, the notion of a special, God-promised land was seen as an unworthy relic of a narrow, particularistic religion (namely Judaism), which they believed had been made nonessential by the more enlightened universalism of Christianity. Such a false view continues to cripple Christian thinking on land issues.

If real land is at stake, however, then borders become important, and here the Bible is less than precise. Some contemporary Jews and Christians contend that modern Israel has a right to the territory claimed at the time of Solomon's kingdom. But even if this were granted, the boundaries are not so clear. How far north did the kingdom extend? Where exactly was Dan? What about the Philistine cities on the plain that were not under Solomon's control in the tenth century B.C.E.? What about the southern border in the Negev? The phrase "from Dan to Beer-sheba" (Judges 20:1; 1 Samuel 3:20) sounds good as a boundary definition, but it leaves many unanswered questions (cf. Exodus 23:31; Numbers 34:1–12; Joshua 15:1–63; 19:40–48; 2 Samuel 24:5–7; 1 Kings 5:1–12; 9:10–14, 26; 11:5–7, 14–25). Or if the land in question is that traversed by Abraham and Sarah, just what did their travels include? Modern Syria? Egypt? Or perhaps only the land ten miles to each side of their route of travel? Thus, land, real land, may have been promised to ancient Israel, but the exact borders of that land are not clear.

There are at least two additional arguments advanced in identifying modern *eretz Yisrael* as the land promised by God to Abraham, Sarah, and their progeny. First, it is argued by some that this must be done to protect the trustworthiness of God. The integrity of God is claimed to be at stake. But the promises can be interpreted as having been kept already at the time of Israel's entry into the land of Canaan. Or, as many Christians in the second century c.e. concluded, the promises were intended for the Church anyway and not for Israel. On the other hand, some more "eschatologically" oriented Christians and Jews today contend, God's trustworthiness is still sound because these promises will surely be "fulfilled" at the end of time. If so, it seems to me, their point is moot.

The second issue is probably more important. For some, the material character of the promise of land is important testimony to the actual involvement of God in human history. But a specific set of borders and an actual government in modern Israel does not guarantee or demonstrate the relation of God to human affairs. Judaism has proven that it does not require one specific place in which to live in order to demonstrate religious integrity, vitality, and conviction. Certainly, Jerusalem has long had special significance to Jews and certain commandments can be fulfilled only there, but the authenticity of Judaism, per se, does not finally depend upon the establishment or continuation of the government of modern Israel.

Judaism prospered for nearly two thousand years without such a concrete geopolitical center. Numerous communities flourished and the richness of Judaism increased. Certainly, Jews continued to live in and near Jerusalem across the centuries from the time of the Romans to the rule of the Ottomans, though they frequently faced tremendous hardship and intermittent discrimination. Certainly, Jews from all around the world continued to yearn for Zion, liturgically and personally, and on occasion returned there from far, distant places to live once again in the place of their beginnings. And certainly, the renewed commitment and hope that modern Israel has brought to countless Jews should not be denied or underestimated. Nonetheless, Judaism has already demonstrated a resilience and authenticity that bodes well for its continuation no matter what may happen in the course of human affairs.

What is required for the material character of the divine promise to be realized, it seems to me, is a concrete place in a real world where decision is called for and righteousness and justice can be practiced. To affirm this is to acknowledge the significance of a land-promise without using it to justify the political claims for autonomy over a particular territory by any group. Political autonomy may certainly assist in ensuring this possibility, but it is not absolutely required. The goal is for every group to have a secure place in which to practice its religion and enjoy the opportunity for a fulfilling life.

The State of Israel

The significance of the modern state of Israel is crucial to consider. I am certain that in the course of our consultation we will have much to say to one another on this subject. Here I intend to register some basic convictions about modern Israel that are related, at least indirectly, to what has been said thus far about "land" and "the land."

First, the modern state Israel is not to be simply equated with the territory or people of ancient Israel any more than Iran should be identified as a direct continuation of ancient Persia, or Italy the reestablishment of the Roman Empire. Modern Israel was named with some intention of claiming that it was the rightful reconstitution in Palestine of a long-absent people. And modern Israel is situated on land once occupied by another Israel. But that does not mean modern Israel is that biblical people. Modern Israel was created, at least in part, to provide a much-needed haven for Jews and a place where Judaism could be lived without hindrance. Nonetheless, modern Israel is not biblical Israel, and any "rights" held by biblical Israel do not automatically transfer to modern Israel.

Second, if modern Israel is not to be equated with ancient Israel, neither is the Church! For centuries, Christian doctrine has asserted that Christianity replaced, or superseded, Judaism and became God's Israel (e.g., Galatians 6:16). Because the Jews rejected Jesus, supersessionism has claimed, God rejected the Jews and put the Church in its place. Now, the oppression, discrimination, injustice, and evildoing that this teaching has been used to justify is well-known to all here (though it is still denied as "actual" by some Christians and non-Christians).

The Presbyterian Church (U.S.A.) has been on record since 1987 as disavowing this teaching and has tried diligently to make certain that our curricula, for instance, do not transmit this terrible, deadly virus. New insights into the formative history of both Christianity and Judaism following the destruction of the Temple in 70 C.E. have led to a new understanding. Consultations such as ours have required a rethinking of old, well-ensconced beliefs that are simply wrong. We are changing our worldview in many ways. Progress is slow, but I think we are making headway. It may not sound important to some, but it is critical that Christians recognize that they are not God's Israel in any singular sense and that we, at best, share a heritage with Judaism to the promises made to ancient, biblical Israel.

Third, modern Israel has every right to political autonomy that includes the right of self-defense with secure, internationally recognized borders. The United Nations authorized and recognized Israel as a nation with all the rights and obligations thereby attendant. There should be no debate on this issue. But some Christians and Jews go further and attribute the creation of modern Israel directly to God. They see the creation of the nation as an ingathering of the Diaspora and thus as a "fulfillment of prophecy." Some use such scriptural references as a way to validate the existence of modern Israel, as if it needed such sanction. These texts, however, are usually taken out of their literary and historical contexts and understood as "predictions," ignoring the fact that they were words of accusation and hope directed to audiences of real people several thousand years ago. They were not secret messages that only some distant generation would finally be able to "decode." Many such Christians see the return of the "Jews" to modern Israel as a sign of the imminent end of the world. For them, modern Israel is merely a means to an end, namely their own "rescue" from this world. The Presbyterian Church (U.S.A.) does not endorse this theology, but there are certainly large numbers of individual Presbyterians who have accepted this position uncritically.

Fourth, though not the result of direct divine intervention, the existence of modern Israel has provoked much reflection. By declaring itself a "Jewish nation" modern Israel raises the issue of spiritual or religious significance. For some Christians, this must be carefully unpacked. Modern Israel is a real, concrete, national entity located in a particular, geographically specific place in this world. For some Christians, this must be emphasized, because for centuries we have expressed theologically a preference for things "spiritual" and "universal" over things "material" and "particular." Thus, for some Christians, "things Jewish," including modern Israel, are, in principle, inferior and of little significance.

But for many Jews the reality of modern Israel has a great spiritual importance precisely because of its particularity. Modern Israel offers, for the religious, a place where all the commandments can be followed and, for all its citizens, the promise of justice as called for in the Bible. In a world where anti-Jewish attitudes continue to thrive and wreck havoc, modern Israel offers the possibility of a safe haven, whether used or not. What's more, by claiming at least in part a religious dimension, modern Israel has taken on the burden and the glory of pointing beyond itself as a light for others to a divine spiritual significance to be found in the affairs of this world. In its own right, then, modern Israel has true significance.

Finally, is modern Israel's land God-given? There are some Christians and many Jews who answer this question in the affirmative. In support of such an assertion, a long list of biblical passages can be put forward. These passages, however, seem to me to fall into three categories:

1. texts "fulfilled" with the entry of ancient Israel into the land of Canaan (Genesis, Exodus, Joshua);
2. texts "fulfilled" by the return of the Babylonian exiles to Judea (Isaiah, Jeremiah, Haggai, Zechariah);

3. passages referring to the end time that can be "fulfilled" only by the appearance of a new heaven and earth (Isaiah, Ezekiel, Joel, Daniel, Revelation).

None of these texts, in my opinion, support land claims now. Because God may have granted land in the past does not mean that modern Israel, on that basis, has a legal justification for occupying the land now. It seems to me that the founders of modern Israel acknowledged this by intentionally buying land. While today, for the religious, some divine right to the land might seem obvious, the founders knew that in the courts of law such claims would be insufficient. Of course, Israel does have rightful claim on much of its territory because that was granted by the United Nations and that should be totally honored. Changes in that original territory should be negotiated as necessary under the universally recognized principles of international law.

Land Rights and Responsibilities

The issue of land rights is central to many who live in or are concerned about the Middle East and especially modern Israel. Who has a "right" to be there? How shall land rights be determined? Is there such a thing as a "moral" claim on the land based on historical connection to the land? When do the interests and needs of a community supersede individual claims? What shall be done to compensate for land taken as a result of war? Who will determine fairness and justice? How long should these concerns remain unresolved?

We have already acknowledged the concept of "promised land" and have denied such a tradition as a basis for legal claims in the modern era. In fact, the Bible does not answer most of our pressing land questions directly. It does, however, offer a framework that can assist those constrained to deal with land issues. But it must be admitted that the biblical perspective is disturbing to many because it places much greater emphasis on land responsibilities than on land rights. Where we might want boundaries, we are given obligations.

The Bible stresses that ancient Israel was *given* the land. Deuteronomy makes this especially clear. While the promise of land is explicit (see 6:23; 7:8; 8:1), the emphasis is on the utter graciousness of the divine act. The people led by Moses were without merit (see 7:7; 9:5–6). The Lord showed deep regard for the people by delivering them from Egypt and by guiding them into a rich land (see 6:10–11; 7:19; 8:7–10). Even though the people were stubborn and rebellious, God's graciousness prevailed (see 8:15–16; 9:6–14).

A corollary to God's giving the land to Israel is God's expelling of the prior occupants. Some, particularly some Christians, find this unfair, but the matter is expressed in moral terms difficult to ignore. Though there are military "victories" recounted (see Joshua 11:23; 12:7), the emphasis remains on God giving the land (see Joshua 1:2; 2:9, 24; 8:1). In Deuteronomy the responsibility for removing the Canaanites belonged to God (see 7:1, 17–21; 8:17–18). The reason? The wicked behavior of the Canaanites (7:23–26; 9:4–5)! What's more, Deuteronomy warned, if the Israelites disobeyed the Almighty as had the Canaanites, they too would be punished and perish (8:11–20). To keep the land, the Israelites were expected to keep God's commandments (see 4:25–26; 30:15–20; cf. Leviticus 18:2–5; 20:22–26; 26:27–33; Joshua 23:6–13; 1 Kings 9:6–9).

The rules regulating life in the land were varied, extensive, and detailed. They governed ritual, lending and commerce, family matters, warfare, relations between the rich and the poor, treatment of captives and slaves, and many more aspects of life with the aim of establishing a society pleasing to God. The essence of these commandments can be stated as serving one God loyally and humbly and working for justice and compassion within the human community (see Deuteronomy 10:12–22; Micah 6:8). Jesus was remembered as having summed up the law and commandments in much the same way (see Matthew 22:34–40; Mark 12:28–34; Luke 10:25–28).

From the biblical perspective, therefore, land rights are quite subordinate to land responsibilities. Ancient Israel displaced the former inhabitants of the land because the Canaanites had lived in ways inappropriate before God. Israel had no right to the land as such, though a promise had been given. The divine promise did not title Israel to Canaan, but rather called for obedient living in expectation that God would eventually provide a proper inheritance for God's people. Life in the land for Israel was explicitly contingent upon allegiance to God and the faithful, loving establishment of justice and peace within the community.

The message of the passages about the land, it seems to me, is that ancient Israel was given stewardship of the land. Occupation and responsible action were inseparably bound. A place was graciously provided for Israel to develop a community that could show the world what God intended for humanity. God's aim was not to make a perpetual land grant but to offer a place for a society to emerge in which God's way was paramount.

Many Jews admit that a special land today may not be absolutely essential for faithful Jewish living. Nonetheless, it is only in a place of safety, where the social structure can be arranged to allow a rigorous pursuit of the ordinances, that the full possibilities can be realized. This does not mean that Jews must be allowed a land at the expense of others, but it does help explain the special regard that most Jews hold for modern Israel. The full possibilities for justice can be realized only in a community that controls its own space. The full possibilities of faithfulness before God, therefore, can be demonstrated only when choices are freely made and policies appropriately established.

From a biblical perspective, then, life before God always involves human community, and human community always involves specific space (i.e., land) where community life can be ordered and experienced. Too many Christians, particularly in the West, disdain or disregard the significance of the reality that we are flesh. They become susceptible to an individualized, privatized, spiritualized form of Christianity that is quite alien to the biblical tradition, with its insistence upon land, incarnation, corporeality, and God's concern for the whole of creation, the world in all its concreteness.

The Presbyterian Church (U.S.A.) has sought to review the policies and actions of the United States, first of all, and those of other governments as well, with such considerations in mind. We have often been most critical of those we consider to be in the best position to work out the claims for justice. While modern Israel is the focus in this paper, the Palestinian Authority, now under the leadership of Hamas, is no less responsible for its use of land. The PA has no automatic guarantee of autonomy that disregards the requirements of justice and peace within its own borders and with its neighbors, including modern Israel. Difficult times in the past do not justify irresponsible, immoral, unjust action in the present on the part of any government.

Summary Remarks

Reflection upon land as based upon the Bible begins with a basic premise: God is creator of all and thus "owns" the world. As Creator, God has a rightful claim on earth, a claim that no individual or government can appropriate or invalidate. As Creator, God can and has set the rules and intends that human beings will respect and live within them. Earth is to be responsibly tended as a luxurious garden for the benefit of the whole human family. Earth is not to be exploited by or for anyone. Earth, God's good land, has been placed in human hands by a loving Creator who desires that all live in harmony and prosperity—that is, in *shalom,* in peace.

In itself, earth is not holy or sacred. The earth is God's creation; God alone is holy. God, not the earth, is to be worshiped. Similarly, human beings are God's creatures and in no way divine. Certain places may be regarded as holy because God's interaction with humankind is commemorated there, but this is only a functional sacredness and not absolute.

That the earth is not holy does not mean it is valueless. Quite the contrary! The earth has been assigned to humankind as a sacred trust. Each human and every human community is responsible to exercise responsible care for the earth. Israel and all the other nations in the Middle East are set under the same mandate by God to care for the land, for earth. Likewise, and even more urgently because of their size and capacity to affect the environment, the wealthiest industrialized nations—the United States, Germany, Japan, and others—are responsible to God. Humans are to care for planet Earth! Water, air, and soil are to be shared and enjoyed, not hoarded, polluted, used wastefully, or used for the advantage of one over another.

The opening chapters of Genesis are not about Israel alone but about humanity and the larger creation to which all humans belong. From the standpoint of Genesis, all humans have the same God, the only God of the universe, as their Creator, whether they acknowledge this or not. The affirmation that God, the God of the Bible, is creator of all is fundamental. Each individual and each group needs land, a part of the earth, for support and development. In the Bible, God is described as allocating land for each of the peoples of earth. Such a notion becomes hopelessly complex if literally applied within the modern context. But the point is clear: Land is essential for humans to have a full life.

The difficulty comes, obviously, when the needs and claims of one person or group conflict with the needs and claims of another. Within modern Israel, for instance, conflicting claims have created great tension and strife. The same is true in Ireland, Bosnia, Azerbaijan, and between some communities within the United States. While it is convenient to claim a God-given right to land, such a claim is invalid unless it includes the conviction that others have the same God-given right to land. The tradition of God's land allotment cannot, it seems to me, be used to settle boundary disputes. The tradition asserts only God's fundamental intention that all people should have a land, a place, in which to live freely and fully.

The residents of modern Israel have a right to a secure land in which to live and develop their culture. Their rights are no greater than those of others, but they are real and justified. Israelis do not have a divine right to any land, however, unless it is understood that all peoples have such rights. The needs and dreams of each person and group are at stake when anyone is deprived unjustly. While the recognition of God's intention that all have a secure place to live is not easily actualized, earth's caretakers cannot rest until just solutions are found and implemented.

Christians have for the most part recognized that human beings have been given freedom and responsibility. Humans are not choice-less puppets, automatons programmed for unthinking, uncaring, irresponsible existence. Rather, human beings have been created with the capacity to discern and to choose better over worse. We don't always do what we are capable of doing, but we are not invariably bound to make wrong choices either. God desires justice among peoples so that all may prosper in peace. We must continue to remind ourselves, and others, that the earth belongs to God and that we are expected to be careful, generous, just, respectful caretakers of God's precious world.

Land as Divine Gift and Human Responsibility: Response to Eugene March

Vernon Kurtz

Abraham Halkin, in an essay titled "Zion in Biblical Literature," has written:

> It is hardly an exaggeration to assert that Zion is the central theme of the Bible. From the moment that God instructed Abraham, 'Go forth from your land,' the Holy Land became the subject along with the people of Israel.

For the Jewish people of today, this statement rings true. We may have been exiled from the Land, but we have never forgotten its place in our religious system.

W. D. Davies, a professor of Christian origins at Duke University, in his book *The Territorial Dimension of Judaism* has written:

> The promise to Abraham was so reinterpreted from age-to-age that it became a living power in the life of the people of Israel. Not the mode of its origin matters, but its operation as the formative, dynamic, seminal force in the history of Israel. The legend of the promise was so deeply entrenched in the experience of the Jews that it acquired its own reality.

Davies discusses in his book the manner in which the attachment of the Jews to the Land has penetrated all aspects of Jewish life. "It cannot properly be seen," he writes, "except through Jewish eyes, not felt except through Jewish words."

I want to thank the Rev. Dr. March for his paper. It is fair, it is concise, and it creates a paradigm of discussion for the difference between "land" and "the Land." I had the opportunity to gain access to his book *Israel and the Politics of Land,* which I enjoyed greatly. His learned reflections in his paper are really a summary of the message of his book. The book, however, also goes into the realities of history and discusses modern Zionism and the modern history of the State of Israel. The book also spends some time on what the Rev. March terms "Earth-keeping." This concept—which the Israelites, and, in fact, all humanity, have a responsibility to uphold—reflects the fact that the land is a gift from God to all of humanity and we have a responsibility to care for it. Thus, modern ecology, land preservation, water preservation, concerns for our climate, and environmental policies can be seen as a religious imperative not only for the Israelite people of old, but, I would suggest, for all of us who attempt to follow God's word.

My problem with Dr. March's paper is that it ends with the Bible. Judaism is not the religion of the Bible. It is the religion of the Bible as interpreted by the rabbis. It is very difficult to separate what we term the Written Law from the Oral Law. However we understand the origins of revelation and however we might comprehend rabbinic commentaries on it, it is impossible to separate one from the other. Thus, the biblical promise of the Land should be seen, as suggested by Davies, through Jewish eyes but as understood by rabbinic interpretations.

It is the attachment to the *Land* that has made us turn to Zion no matter where we may have lived. Our religious calendar follows it, our prayers talk of our return to Zion, and our rituals bespeak a longing for the Holy Land. It is that same spirit that informs the Zionist movement of modern times. Though Zionism, as has been claimed, may be a break from the Jewish history of exile and dispersion, it is, at the very same time, a continuation of the Jewish tie to the Land. When Theodor Herzl, who believed in the need to solve the Jewish problem by the establishment of a state for the Jews, recommended that Uganda would serve the purpose as well, he was overruled. The continuous presence of Jewish religious tradition, with its concentration on the Land of Israel, made the choice for the locale of the Jewish homeland inevitable. As Davies writes, "The Land is ultimately inseparable from the State of Israel, however much the actualities of history have demanded their distinction."

It is true that the difference between the concept of the Land and modern realities of the Land is uncertain and in some ways controversial. It is true that one cannot and should not dictate the borders of the Land from the biblical story. It is true that it is the responsibility of the modern state of Israel to care for its minority populations and to express in action the biblical attitudes of respect for the stranger, concern for the welfare of all humanity, and justice and equality for all. It is true that the ancient Israelites and the modern Jew have responsibilities for the stewardship of the Land. And it is true that modern politics cannot always be dictated by ancient texts.

However, to end the story of attachment of the Jewish people to the Land with the Bible is simply unfair. It is essential to look at all of Jewish history from its religious practices to its cultural ones, from its liturgy to its legal sources, from its legends to its poetry. There, we can see that its attachment to the Land conveys much more than a simple promise in an ancient book and is a living, vibrant, and essential part of our covenant with God. I appreciate Dr. March's concern with the fate of the Jewish people in modern times and the need for them to have a place of their own. I understand the difficulty of the leap from a Balfour Declaration to a United Nations resolution from a biblical mandate. However, it is essential to look at past aspects of that long history that the Jewish people had with the Land and not simply cut the tie at the end of the biblical era.

Walter Brueggemann, professor of Old Testament at Columbia Theological Seminary writes in his book *The Land:*

> It is clear that, since the recent wars of the State of Israel, Christians cannot speak seriously to Jews unless the acknowledged Land can be the central agenda. While the Arabs surely have rights and legitimate grievances, the Jewish people are peculiarly the pained voice of the land in the history of humanity, grieved Rachel's weeping. And unless we address the land question with Jews, we shall not likely understand the locus of meaning or the issue of identity. The Jewish Community in all its long, tortuous history has never forgotten that its roots and its hopes are in storied earth, and that is the central driving force of its uncompromisingly ethical faith.

Land, the Land, and the modern State of Israel are inextricably tied together for the Jewish people. I understand, based on his Christian faith and biblical scholarship, that Dr. March is careful not to make a continuum from one to another. However, as expressed in the words of Ecclesiastes 4:12, "A threefold cord is not readily broken." It is impossible to address the Jewish people of today without understanding their attachment to the Land, its promise, and its reality. It is impossible to understand Jewish identity today without comprehending the tie of the Jewish people to the modern State of Israel. It is impossible to truly have a religious dialogue with Jews today without appreciating their concern, their love, and their attachment to *eretz Yisrael,* the Land of Israel, and *Medinat Yisrael,* the State of Israel.

The Historical, Theological, Liturgical Significance of *Eretz Yisrael*

Reuven Hammer

In the month of May, Jews throughout the world gather in synagogues to celebrate the newest holiday of the Jewish year, Yom Ha-Atzmaut, Israel Independence Day. More than sixty years after the founding of the Jewish state, the first independent Jewish state to exist in nearly two thousand years, the Hebrew date of 5 Iyar has found its place together with such holidays as Purim and Hanukkah on the religious calendar of Judaism and has been given liturgical expression in our prayer books. This fact alone says volumes about the historical, theological, and liturgical significance of *eretz Yisrael*.

True, a distinction is to be made between *eretz Yisrael*—the Land of Israel—and *Medinat Yisrael*—the State of Israel. The state is a secular-political entity that is a creation brought about by the Zionist movement through the offices of the United Nations. It is, nevertheless, the modern embodiment of Jewish sovereignty (even though not all its citizens are Jews and not all Jews are its citizens) and as such is the inheritor of the status of the ancient kingdoms of Israel and Judah and then of the postexilic State of Judea. The Land of Israel, on the other hand, is a geographic designation, the exact borders of which are difficult if not impossible to define since there are different definitions found in Scripture. It has theological implications in that it is the land promised by God to the descendants of Abraham, Isaac, and Jacob. Certain religious obligations exist only within it, and it has the status of holiness both according to Scripture and to rabbinic tradition. The Mishnah, for example, speaks of "ten degrees of holiness," for "the Land of Israel is holier than all other lands" (*Kelim* 1:6). Of course, the holiest of them all is the Holy of Holies within the Temple (*Kelim* 1:9).

There is no holiness to the state as a political entity; therefore, theoretically it would seem that there is no religious significance to the state. Nevertheless, in the perception of most Jews, these distinctions are—to put it mildly—blurred if they exist at all. Yom Ha-Atzmaut, after all, celebrates the creation of the state—within the Land. Thus Moshe Greenberg, one of the most distinguished Jewish biblical scholars, writes:

> As the sole political entity created by the combined and concentrated efforts of the Jewish people, the State of Israel is willy-nilly the most salient achievement of the Jewish people in our time . . . Jews in Israel and outside it share, then, the estimate of the state as somehow expressing the essence of the Jewish people. Jewish identity is inextricably bound up with the state. This is a new thing in the history of Jews and Judaism . . . Indeed one may play with the notion that for the health of Judaism the state is dangerous.[1]

Greenberg recognizes at one and the same time that a person cannot equate Judaism with any political entity and yet that the two are today inextricably intertwined.

Abraham Joshua Heschel, surely one of the most important theological figures—Jew or Christian—of the twentieth century, wrote an entire book about the state, *Israel: An Echo of Eternity*. The title says it all. He wrote there:

> What is the meaning of the State of Israel? *Its sheer being is the message.* The life in the land of Israel today is a rehearsal, a test, a challenge to all of us. Not living in the land, nonparticipation in the drama, is a source of embarrassment. The ultimate meaning of the State of Israel must be seen in terms of the vision of the prophets: the redemption of all men. The religious duty of the Jew is to participate in the process of continuous redemption, in seeing that justice prevails over power, that awareness of God penetrates human understanding.[2]

Therefore, although there is a definite distinction between the two—state and land—and from now on I will speak only of the land, it is obvious that for the Jewish people today the state has a status more important than a mere political entity. And although the state can be challenged and criticized, since as a human creation it can be wrong, as were the rulers of the ancient states of Israel and Judah, its existence is nevertheless crucial to Jews and Judaism.

For many Jews, including many Zionist thinkers, the raison d'être for the creation of the state includes the need for a place of refuge, a place to escape anti-Semitism (even long before the Holocaust). But for some it also includes the need for a place in which Judaism and Jewish culture would be the majority culture, thus strengthening Judaism and Jewish communities throughout the world. In some cases, this also includes a religious—almost messianic—vision as we see in these quotations from two early Zionist leaders at the beginning of the twentieth century in America:

> The rebirth of Israel's national consciousness, and the revival of Israel's religion, or, to use a shorter term, the revival of Judaism are inseparable . . . The selection of Israel, the indestructibility of God's covenant with Israel, the immortality of Israel as a nation, and the final restoration of Israel to Palestine, where the nation will live a holy life on holy ground, with all the wide-reaching consequences of the conversion of humanity and the establishment of the Kingdom of God on earth—all these are the common ideals and common ideas that permeate the whole of Jewish literature . . . History may, and to my belief, will repeat itself, and Israel will be the chosen instrument of God for the new and final mission; but then Israel must first influence its own redemption and live again its own life, and be Israel again, to accomplish its universal mission. . . . "Out of Zion shall go forth the law and the word of the Lord from Jerusalem."
> —Solomon Schechter

> Palestine is the land of Promise not only to the Jew but to the entire world—the promise of a higher and better social order.
> Upon the gates of the Third Jewish Commonwealth will be inscribed the same prophetic words which greeted the establishment of the Second Jewish Commonwealth:
> "Not by might, nor by power,
> But by My spirit, saith the Lord of Hosts."
> —Israel Friedlander

In this approach, these thinkers come close to what I believe to be the biblical view of the importance of the land, seeing it neither in terms of how it benefits other Jewries nor as a physical haven for Jews in danger, but in terms of its intrinsic value. The Torah envisions the creation of the kingdom of God in the land as a necessary component of the fulfillment of God's divine plan. This is a utopian, not a utilitarian, concept in which Jewish sovereignty in the land becomes an end in itself.

To begin with, the story of the book of Genesis is the story of God in search of a people that will be His people and actualize His will on earth. It begins with the search for an individual. The first to be chosen is Noah, but his descendants disappoint and again one person is singled out for the task: Abraham. "I have known him so that he may command his children and his household after him, and they shall keep the way of the Lord, to do justice and judgment" (Genesis 18:19). This is then passed on through Isaac and his son Jacob, after whom all Jacob's progeny become the bearers of this promise and this task, becoming a people—the children of Israel (Jacob), the people Israel. The task assigned to that people is reiterated over and over again in the Torah and is best summarized in the prologue to the Decalogue itself: "If you will obey My voice and keep My covenant, you shall be My particular treasure from among all the peoples, though all the earth is Mine. And you shall be unto Me a kingdom of priests and a holy nation" (Exodus 19:5–6). The ultimate purpose of this was enunciated clearly by Isaiah: "On that day shall Israel be the third, with Egypt and Assyria, a blessing in the midst of the earth. For the Lord of hosts will bless them, saying, 'Blessed be My people Egypt, and Assyria the work of My hands, and My heritage Israel' " (19:24–25).

The land is an integral part of this promise. Without the land they will not be able to fulfill their task. The greatest punishment that can be envisioned for the people is to be driven from the land (see Deuteronomy 28:36ff). The Sages put it as strongly as possible when they said, "Dwelling in the Land of Israel is equivalent to observing all of the Torah's commandments" (*Sifre* Deuteronomy 80).

An analysis of the Torah, Israel's constitution, shows that the narrative of the Torah is basically the story of how Israel got to the land and what they were to do there. It is entirely the story of a journey. Take away the chapters that deal with getting to the land and you would have a brief book, ending with Genesis 11. According to Judaism's most authoritative traditional commentator, Rashi, even those chapters were included only to indicate that, as the Creator of the world, God had the right and the power to allocate the land of Canaan to whomever He wanted!

The granting of the land is not simply the gift of a place to live. As Amos points out (see 9:7), God has taken other nations out of captivity and given them lands. In the case of Israel, the land is there as a place in which they can live according to the terms of the covenant and actualize the commands that God gives to them. The grant of the land is, in fact, conditional, upon following God's ways. The confession made upon the first fruits (see Deuteronomy 26) makes it clear that the fulfillment of the covenant occurs when one has the fruit of the land in hand. As Heschel wrote, "To abandon the land would be to repudiate the Bible."[3] The extreme position on this matter is the rabbinic saying (*Sifre* Deuteronomy 43) that when exiled "you are to continue to observe the commandments *so that when you return they will not be new to you.*"

Just as the Torah is unfathomable without the emphasis on the land and its meaning, so Jewish prayer is incomprehensible without an acknowledgment of the centrality of the land. Judaism's basic prayer, known in Hebrew as the *Amidah,* recited at each service, three times a day, more on holy days, is a prayer for the restoration of life and sovereignty in the land. In it, we recite such phrases as: "return to Your city, Jerusalem," "sound the great shofar for our freedom," and "gather us together from the four corners of the earth." At the conclusion of Yom Kippur and the Passover Seder, we recite, "Next year in Jerusalem." At a wedding, we break a glass and recite, "If I forget you, O Jerusalem, may my right hand lose its cunning."

The centrality of Israel, then, lies primarily not in providing a safe place for Jews but in being the focus for the realization of the Torah's ultimate goal, as reiterated by the prophets and reaffirmed in rabbinic literature: God has found this people and appointed them His people, and they will be able to fully fulfill His will only in the land, the end result of which will be the establishment of the Sovereignty of God on earth.

James Carroll, the Catholic author of *Constantine's Sword,* recently wrote a column in the *Boston Globe* (*International Herald Tribune,* April 4, 2006) in which he briefly traced Christianity's historic attitude toward Jewish settlement in the Land of Israel. He wrote, "Christian theology . . . required the exile of Jews from the Holy Land precisely as a proof of religious claims." Augustine, he continues, argued that Jews must be scattered throughout the world to give witness that Jesus fulfilled the ancient promises. This evolved into an understanding of exile as punishment for Jewish rejection of Christian claims. He points out that Pope Pius X replied to Theodor Herzl, who asked for support for Zionism: "If you come to Palestine and settle your people there, we will be ready with churches and priests to baptize all of you." How different this is from the Church's recent actions and statements, as demonstrated by the visit of John Paul II to Jerusalem and the Western Wall. Nevertheless, Carroll concludes with this warning,

> "Contempt for Jews and Judaism is ancient. Such impossible threads weave invisibly through attempts to reckon with Israel's dilemma, forming a rope that trips up the well-intentioned and the unaware, even as others use it, as so often before, to fashion a noose."

It should be noted that several Christian theologians have written with understanding about the importance of the land to Judaism. Perhaps no one better than Walter Brueggemann in *The Land:*

> The land for which Israel yearns and which it remembers is never unclaimed space but always *a place with Yahweh,* a place well filled with memories of life with him and promise from him and vows to him. It is land that provides the central assurance to Israel of its historicity, that it will be and always must be concerned with actual rootage in

a place which is a repository for commitment and therefore identity. Biblical faith is surely about the life of a people with God as has been shown by all the current and recent emphases on covenant in an historical place. And if God has to do with Israel in a special way, as he surely does, he has to do with land as an historical place in a special way. It will no longer do to speak about Yahweh and his people but we must speak about Yahweh and his people *and his land*.[4]

In the post-Emancipation days of the 1800s, there were attempts by certain Jewish groups, eager to establish citizenship and equality for Jews in Western Europe, to reinterpret Judaism in such a way as to eliminate the place of the land within Judaism. Slogans such as "Berlin is our Jerusalem" were coined. Zion was eliminated from the prayers. The irony of these misguided reformations is bitter and obvious. The centrality of the land to Jewish belief has been restored and with it the responsibility of those who live there, those who govern there, and those who look to it to make certain that its meaning and its promise are fulfilled. It is vital that Christians understand and appreciate this as well and see the Return to Zion as a normative and positive part of Judaism.

In conclusion, I cite a poem by Judah Halevi, a medieval poet and theologian (1075–1141), who expressed in many of his writings the feelings of Jews throughout the ages for the land of Israel. Living in Spain at the height of the Golden Age of Spanish Jewry, he nevertheless longed for the land:

> My heart's in the east and I languish on the margins of the west.
> > How taste or savor what I eat?
> How fulfil my vows and pledges while Zion
> Is shackled to Edom and I am fettered to Arabia?
> I'd gladly give up all the luxuries of Spain
> If only to see the dust and rubble of the Shrine.
>
> Happy is he who waits
> And lives to behold your lights rising as dawn
> breaks over him and he sees
> your chosen prospering, and thrills
> at your joy, when you regain the vigor of youth.[5]

For Judaism, the establishment of an independent Jewish society in the land of Israel stands at the core of the message of Scripture. It is both the purpose of the Exodus and the means of fulfilling the Divine purpose. For the Jew, it is the dream that has never died and the hope that is eternally new.

1. "The Task of Masorti Judaism," in *Zionism and the Conservative Movement,* ed. John S. Ruskay and David Szonyi (New York: The Jewish Theological Seminary, 1990), pp. 137–139.
2. Abraham Joshua Heschel, *Israel: An Echo of Eternity,* pp. 224–225.
3. Heschel, p. 44.
4. Walter Brueggemann, *The Land,* pp. 5–6.
5. Judah Halevi, trans. Gabriel Levin.

The Significance of *Eretz Yisrael:* Response to Reuven Hammer

Rebecca Weaver

I would like to express my appreciation to Rabbi Hammer for his elegant and provocative paper on "The Land." His careful linkage of historical, theological, and liturgical issues calls our attention to the complexity of the matter with which we are engaged. It also serves as an oblique reminder to those of us who are Christians that our own views on the land of Israel and the state of Israel are similarly complex: Our history, our theological commitments, and our worship interpenetrate each other in ways that can render our own words and actions opaque not only to the non-Christian but also to ourselves.

To hear Rabbi Hammer's presentation is for this Christian to be confronted with two difficult questions.

First, what is meant when the Land of Israel and the State of Israel are distinguished yet at the same time considered inextricably connected? Contained within that overarching question are some subordinate questions. For example, are there two Israels being spoken of here? And are the land and the state two actual entities, or is the state an entity and the land a concept, a dream, a promise? I think that the relationship between Land and State, Israel and Israel, must be the heart of our discussion later this morning. In a moment, I shall point to several elements in Rabbi Hammer's paper that may serve as entry points for our discussion of this relationship.

There is, however, a second question that Rabbi Hammer raises for me, and for Presbyterians more generally: Why is it so difficult for those of us who are Christians to grasp your meaning? What is it in our history, our theology, and our worship that makes it so difficult for Christians, for Protestants, for Presbyterians to understand what *you* mean? Why are we so baffled? Why do I always have the feeling that in your eyes we are missing the point? By raising this second question, I want to suggest that there are aspects of Christian history, theology, and worship—certain ancient elements—that, however much we may discount them today or even be unaware of them, continue to shape Christian views on the Land of Israel and, now, on the state of Israel. I shall discuss some of these ancient elements in a moment.

First, however, let's return to Rabbi Hammer's paper and the complex relationship that he is describing between the Land of Israel and the State of Israel. To help us think about that, I want to underscore a few elements of his paper that I hope we will consider as we explore the complex relationship between Land and State that Rabbi Hammer has so beautifully described.

For example, we might find it fruitful to discuss the meaning of the "newest holiday of the Jewish year, Yom Ha-Atzmaut, Israel Independence Day." It is a holiday that, in Rabbi Hammer's words, "celebrates the creation of the state—within the Land." This sounds to me like a liturgical celebration of a secular reality, the meaning of which, for Jews, is fundamentally theological. The holiday is a marvelous illustration of the intertwining of history, theology, and liturgy about which Rabbi Hammer speaks. It is a splendid example of the complexity of the problem. For it is not at all clear that any of the three dimensions (liturgy, secular history, theology) can be extracted without the destruction—or at least the distortion—of the whole.

I think that we also might want to consider Rabbi Hammer's claim that the State of Israel "is the inheritor of the status of the ancient kingdoms of Israel and Judah and then of the postexilic State of Judea." That claim is one that many of us in the Reformed tradition (the theological tradition of Presbyterians) would have difficulty embracing, as Gene March's paper indicates. We Presbyterians would certainly grant the historical and theological significance of those ancient kingdoms, but if you are suggesting that the theological significance of those biblical kingdoms can be transferred to the State of Israel, we would have to question the basis on which such a claim can be made.

Carrying that point further, I would say that Presbyterians can certainly agree that Jews are bound in a covenantal relationship with God that requires an obedience to commandments whose ultimate purpose is the fulfillment of the divine will, the accomplishment of the divine purpose for all of humanity. But that the State of Israel has the same or similar role in the covenant as did the ancient kingdoms of Israel and Judah, that the State of Israel is necessary for the fulfillment of that obedience or the accomplishment of the divine purpose—that we simply do not understand. Help us.

Another issue to be considered: Rabbi Hammer utilizes a quotation from Moshe Greenberg that can give us all pause:

> Jewish identity is inextricably bound up with the state. This is a new thing in the history of Jews and Judaism . . . Indeed one may play with the notion that for the health of Judaism the state is dangerous.

Rabbi Hammer interprets Greenberg's statement to mean "that one cannot equate Judaism with any political entity and yet that the two are today inextricably intertwined." I take the term *Judaism* as used here to refer to a people with its Scriptures, its practices, its worship, its history. I understand Greenberg and Hammer to be saying that the Jews' sense of being a people is a complex phenomenon in which the theological cannot be isolated from the secular or political. If I have understood correctly, then, yes, the state must surely be a danger for the health of Judaism. Help us think about this.

Finally, although Rabbi Hammer attests that the State of Israel is a human creation that is appropriately subject to criticism, throughout the paper there appears to me to be an absence of differentiation between Jews scattered throughout the world and Jews who are the citizens of Israel. The result, I feel, is that any criticism that a non-Jew, a Presbyterian, might make about Israel is understood to be a criticism of all Jews. Surely, you can help us make some distinctions here.

What I have just noted is a series of questions that Rabbi Hammer's paper has raised for us. There are other issues that all of you will want to call attention to. We must attend to them.

In the time that remains to me here, however, I want to explore briefly the second large question that Rabbi Hammer's paper raised for me. That is, what is there within the heritage of Presbyterians (and perhaps of Western Christians more generally) that interferes with our ability to accept or, more fundamentally, to understand the relationship of Land and State that is self-evident to our Jewish neighbors? Perhaps just noting some of the obstacles to our understanding will be a useful start.

I think that these obstacles to Christian understanding are of two kinds. The first kind or category of obstacles has to do with issues of interpretation: interpretation of Scripture and interpretation of events. The second category has to do with evolving Christian perception and practice in relation to the land. The first category downplays the concrete, the historical; the second emphasizes the concrete, the historical. Thus, it may be that in the heritage of Christians there is a contradiction that lies at the heart of our dilemma in relation to the land of Israel.

First, there is a cluster of issues relating to the interpretation of Scripture and events. To identify these, we must go back almost two millennia.

In the second century of the Church's history, it became obvious that Christianity was not to be a sect within Judaism but a religion distinct from Judaism. The Church, predominantly Gentile by this time, had to decide what elements within Judaism were essential to the core of Christianity and what was nonessential and could be left behind.

I believe that the most important decision those second-century Christians made pertained to the Scriptures taken from Judaism. The view that prevailed was that the Scriptures (in Greek) were essential to Christian identity but that they had to be interpreted through a particular lens: the life, death, and resurrection of Jesus of Nazareth. What would come to be called the Old Testament was to be understood in its entirety as prophecy to Christ. To read all of these documents as prophecy meant, of course, that they could not necessarily be taken at face value. Often it was a nonliteral, allegorical meaning that seemed to be the Christian, thus the true, meaning.

Christians could claim that the groundwork for such a move had been laid by the apostle Paul when in his letter to the Galatians he contrasted the sons of Hagar and Sarah:

> This is an allegory: these women are two covenants. One woman . . . is Hagar, from Mount Sinai, bearing children for slavery. Now Hagar is Mount Sinai in Arabia and corresponds to the present Jerusalem, for she is in slavery with her children. But the other woman corresponds to the Jerusalem above; she is free, and she is our mother. . . . Now you, my friends, are children of the promise, like Isaac (4:24–28).

As troublesome as this passage may be, it was read as an endorsement of the allegorical interpretation of the Scriptures inherited from Israel. Through this method of interpretation, Christians could claim that they had located the true meaning of the texts, the christological interpretation.

The point that needs to be made here is that this prophetic reading of the Old Testament prevailed among many Christians into the nineteenth century when it came up against the spread of the historical-critical study of Scripture. That scientific method of studying Scripture made clear that the book really is about an ancient people who were located firmly in time and space. The historical-critical study led to the conclusion that the Old Testament, at its core, is about ancient Israel and its God.

Of course, that understanding creates a problem. If these documents can no longer be read as entirely or even primarily prophecy to Christ, what is their meaning for Christians, specifically for Presbyterians, who try to take them very, very seriously as the Word of God for Christians as well as for Jews? If the historical is made to prevail, the inevitable question becomes: Is there a theological meaning for Christians?

This could go much further. The point I would make is simply that we Presbyterians (and many other Christians) are at an awkward time in our appropriation of your text. As I was studying Rabbi Hammer's paper, I had to face up to the fact that, although the historical understanding may be necessary, it is not sufficient for us. And that conviction I, along with other Christians, have inherited from the second century. The literal is simply not the point of the Old Testament for most Christians. Nevertheless, when we do look at it literally, historically, we are led to conclude that the text refers to an ancient people, not a twenty-first-century people, as the rightful possessors of the land.

In the early fifth century, a monk by the name of John Cassian provided a telling example for the interpretation of Scriptures, particularly the Old Testament. He spoke of Scripture as having two primary levels of meaning: a historical or literal level and a spiritual level. The spiritual level had within it a variety of meanings: allegorical, anagogical, and tropological or moral. The biblical example that Cassian used to illustrate his scheme is telling for our purposes: It was simply the word *Jerusalem*. Literally or historically, Cassian argued, the word referred to the city of the Jews. Allegorically it referred to Christ and the Church, anagogically it referred to the heavenly Jerusalem, and tropologically or morally it referred to the soul. The literal or historical meaning was the least interesting to him. That meaning was available to anybody. Access to the deeper meanings of the text required spiritual growth.[1]

When Presbyterians study the Old Testament today, we do not go through any checklist of types of meaning, but our primary interest is in what the text has to say to us today. Its meaning in antiquity, what the author(s) intended, is important. Nevertheless, once a pastor or teacher has determined, to the best of his or her ability, what that historical meaning is, then the next question is: What difference does that make for Christians today? We believe, on one hand, that further interpretation must be anchored in the historical if it is to be responsible; on the other, we also believe that further interpretation is necessary. To stop with the historical is to render the text irrelevant to us. If the text has no christological meaning, no ecclesiological meaning, no moral meaning, then there is not much reason for us to bother with it. And if we don't care about it, we are going to lose our sense of affinity with you and with the land of Israel, as well.

A second issue of interpretation pertains to extrabiblical events. Here, I think that we Presbyterians run up against another difficulty. We are reluctant to interpret theologically extrabiblical events, even events today, such as the creation of the State of Israel. In this regard, I think that many of us are shaped, however unknowingly, by the skepticism of a theologian of the fifth century C.E., Augustine of Hippo Regius in North Africa. Augustine is of vast importance in the theological heritage upon which we draw.

Significantly, he was convinced that the theological meaning of extrabiblical events is not available to us. The events of Scripture are provided to us with their own divinely inspired interpretation built in, however much we have to struggle to identify and understand that interpretation. In contrast, we are not privy to the theological meaning of events outside the Bible. We must exercise a humble agnosticism in the interpretation of these events. We really do not know what God is doing with them.[2]

Perhaps even more influential than Augustine's warning is our own experience. We have learned through our own history that when Christians seek to equate or connect the fulfillment of the divine will with a particular event or political entity, whether that entity be the Roman Empire, the Holy Roman Empire, or the United States, we Christians have always been proved wrong. It is one thing to speak of the role of the biblical Israel and Judah in God's will; it is quite another to speak of the role of Roman emperors or the United States in the divine plan. We have learned that we cannot faithfully do that. Getting that concrete has never worked for us.

Thus, I must say here that we are baffled when you claim that you know what God is doing with the State of Israel in the Land of Israel. On what basis do you make this claim?

If these are some of the interpretive issues involved in our difficulty in understanding your claims, there is another side to the problem. I will treat it only briefly. It may seem to contradict all that I have just said. What I am referring to now is the historical process by which Christians, scattered over the world, came to claim as their own "Holy Land." Robert Wilken, a Roman Catholic scholar, in a wonderful book titled *The Land Called Holy* has traced the evolution of the notion of "holy land" in the early centuries of Christianity.[3]

I will sketch a brief outline here. At the heart of the Christian faith is the conviction that in Jesus of Nazareth God became flesh. Thus, however great a preference Christians have had for spiritual or allegorical interpretations of Scripture, we can never escape the historical, the concrete, the particular, the material. The material world is somehow fundamental to our understanding of God's work of salvation.

It is not at all remarkable, therefore, that Christians, from the first century C.E., have worshiped at the tombs of the martyrs and venerated the bones and relics of saints and martyrs. It was in these places, in these bones, that God acted.

In the third and fourth centuries C.E., sites of biblical history became the goal of pilgrimages by Christians. Significantly, the itineraries of Christian pilgrims included not just places that were important in the history of Jesus and the Church but also places that were important in the history of Israel. The emperor Constantine contributed significantly to the construction of churches at these locations. Thus, Christians came to venerate not just holy objects but also holy places.

This range of holy locations created the sense of holy territory or holy land—a land that Christians not only visited but also inhabited. Beginning in the late fourth century and for several centuries thereafter, the majority of the population of Palestine was Christian. Later, in medieval Europe, the notion of the holy land as property, Jesus' property, inspired Crusades.

The point that I am trying to make is that matter, the material realm, the land of ancient Israel, is part of who we are, too. Christians claim that land. We are quite willing to grant that it is your holy territory, but we will insist that it is ours as well. The foundational events of our faith took place there. We continue to go there on pilgrimage. It is crucial to our memory of who we are, as it is crucial to your memory of who you are. But there is a significant difference. From Rabbi Hammer's paper, I get the distinct impression that the land for you represents far more than memory. It represents hope. And that is a crucial difference, one that we need to explore.

Rabbi Hammer, I would like to thank you again for an elegant—and very helpful—paper.

1. John Cassian, Conference 14.8.4 ("On Spiritual Knowledge"), *The Conferences,* trans. Boniface Ramsey, O.P., Ancient Christian Writers, No. 57 (New York: Paulist Press, 1997), p. 510.
2. I am relying here on the excellent work of R. A. Markus, *Saeculum: History and Society in the Theology of St. Augustine* (Cambridge: Cambridge University Press), pp. 9–21, 157–166.
3. Robert L. Wilken, *The Land Called Holy: Palestine in Christian History and Thought* (New Haven: Yale University Press, 1992).

Evangelism

A Presbyterian Understanding of Evangelism

Robert J. Weingartner

Introduction

My assignment is to describe a Presbyterian understanding of evangelism from the perspective of one who is engaged in evangelistic work. As an ordained Presbyterian minister who pastored congregations for twenty years, I now serve as the executive director of a validated mission support group of the Presbyterian Church (U.S.A.), whose mission is "to engage Presbyterians in Christ-centered evangelistic mission for the salvation of humankind." The Outreach Foundation is an independent mission agency, but we work in a covenant relationship with the PCUSA, seeking to build the capacity of Presbyterian global church partners for their own evangelistic work.

There is disagreement among some Presbyterians today about the nature of evangelism and even the appropriateness of evangelistic activity. This disagreement exists despite substantive and coherent denominational policy statements and other evangelism-related actions by the General Assembly over the past twenty-five years. I will draw upon these statements that express well the core convictions of our Church, convictions with which I personally agree. Much of what I write will reflect themes articulated in *A Theological Understanding of the Relationship between Christians and Jews,* a document that describes contours of the challenge that Presbyterian evangelistic work poses for that relationship.[1]

Defining Evangelism

The English word *evangelism* originates in the Greek word *evangelion,* meaning "good news" or, more commonly, "gospel." A related form is the Greek word *angelos,* usually translated as "messenger" or "angel." Although no Greek word that would be translated as "evangelism" appears in the New Testament, the text is filled with references to the gospel about Jesus Christ and bearing this good news to others—e.g., announcing the gospel, proclaiming the gospel, confessing the gospel, declaring the gospel. This gospel in the New Testament is most frequently designated the "gospel of the kingdom of God." Because the word *evangelism* connotes to some a programmatic and formulaic approach to the bearing of the gospel, a number of Presbyterians have recently taken up the more dynamic term long preferred by Roman Catholic missiologists: evangelization.

The fundamentally evangelistic character of the Church's mission is evident in each of the New Testament Gospels and in all of the Pauline writings. One finds texts such as Matthew 28:18–20:

> And Jesus came and said to them, "All authority in heaven and on earth has been given to me. Go therefore and make disciples of all nations, baptizing them in the name of the Father and of the Son and of the Holy Spirit, and teaching them to obey everything that I have commanded you. And remember, I am with you always, to the end of the age."

This passage, often referred to as the Great Commission, has parallels in Mark 16:15ff and Luke 24:44–49. In the Gospel of John, Jesus also commissions his disciples, following his resurrection, to go into the world on his behalf. "Jesus said to them again, 'Peace be with you. As the Father has sent me, so I send you' " (20:21). This commission text lifts up not only the fact that the disciples are being sent but also the manner in which Jesus' followers are to go—like Jesus. But for what purpose are they sent? What is the good news, the gospel, that Jesus' disciples are called to share? And how shall the gospel be proclaimed?

An excellent Presbyterian summary of the evangelistic mission of the Church is found in Chapter 3 of the "Form of Government" in the *Book of Order,* the second volume in the *Constitution of the Presbyterian Church (U.S.A.):*

a. The Church is called to tell the good news of salvation by the grace of God through faith in Jesus Christ as the only Savior and Lord, proclaiming in Word and Sacrament that
  1. the new age has dawned.
  2. God who creates life, frees those in bondage, forgives sin, reconciles brokenness, makes all things new, is still at work in the world.

b. The Church is called to present the claims of Jesus Christ, leading persons to repentance, acceptance of him as Savior and Lord, and new life as his disciples.

c. The Church is called to be Christ's faithful evangelist
   1. going into the world, making disciples of all nations, baptizing them in the name of the Father and of the Son and of the Holy Spirit, teaching them to observe all he has commanded;
   2. demonstrating by the love of its members for one another and by the quality of its common life the new reality in Christ; sharing in worship, fellowship, and nurture, practicing a deepened life of prayer and service under the guidance of the Holy Spirit;
   3. participating in God's activity in the world through its life for others by
      (a) healing and reconciling and binding up wounds,
      (b) ministering to the needs of the poor, the sick, the lonely, and the powerless,
      (c) engaging in the struggle to free people from sin, fear, oppression, hunger, and injustice,
      (d) giving itself and its substance to the service of those who suffer,
      (e) sharing with Christ in the establishing of his just, peaceable, and loving rule in the world.

The Church is called to undertake this mission even at the risk of losing its life, trusting in God alone as the author and giver of life, sharing the gospel, and doing those deeds in the world that point beyond themselves to the new reality in Christ.[2]

The Church's evangelistic mission of bearing the good news to others is first Christ-centered. " 'God loved the world so much that he gave his only Son, that whoever believes in him might not perish but have everlasting life' " (John 3:16). "For our sake he made him to be sin who knew no sin, so that in him we might become the righteousness of God" (2 Corinthians 5:21).

This evangelistic mission is also invitational. The one who came proclaiming the kingdom of God was himself Lord and Savior, and those who witness to his life, death, and resurrection, in so doing, invite others to yield their lives and their futures to him.

This mission is incarnational. The Church is called to be a provisional demonstration of the kingdom of God, standing amid the death and decay of the world as an alternate reality, witnessing to the reality of God's love revealed in Christ Jesus by means of the Church's own transformed life, its proclamation of the gospel, and its demonstration of the gospel as it plunges into the realities of a broken creation. Such an incarnational witness has both personal and social implications. The gospel is about the new life that comes to individuals as they place their faith in Jesus Christ. It offers authentic hope for the age to come. It is also about the work of God's covenant community as they serve others in Christ in this age, seeking to promote social righteousness.

Evangelism characterizes a Church that recognizes there is only one thing to do with good news: to share it with others! As a community of faith declaring the mighty acts of God, the Church is to be oriented toward the needs of the world and not toward its own needs. The Church is to be a sign pointing others to Christ.

Few Presbyterians have read the *Book of Order* description of the Church's evangelistic ministry. While some would affirm that the words generally fit the content of the preaching and teaching that they hear in their congregations, most Presbyterians would say that they are uncomfortable with the whole notion of evangelism and do not often personally share their faith with others who are not Christians. When evangelism is publicly affirmed as a priority in Presbyterian congregations, it often has more to do with programs to gain new members and institutional survival goals than it does with a commitment to engage in God's redemptive purpose in the world. A huge disconnect exists between what our Church says we believe about evangelism and what we do in practice.

A few years ago, a brief definition of evangelism was approved by the General Assembly: "Evangelism is joyfully sharing the good news of the sovereign love of God and calling all people to repentance, to personal faith in Jesus Christ as Savior and Lord, to active membership in the Church, and to obedient service in the world."[3] It is a sound definition. While not wishing to put too fine a point on it, I would submit that the need to approve such a definition reflects the Church's lack of consensus around and lack of commitment to the joyous privilege of bearing witness to the gospel.

A Look Back

A recent Faith and Order paper of the World Council of Churches affirms, "The Church is not an end in itself, but a gift given to the world in order that all may believe (John 17:21). Mission belongs to the very being of the Church."[4] But this missional understanding of God's purpose for the Church is not so evident in the writing and work of the early Reformers. Stephen Neill asserts that there is little evidence that mission, in the sense of being sent by God out into the world, was important to the Protestants of the sixteenth century,[5] and he points out that the Reformers' thinking about mission was profoundly shaped by their primary focus upon efforts to reform the Church.[6] Moreover, the manner in which the Protestants thought about regional churches reflected the predominant understanding of the connection between a ruler's faith and the spiritual welfare of those ruled—*Cuius regio, eius religio.* For the most part in post-Constantinian Europe, the faith of the people of a region was the faith of their ruler. The question, then, was not whether or not one was Christian but what kind. People of other religions were obviously present, to one degree or another, but sharing the gospel with those persons was not a priority for the churches.

While there were a few exceptions to this historic preoccupation with the Church's own theological and organizational life, Presbyterians generally "discovered" evangelism with the other Protestant denominations as Western nations moved out into the world for conquest and commerce. The Church, confronted by unfamiliar peoples and seeking to understand their place in the purposes of God, began to look outward in new ways. Still, for centuries mission "basically meant the Western expansion of its own culturally conformed Christianity, carried out in a complex relationship with colonialism."[7] In fact, the great push for mission by the Reformed churches closely parallels British and Belgian colonial expansion, entwining commerce and conversion in an awkward alliance that confused the extension of the kingdom of God with national and economic expansion. While Catholic mission efforts, largely through the work of Catholic orders, had begun a few centuries earlier, they also often functioned in collaboration with the "discovery" of new lands and complicating colonial interests.

American Presbyterians first became broadly involved in evangelistic mission through the vehicle of the independent, ecumenical mission boards that flourished during the early nineteenth century. The Presbyterian Board of Foreign Mission was soon established in 1837, in part because Presbyterians wanted to bring expanding mission initiatives under denominational control. Presbyterians undertook evangelistic mission work at home and abroad that linked preaching, education, and health work as expressions of the love of God revealed in Jesus Christ.

A century later, many Presbyterian mission leaders embraced the conclusions of the 1930 Hocking Report, a controversial review of mission values and commitments that critiqued much of the Church's mission practice, and they labored to shape a mission enterprise that was less focused upon salvation from the world and more committed to transformation of the world.[8]

This shift was shaped by fallout from the modernist-fundamentalist battles and the recognition that the Church had, too often, imposed Western culture on those whom the Church had purposed to serve in Jesus' name. The Western churches had sought to dominate and control. During the decades that followed, the Presbyterian Church continued to engage in mission activities, both locally and globally, but a definite shift away from evangelism and toward social transformation had occurred. Presbyterians shifted so completely from proclaiming the gospel to demonstrating the gospel via concrete, compassionate action and advocacy that the Church eventually lost much of its capacity to articulate why it was doing the good things that it was doing. This de-emphasis on verbal evangelism contributed to a passionate debate about proper Presbyterian priorities.[9]

Thus, one factor shaping Presbyterian evangelistic theory and practice from the mid-twentieth century onward was the diminishing consensus among Presbyterians about the nature of the Church's mission. A 1998 Presbyterian Panel survey on the topic of world mission showed that Presbyterian Church members identified "leading people to faith in Christ" as the top priority. But a few years later, in a 2002 Presbyterian Panel survey, 35 percent of respondents said, "All different religions are equally true." After a fractious debate about the person and work of Jesus Christ, the 213th General Assembly, sensing the need for the Church to articulate again its faith in a clear and concise manner, directed the denomination's Office of Theology and Worship to prepare a statement that would lift up the central affirmations of the faith about which we witness to the world. The resulting statement, *Hope in the Lord Jesus Christ,* focuses on salvation and the role of Jesus Christ in our salvation. The paper affirms that humans are utterly dependent upon the triune God for their salvation and that God has come among us in terms we can understand only in Jesus Christ. Jesus Christ is Lord of all and the only Savior.[10]

The fact that the affirmations of this document, which received nearly unanimous approval by the General Assembly in 2002, are at odds with the convictions of some in the PCUSA is evident when one considers a work such as the recent book by W. Eugene March, retired professor of Old Testament at Louisville Presbyterian Theological Seminary, in which he describes three positions that Christians might take vis-à-vis other religions: exclusive (Christianity is the only valid religion), inclusive (Christianity is the best religion but allows that others could be saved), and pluralist (Christianity is one valid religion among other more or less equally valid religions). Although this scheme is a bit simplistic and not reflective of the nuanced convictions of many Presbyterians, his affirmation of what he terms the "pluralist" position is illustrative. March writes, "Fewer people who are actively engaged in a faith community tend to adopt the pluralist position. Because of their involvement in a particular faith they tend to assume that their religion alone is valid (exclusive) or that among all the other possibilities it is the best (inclusive). But a growing number of people who have carefully studied the religions of the world find the pluralist position the most honest in light of the evidence."[11]

I find the pluralist position to be incompatible with the official teaching of our Church, with its constitution and other statements; nevertheless, some of our clergy and church members espouse March's view. In this increasingly pluralistic age, at a time when increasing diversity exposes Presbyterians to new ideas and new neighbors and philosophical shifts that affect how truth claims are viewed, some in our Church are struggling with basic historic theological affirmations. Moreover, some wrestle deeply with evangelistic commitments that assert we should invite people of other faiths to give their allegiance to Jesus Christ as Lord and Savior and to become a part of a Christian community of faith. Sometimes this reflects not only theological uncertainty but also a discomfort with others' evangelistic methods that are deemed offensive.

Four Recent Shifts

1. While today's context raises questions for some Presbyterians about evangelism, developments during the past fifty years are proving to be very helpful as Presbyterians seek to deepen their understanding of the Church's evangelistic calling. The first shift has to do with the theological position for mission.

In this new approach, especially championed in the mid-twentieth century by Karl Barth, mission is understood as being grounded in the nature of God and is thus located in the context of the doctrine of the Trinity rather than in the doctrines of the Church (ecclesiology) or salvation (soteriology). The classical doctrine of the *missio Dei* as God the Father sending the Son, and God the Father and the Son sending the Spirit, is expanded to include yet another "movement": Father, Son, and Holy Spirit sending the Church into the world.[12] Mission is then, fundamentally, a matter of the doctrine of God. This shift is reflected in how much of the theological conversation has moved away from a discussion of the mission of the Church and refocused on the missionary God or God's mission, the *missio Dei*.

What is emerging is a missional ecclesiology, grounded in the Church's doctrine of God that moves beyond a consideration of the Church's institutional structures and forms to explore what it is that the Church is called to be in the purposes of God. Biblical history is viewed as the story of the unfolding of God's saving purpose, God's plan to bless all of the peoples of the earth through the Son. "With all wisdom and insight he has made known to us the mystery of his will, according to his good pleasure that he set forth in Christ, as a plan for the fullness of time, to gather up all things in him, things in heaven and things on earth" (Ephesians 1:8b–10). The blessing in Christ is for all people. God desires to gather up all things in Christ. The focus of the Church's sharing of the gospel of the kingdom of God, therefore, is the kingdom and not the Church.

To affirm that the Church exists for participation in God's mission to the world is to articulate an instrumental view of the Church that relativizes its institutional forms. What God is doing in the world determines what the Church must give itself to, why it exists. The trajectory of the Church's mission reflection becomes, therefore, not how to "take" the gospel to the world but how to discern where God is already at work and to join God there. At The Outreach Foundation, we summarize these themes in this manner: Mission is not a program of the Church but the purpose of the Church. Evangelism is not just a part of mission; it is the heart of mission. And it is not the Church's mission; rather, it is God's mission into which we are invited. God did not create mission to give the Church something to do.

The God who sent the Son out of love for the world and sent the Spirit upon the disciples now constitutes the Church to be sent into the world for God's own redemptive purpose.

2. A second shift that is shaping how Presbyterians think about evangelism and mission might be described as the embrace of a new favorite mission text. For Protestants, the modern mission movement, which was largely evangelistic at heart, can be said to have begun with the ministry of William Carey, a cobbler and linguist in England who in the 1790s tried to convince his Baptist colleagues that the Great Commission in Matthew 28 was as much the responsibility of Christians in their day as it was for the first disciples in Jesus' day. For more than a century to follow, this was the text that most profoundly shaped the character of Christian mission—going out, making disciples, baptizing, teaching. Actually, the Church often did not do so well "teaching them to observe all that I have commanded you," as Jesus said. If the Church had done that, called Jesus' followers truly to obey him, many of the mistakes of the past might have been avoided. We have not faithfully heeded Jesus' teaching ourselves, and we have failed to pass from one generation to the next a clear, compelling set of religious beliefs.

John 20:21 has today replaced Matthew 28 in many circles as a favorite formative mission text: "As the Father has sent me, so I send you." The double meaning of the text is what has made it so fruitful. Not only is Jesus sending his followers into the world as the Father sent him into the world, but also he is teaching them that the way in which they go, the manner in which they take up this work, should be according to the character of Jesus' own ministry. This conviction has been framed by the World Council of Churches and the Presbyterian Church (U.S.A.) in terms of evangelizing "in Jesus Christ's way."[13]

Our obedience in mission should be patterned on the ministry and teaching of Jesus. He gave his love and his time to all people. He praised the widow who gave her last coin to the temple; he received Nicodemus during the night; he called Matthew to the apostolate; he visited Zacchaeus in his home; he gave himself in a special way to the poor, consoling, affirming, and challenging them. He spent long hours in prayer and lived in dependence on and willing obedience to God's will. An imperialistic crusader's spirit was foreign to him.[14]

The PCUSA resolution *Turn to the Living God: A Call to Evangelism in Jesus Christ's Way* identifies a number of characteristics of the way in which Jesus proclaimed and lived the good news. He lived with the people among whom he evangelized. His offer was universal and inclusive. Jesus evangelized as a servant. His healing ministry went hand in hand with evangelism. Prayer undergirded his actions. A sense of urgency marked his life. And Jesus multiplied his evangelistic efforts as he shared the ministry with others.[15]

The point is that those who share the gospel should consistently relate to others in a manner that reflects the grace and goodness of God to which they bear witness. Evangelism, if it is to be done in Jesus' way, must be invitational without being coercive, passionate without being manipulative, confident without being triumphalistic. Too often, the good news has been made to sound like bad news, and the Church's witness to the gospel has been crippled by those who express toward others a spirit of judgment and hostility that is inconsistent with the grace that they themselves profess to have found through faith in Jesus.

3. A third shift, and it relates to doing evangelism in Jesus' way, is the rejection of a false bifurcation of the gospel into either evangelism *or* compassion and social action. In too many Presbyterian congregations, leaders and members still contend over whether the mission Christ calls us to is evangelism *or* justice, saving souls *or* acting with compassion and seeking social transformation in ways that disclose God's intention for creation. But if one takes seriously Jesus' words and his life, one must conclude that this is a false division. Those who would spiritualize the gospel and reduce it to the private areas of life ignore Jesus' teaching about God's loving lordship over all of life and human history. Those who would reduce the gospel to political and economic schemes ignore the promise of a love that is stronger than death and a life hidden with Christ that nothing can take away. "A proclamation which does not hold forth the promises of the justice of the kingdom to the poor of the earth is a caricature of the gospel. A Christian participation in the struggle for justice which does not also point to God's gracious offer of reconciliation and salvation to the poor is likewise a caricature."[16]

Congruence between what we proclaim and how we proclaim it, both at the personal and the denominational level, can free us from the too narrow view of salvation of souls as the end of evangelism, a view that on its own can lead to all kinds of mischief, even violence. Those who would speak of love must seek to love and work for social righteousness. "It is . . . impossible to talk about God's love for the poor, the outcast, the marginalized, and not to incarnate that love in the ways that demonstrate that God's kingdom is, in fact, coming now. One cannot communicate a gospel of love without letting that love become the dominant agenda of one's own life and the life of the community."[17]

Evangelism in Jesus' way is incarnational. The Gospel of John declares, "The Word became flesh and lived among us, and we have seen his glory, the glory as of a father's only son, full of grace and truth" (1:14). The Son entered into human existence to disclose the glory and grace of the Father. In the same way, those who witness to the Son enter into the realities of this broken world to demonstrate God's love. As the evangelism passage from the *Book of Order* puts it, an essential dimension of the Church's evangelistic calling is "participating in God's activity in the world through its life for others by healing and reconciling and binding up wounds; ministering to the needs of the poor, the sick, the lonely, and the powerless; engaging in the struggle to free people from sin, fear, oppression, hunger, and injustice; giving itself and its substance to the service of those who suffer; and, sharing with Christ in the establishing of his just, peaceable, and loving rule in the world." Evangelism at its best always involves both telling people about Jesus and more than only telling people about Jesus.

4. The fourth shift has to do with the relationship between gospel and culture. The biblical vision for the outcome of the Church's evangelistic activity is described by John in a vision from Revelation: "After this I looked, and there was a great multitude that no one could count, from every nation, from all tribes and peoples and languages, standing before the throne and before the Lamb, robed in white, with palm branches in their hands. They cried out in a loud voice, saying, 'Salvation belongs to our God who is seated on the throne, and to the Lamb!' " (Revelation 7:9–10).

This is a further dimension of how the Church's mission is to be shaped by the reality of the incarnation of God in Christ Jesus. Every culture is a fit vehicle for the expression of the gospel. Yet at the same time, the gospel stands in critique of aspects of every culture. Western churches have been arrogant in the confidence that we placed in our own culture, too often conflating the gospel with democratic capitalism, consumerism, patriotism, or some other -ism. We failed to recognize that the incarnational nature of the Christian faith demands the cross-cultural transmission of the gospel.

D. T. Niles, the Ceylonese mission leader, put it this way. "The Gospel is like a seed, and you have to sow it. When you sow the seed of the Gospel in Palestine, a plant that can be called Palestinian Christianity grows. When you sow it in Rome, a plant of Roman Christianity grows. You sow the Gospel in Great Britain and you get British Christianity. The seed of the Gospel is later brought to America, and a plant grows of American Christianity. Now, when missionaries come to our lands they brought not only the seed of the Gospel, but also their own plant of Christianity, flowerpot included! So, what we have to do is to break the flower pot, take out the seed of the Gospel, sow it in our own cultural soil, and let our own version of Christianity grow."[18]

The gospel is bearing fruit in soil all around the world and the majority Church is now outside the West. In 1900, Africa had 10 million Christians, or about 9 percent of its population. Today, that continent is home to 360 million Christians out of 784 million people, or 46 percent. Latin America has 480 million Christians and Asia another 313 million. By 2025, Christianity will be by far the world's largest faith with 2.6 billion Christians, with half of those in Latin America and Africa, and another 17 percent in Asia.[19] Andrew Walls notes the incredible experiences of the churches around the world, all that they have been through, and writes, "It is now the Churches of the non-Western world that have the accumulated and ripened experience of God's salvation."[20]

Harold Kurtz, who for years led Presbyterian Frontier Fellowship, a group that focuses upon sharing the gospel among unreached peoples (ethnologically distinct groups within which is no indigenous Christian witness), affirms that we need not only to become comfortable with what God is doing in the world; we need to learn once again the lessons that Peter and Paul learned and that we have forgotten in our misguided attempts to hold the gospel captive to Western culture. We not only need to give people the Bible in their mother tongue; we need to be the messengers of Jesus who do and say everything we can to encourage those people to live out their discipleship in their mother culture.[21]

For The Outreach Foundation, this means that as we build relationships with mission partners around the world we must strive to listen deeply, speak softly, hold things loosely, learn from others, and trust the Spirit of God to direct the life and growth of the Church. We do not have to be and should not seek to be in control.

Evangelism and Other Religions

The Presbyterian Church (U.S.A.) and ecumenical partners officially affirm, "the proclamation of the gospel includes an invitation to recognize and accept in personal decision the saving lordship of Christ. . . . Christians owe the message of God's salvation in Jesus Christ to every person and every people."[22] This responsibility to share the good news of how God has acted uniquely in Jesus for the salvation of the world is grounded in the faith of the Church. But how should we relate to people of other religions? The PCUSA's *Study Catechism* includes a helpful question and answer in this regard.

> Q: How should I treat non-Christians and people of other religions?
> A: As much as I can, I should meet friendship with friendship, hostility with kindness, generosity with gratitude, persecution with forbearance, truth with agreement, and error with truth. I should express my faith with humility and devotion as the occasion requires, whether silently or openly, boldly or meekly, by word or by deed. I should avoid compromising the truth on the one hand and being narrow-minded on the other. In short, I should always welcome and accept these others in a way that honors and reflects the Lord's welcome and acceptance of me.[23]

Policies and catechisms notwithstanding, mission history, including the history of our relationships with Jewish neighbors, makes it clear that we have often failed at this. The study paper *A Theological Understanding of the Relationship between Christians and Jews* affirmed this. The authors wrote, "The study has helped us to feel the pain of our Jewish neighbors who remember that the Holocaust was carried out in the heart of 'Christian Europe' by persons many of whom were baptized Christians. We have come to understand in a new way how our witness to the gospel can be perceived by Jews as an attempt to erode and ultimately to destroy their own communities."[24] If we are to be faithful to the gospel as followers of Jesus Christ, an essential dimension of our witness to the gospel must be our own willingness to repent and to seek the forgiveness of those whom we have wronged.

It is true that we Presbyterians believe that there is much that we can affirm as true about how God has acted in Jesus Christ for our salvation and for the salvation of the world. But even as we confess our faith, it is important for us not to claim too much. This combination of clarity and humility can be found in *Hope in the Lord Jesus Christ:*

> Jesus Christ is the only Savior and Lord, and all people everywhere are called to place their faith, hope, and love in him. No one is saved by virtue of inherent goodness or admirable living, for "by grace you have been saved through faith, and this is not your own doing; it is the gift of God" (Eph. 2:8). No one is saved apart from God's gracious redemption in Jesus Christ. Yet we do not presume to limit the sovereign freedom of "God our Savior, who desires everyone to be saved and to come to the knowledge of the truth" (1 Tim. 2:4). Thus, we neither restrict the grace of God to those who profess explicit faith in Christ nor assume that all people are saved regardless of faith. Grace, love, and communion belong to God, and are not ours to determine.[25]

As participants in God's continuing mission to the world, we are called to be witnesses to what we have seen and heard, what we have experienced in Jesus (see Acts 1:8). We are called to be servants of the last, the least, and the lost of this world with whom Jesus' identifies (see Matthew 25:31–46). As ones sent out by Jesus into the world, "We are ambassadors for Christ, since God is making his appeal through us" (2 Corinthians 5:20). We are called to be people of the Great Commission and the Great Commandment. We are not called to be judges. Some things, indeed, are not ours to determine.

Examples of Our Evangelistic Work

What does this understanding of evangelism look like in the ministry of The Outreach Foundation? To be sure, our work reflects our own sinfulness and the struggles of the Church of which we are a part. But we do believe that we are called to witness to the saving work of Jesus Christ, proclaiming the good news among all the peoples in word and deed.

Tete Province

In the mid-1990s, people began returning to Tete Province in northwestern Mozambique, a region previously devastated by a decade of revolution and civil war. Some were Christians; many were not. They had fled across borders seeking safety, often finding themselves in refugee camps. When they returned home, their villages were gone. The needs, both spiritual and physical, of the people were great and, in partnership with the Presbyterian Church of Mozambique, The Outreach Foundation undertook the development and support of a holistic evangelistic initiative. Although financial support for the work comes from U.S. partners, the project is entirely carried out by African Christians. The work is led by a Zambian minister who directs the work of two ordained pastors and a health specialist. They, in turn, work with scores of evangelists and congregational leaders. Outreach is working to build the capacity of our church partner in Mozambique for its own evangelistic mission.

Since this project's inception, fifty-eight new congregations have been founded. The work of sharing the gospel takes different primary forms. First, most church members recognize their responsibility to share the gospel with others in word and deed. They are actively engaged in sharing their faith with their families and neighbors. Second, a cadre of evangelists who come from the village churches are trained to share the gospel. They serve as part of an intentional strategy of sharing the gospel in communities where no church exists. Third, rallies are held from time to time in new areas using *The Jesus Film* as a means to share the basic story of Jesus and invite others to follow him. The congregations that have been formed through this project worship, study, and witness in cultural forms that are their own, using their mother tongue and indigenous music. For the most part, training takes place in the communities of the province, rather than extracting leaders to another context that might disconnect them from the people whom they are serving.

The initiative goes beyond verbal proclamation of the gospel as it seeks to flesh out the gospel in concrete caring ministries, such as public health. The project's health specialist, a Zambian nurse, is actively engaged in training persons in first-aid skills and to be village health assistants. With the help of these workers, and often utilizing a drama team, the ministry has undertaken an HIV/AIDS awareness campaign and a cholera- and malaria-prevention campaign. The lack of potable water is a problem throughout the region, and the evangelism initiative has put wells in many of the communities. These wells are typically under the oversight of a church elder. The water is used by church members and shared by the church with those who are not believers as an expression of God's love. Along with the availability of good water, instruction in sanitation, better drainage, and the use of mosquito nets are greatly improving the lives of the villagers.

With only three ordained leaders for nearly sixty congregations, equipping lay leaders through seminars and workshops is essential. In this context, leaders at every level understand that their responsibility is to equip others for ministry and mission.

A further dimension of this project, with the participation of many U.S. Presbyterian congregations, has been church building projects. The typical pattern is that a church will outgrow the grass hut in which they have been worshipping. They will obtain land, prepare and bake bricks, and put up the walls, and we will assist them in obtaining a metal roof. We have also built numerous schools, several grinding mills, and two village health clinics. Most of the financial resources for the project in Tete Province come from the United States, but the believers in Tete are giving sacrificially to support the work.

Portuguese Language Ministry

The Outreach Foundation's Portuguese Language Ministry began in 2002 when Pastor José Carlos Pezini developed a project that focused on sharing the gospel of Jesus Christ through preaching, leadership training, teaching, and the practice of the gospel in the Brazilian community in the United States, within the context of the Presbyterian Church (U.S.A.). Pezini had previously served for eleven years in Brazil as a Presbyterian pastor, ministering to two congregations and planting five other churches. He also taught theology at the Isbel Theological Seminary in Londrina.

Three basic strategies shape the evangelistic character of this ministry. First, the ministry focuses on church planting, preaching the gospel, and forming new fellowships and churches. This strategy among Presbyterians is typically referred to as new church development. The second principle, training, involves equipping leaders in evangelization so they can share the gospel with others in order to gather a community for worship, discipleship, and mission. Leaders are equipped with biblical and theological knowledge and receive training in the skills that they will need for discipleship and the promotion of spiritual growth in other believers. The third principle, resourcing, involves the production of resources to support the leaders and the Brazilian congregations. These resources include printed material such as curricula, books, pamphlets, magazines, videos, and a Web site. A recent project involved translating the *Book of Confessions* of the Presbyterian Church (U.S.A.) into Portuguese.

The focus of the ministry is twofold: ministering to believers who have come to new communities and who are seeking a church home, and reaching out to share the gospel with new neighbors who are not followers of Jesus. The traditional model of immigrant ministry involves bringing in pastoral leadership from the country from which the immigrants emigrated, but we have found that this model has several weaknesses. In the first place, it is expensive. It also often fails to connect culturally; a pastor from the old country does not necessarily have the cultural skills to assist immigrants with assimilation into their new environment. And we have observed that the pastoral skills needed to plant a new congregation are different from the skills needed to lead an established church. Our strategy involves identifying immigrant believers from within the community who have leadership gifts and training them for ministry. This makes for more successful church planting in immigrant communities.

Pastor Pezini helps congregations and presbyteries plant new fellowships and churches among Portuguese-speaking immigrants throughout the United States. He has also worked with Columbia Theological Seminary to develop a successful leadership-training program for both Portuguese- and Spanish-speaking immigrants. This training is now being offered at several sites across the country.

Our work among Arabic-speaking immigrants and Native Americans takes much the same form as the ministry described above, focusing on planting new fellowships/congregations and on equipping leaders from within the community for leadership in ministry and mission. Our experience has shown us that successful ministry among immigrants requires a holistic approach to their spiritual, social, and practical needs—and genuine expressions of Christian caring for those being served through the ministry. The lay leaders who are leading the fellowships often find themselves supporting immigrants who are dealing with immigration, housing, employment, and educational issues, and issues of cultural assimilation and identity, even as the leaders deal with those issues themselves. A focus upon saving souls that ignores the concrete realties of the lives of those with whom we are sharing the gospel of Jesus Christ dishonors both them and the Lord we proclaim.

Listening to the Postmoderns

Although most Presbyterians find it is easier to support evangelistic efforts abroad than to share their faith with their friends and neighbors, our Church is discovering that we live on a mission field. Our society increasingly seems to be functionally pagan, filled with people who live their lives without any practical reference to God. Some perceive Western consumer culture to be inimical to matters of religious faith and community. While the Church outside of the West is growing rapidly, most of the Western churches are in patterns of decline, including the Presbyterian Church (U.S.A.). No longer in a privileged social position as part of a hegemony of institutions shaping American society, our Church is striving to understand its context in the same way a missionary with cross-cultural skills seeks to understand a new society into which she has been sent to serve.

Younger Presbyterian Church leaders and members are increasingly raising questions about evangelism that reflect what might be described as postmodern concerns. Some of these leaders are concerned that much of what Christians have undertaken in the name of evangelism—efforts to share the gospel as so many spiritual laws or some simple few steps—reduces the gospel to a formula that is incongruous with the radical, transformational character of the gospel embodied by Jesus and proclaimed by the early Church.

Some in this emerging movement, having left behind a purely rationalistic Enlightenment-style epistemology, want to affirm that faith transcends the rational, is relational, and is therefore "transpropositional." Others come at the question of evangelism using a post-semiotic framework for human communication, taking a much more pragmatic approach to language and focusing upon relational forms of communication. In this approach, the question of whether something is true or relevant is not as important as whether it is real. For many today, experience trumps knowledge, reality trumps reason, spirituality trumps religion; truth is not about propositions but about relationships.

While some contend that it is far too early to define what habits and patterns of thought will follow modernism, contemporary culture is clearly more indifferent to mere words. In the face of a barrage of truth claims and the absence of any unifying interpretive story or metanarrative, it is more crucial than ever that the good news of God's love revealed in Jesus Christ be fleshed out in authentic expressions of community and in genuine service to others. Whatever this particular age is best called, Newbigin is right, "For the Church to live out an intimate engagement with the narrative of God's action in Jesus Christ that shapes its life and thought, it must use personal and communal ways of knowing that reach beyond the merely rational."[26] More than ever, actions speak louder than words.

Conclusion

Evangelism is joyfully sharing the good news of the sovereign love of God and calling all people to repentance, to personal faith in Jesus Christ as Savior and Lord, to active membership in the Church, and to obedient service in the world. This calling is at the heart of God's mission to the world, God's promise to bless all the peoples of the earth, and at the heart of God's purpose for the Church. The Church should undertake this work of proclaiming the good news humbly and patiently, seeking not only by its words but also in its common life and through its service to the world to disclose God's grace revealed in Jesus Christ. Because the history of the Church's evangelistic activity is replete with examples of how the Church has failed to witness to God's grace in gracious ways, it is crucial that the Church learns from the past and from those with whom we share our faith. The Church must care for others so genuinely and so consistently that it is clear to all that what motivates the Church in its work of witness to the gospel is an authentic regard for the well-being of others.

In writing to the church at Corinth, Paul reminds his readers of the transformation that has occurred in their own lives, that their evangelistic vocation is directly linked to the change Christ has wrought in their own lives.

> So if anyone is in Christ, there is a new creation: everything old has passed away; see, everything has become new! All this is from God, who reconciled us to himself through Christ, and has given us the ministry of reconciliation; that is, in Christ God was reconciling the world to himself, not counting their trespasses against them, and entrusting the message of reconciliation to us. So we are ambassadors for Christ, since God is making his appeal through us; we entreat you on behalf of Christ, be reconciled to God (2 Corinthians 5:17–20).

In every age and place the Church's proclamation of the gospel for the salvation of others rightly begins with the Church's recognition of its radical dependence upon God's grace and with its own ongoing transformation.

1. *A Theological Understanding of the Relationship between Christians and Jews,* Minutes of the 199th General Assembly of the Presbyterian Church (U.S.A.), 1987, pp. 417–424.
2. *Book of Order,* Part II of *Constitution of the Presbyterian Church (U.S.A.)* (Louisville: Office of the General Assembly, 2003–2004), G-3.0300–3.0400.
3. Minutes of the 201st General Assembly of the Presbyterian Church (U.S.A.), 1989, Part I, 359.
4. Faith and Order Commission, *The Nature and Purpose of the Church: A Stage on the Way to a Common Statement,* Faith and Order Paper no. 181 (Geneva: World Council of Churches, 1998), p. 15.
5. Even a mission team sent to Brazil, while expressing authentic interest in the culture of the Tupinamba Indians on the coast, was more interested in understanding these natives in the light of the Scriptures than in helping the natives to understand the gospel. Attempts to evangelize were modest.
6. Stephen Neill, *A History of Christian Missions,* 2nd edition revised by Owen Chadwick (London: Penguin Books, 1990), p. 188.
7. Darrell L. Guder, *The Continuing Conversion of the Church,* Gospel and Our Culture Series, ed. Craig Van Gelder (Grand Rapids: William B. Eerdmans, 2000), p. 18.
8. Milton J. Coalter, John M. Mulder, and Louis B. Weeks, *The Re-Forming Tradition: Presbyterians and Mainstream Protestantism* (Louisville: Westminster/John Knox Press, 1992), p. 99.
9. Ibid., p. 228.
10. *Hope in the Lord Jesus Christ,* affirmed by the 214th General Assembly of the Presbyterian Church (U.S.A.), (2002).
11. W. Eugene March, *The Wide, Wide Circle of Divine Love: A Biblical Case for Religious Diversity* (Louisville: Westminster John Knox Press, 2005), p. 28.
12. David Bosch, *Transforming Mission: Paradigm Shifts in Theology of Mission* (Maryknoll, NY: Orbis Books, 1991), p. 390.
13. *Mission and Evangelism: An Ecumenical Affirmation,* World Council of Churches (Geneva: World Council of Churches, 1982); *Turn to the Living God: A Call to Evangelism in Jesus Christ's Way,* adopted by the 203rd General Assembly of the Presbyterian Church (U.S.A.), (1991).
14. *Mission and Evangelism,* p. 14.
15. *Turn to the Living God,* pp. 3–4.
16. "Message" of the San Antonio Conference on World Mission and Evangelism of the World Council of Churches, quoted in *Turn to the Living God,* p. 22.
17. Guder, "Incarnation and the Church's Evangelistic Mission," *International Review of Mission* 83, no. 30 (1992): p. 424.
18. Quoted in Paul-Gordon Chandler, *God's Global Mosaic: What We Can Learn from Christians Around the World* (Downers Grove: IVP, 2000), p. 16.
19. Philip Jenkins, *The Next Christendom: The Coming of Global Christianity* (Oxford University Press, 2003).
20. Andrew F. Walls, *The Cross-Cultural Process in Christian History* (Maryknoll, NY: Orbis Books, 2002), p. 70.
21. Harold Kurtz, personal e-mail, October 21, 2003.
22. *Mission and Evangelism,* pp. 7, 21.
23. Question 52, *The Study Catechism,* adopted by the 210th General Assembly of the Presbyterian Church (U.S.A.), 1998.
24. Minutes of the 199th General Assembly of the Presbyterian Church (U.S.A.), 1987, p. 418.
25. *Hope in the Lord Jesus Christ,* pp. 11–12.
26. Lesslie Newbigin, *The Gospel in a Pluralistic Society* (Grand Rapids: Eerdmans, 1989), pp. 222–223.

Presbyterian Evangelism: Response to Robert Weingartner

Richard Hirsh

I am going to offer a Jewish response to this paper by looking at three issues that it raises, either explicitly or implicitly. In doing so, I know I am overlooking many other important ideas and insights and, insofar as I am sure we share an interest in moving toward discussion sooner than later, hope that you will forgive me for not focusing on the many other issues of interest that are deserving of comment.

The three topics on which I would like to offer a brief response are: (1) the relationship between evangelism and proselytism, and by extension the meaning of conversion; (2) our (Jewish) understanding of Jewish identity and how it relates to the idea of conversion, both into and out of the Jewish people and Judaism; and (3) the larger context within which this discussion is taking place.

The Relationship between Evangelism and Proselytism

By way of stating the obvious, the Rev. Weingartner's paper is titled "A Presbyterian Understanding of Evangelism" and Dr. Berger's paper is named "Reflections on Conversion and Proselytizing in Judaism and Christianity." That the term *conversion* appears in the title of the "Jewish" paper but not in the title of the "Christian" one seems to me more than coincidental.

Suppose we analyze what we know to be so challenging: The Christian ~~ution, particularly the Protestant Christian tradition, and perhaps more particularly the evangelical approaches as described here, believes—as the Rev. Weingartner stated—that "mission is not a *program* of the Church but the *purpose* of the Church" (emphasis added).

Whether refracted through the conversional evangelism that the *HarperCollins Dictionary of Religion* tells me is embraced by Southern Baptist and Pentecostal denominations or through the confessional evangelism of the Reformed churches such as the Presbyterian Church, proclaiming, announcing, confessing the gospel seems to be, if you'll pardon the linguistic boundary-crossing, a *mitzvah,* and in both senses of that term: the elite and linguistically correct sense of "commandment and therefore obligation" and the folk sense of "a good deed." If I understand the Rev. Weingartner's analysis, evangelism is both a "good deed" because it brings the opportunity of salvation, and a "commandment" both because Scripture attributes it to Jesus (whether Matthew 28 or John 20:21) and because a universally sinful humanity stands in need.

When heard from the Jewish side, surely on the folk level and probably to some degree on the elite level, any distinction between conversional and confessional evangelism would certainly be lost. Evangelism as the proclamation of the gospel with an invitation and offering and implicit expectation that one share in salvation is not so much seen as a gift as, at best, an offer of exchange—in which something of implicitly lesser value (or, perhaps more kindly, of incomplete value) has to be surrendered in exchange for something of greater value (or, perhaps more kindly, completed value).

Or, to put it perhaps too simply, when Christians say "evangelical" many, perhaps even most, Jews hear "conversion."

That said, it seems to me that the Rev. Weingartner's paper raises an interesting and nuanced distinction, or at least so it seems to me. I hope our Christian colleagues here will corroborate what I want to suggest here, or, more importantly, correct me if I am off base. I am curious if, as the Rev. Weingartner says, the only thing to do with good news is to share it with others, if the nature of the sharing is open to more than one understanding. That is, is "sharing" the same thing as "witnessing"? And is "witnessing" the same thing as "proselytizing"? And is "proselytizing" the same thing as "missionizing"? Is all of this subsumed under "evangelism"? Or does it depend if one is, to use the distinctions identified by W. Eugene March, an "exclusivist" an "inclusivist" or a "pluralist"?

I think I can safely say that an evangelism that witnesses, testifies, lifts up, and is evidenced in the way one describes how his or her life of faith is shaped, informed by, and given meaning by the gospel is less confrontational and therefore less controversial vis-à-vis many, I imagine most, Jews. But whether that can be considered "an" authentic evangelism, let alone "the" authentic evangelism, is something I cannot address. I would be interested to hear from our Presbyterian colleagues on this subject.

Our (Jewish) understanding of Jewish identity and how it relates to the idea of conversion, both into and out of the Jewish people and Judaism
It happens that one of the courses I teach at our seminary (the Reconstructionist Rabbinical College) is on Jewish identity, viewed historically and then examined as it moves through the stages of the life-cycle. I devote one week to conversion (to Judaism), because conversion is the best prism for breaking up the component pieces of Jewish identity so that the individual refractions can be seen more clearly.

Without taking the time to survey the evolution of Jewish identity from tribal *Hebrews* to national *Israelites* to landed but politically limited *Judeans* to an ethnic-faith community known as *Jews,* let me only identify a key difference between being a Jew and being a Christian. Because, especially here in America, we are so fond of invoking "the Judeo-Christian tradition" and, at least once upon a time, speaking of, in Will Herberg's memorable title of his 1955 book *Protestant, Catholic, Jew,* it is easy to assume that being a Christian or being a Jew is a matter of faith, a question of assent, or an affirmation of a theology.

When I was in graduate school in the religion department of Temple University, I heard from more than one Christian professor, both Catholic and Protestant, the adage that "one is born a Jew, but one becomes a Christian." This is to say that there is a lineal dimension to Jewish identity that involves descent irrespective of assent. A child born to or of a family in which one parent is Jewish (the liberal position) or the mother is Jewish (the conservative position), where the child is identified as Jewish by the parents and there is nothing to indicate anything to the contrary (such as a child being raised in two faiths), is Jewish.

I challenge my rabbinic students to consider what analogy they will use to explain conversion to those seeking to join the Jewish people. Since in America the majority of those doing so come from Christian backgrounds, it is important for rabbis to explain that conversion to Judaism is not so much adopting a faith as it is joining a people; the analogy is more akin to taking out citizenship than to confessing a faith. Clearly, adopting Jewish identity is a religious ritual and Jewish religion is central. But the case of conversion helps us understand that being a Jew is a matter of ethnicity, history, lineage, culture, custom, and content as much as it is a matter of faith.

That said, it seems valuable to put on the table that the approach by a Christian to a Jew for the sake of conversion (and in cases of Jewish-Christian conversion, ultimately "Christianity" and "Judaism" will come down to "this Christian" and "this Jew") is not simply an offering of one faith for another. It is asking a Jew to take the one step a Jew can take that suspends his or her participation and membership in the Jewish people: the accepting of a faith other than Judaism. While Jewish identity allows for multiple ethnic and cultural dimensions, it demands exclusive religious affirmation.

Put differently, a Jewish child may have one parent who is African American and one who is Eastern European, and may be raised in South America, but that child cannot have a Jewish religious identity as well as a Christian religious identity. One scholar puts it this way: A Jew who converts to another faith is a non-Jew for some purposes, and remains an apostate Jew for others.

I am taking the time here because it seems to me any discussion of evangelism, proselytism, and conversion in which the approach is of a Christian to a Jew necessarily becomes entangled in the differing nature of these identities. Dr. Berger raises, at the end of his paper, the question of whether Christian religious authorities can or perhaps should have a different perspective on the question of conversion when the subject is the (potential) conversion of Jews. We may be asking similar questions here, although I recognize I am coming from a different direction to reach what I think may be the same point.

The bottom line is that asking an affirmative Jew to convert is asking him or her to surrender not only his or her faith but also his or her identity. And that involves loss as much as it might mean gain; and, for many Jews, it would involve a betrayal of a somewhat primal, admittedly somewhat tribal, surely in context of our moment in Jewish history somewhat compelling, contribution to the continuity of a people and a tradition whose survival has been so sorely tested.

I am anticipating that our Presbyterian colleagues here might say, "faith *is* identity" but I am not sure; in any event, I would welcome comments and clarifications on that count.

The larger context within which this discussion is taking place

I will make this third comment as briefly as I can. As a former pulpit rabbi and an occasional teacher of homiletics, I know the value of the speaker letting the congregation know that the speaker knows that the congregation is wondering how close the speaker is to being done!

One of my favorite metaphors for my rabbinic students is the wonderful tool offered at the Web site called Google Earth. If you're not familiar with this, you enter an address or location and then you can zoom in and zoom out, pulling back far enough to have, as it were, a satellite view, to understand how small our place is in the context of the big picture. It's a useful tool for gaining perspective.

So all I want to add here is that if we step outside of the Jewish-Presbyterian discussion on evangelism and conversion for a moment, and pull back far enough, it seems to me Jews and Christians have to take a look at the same questions—that we need to think equally about the content and the context of our respective faith traditions. When I look down from way out there, I see a lot of Muslims, Hindus, Buddhists, and Taoists. And I see a lot of other perhaps lesser-known faiths. It surely gives me a different perspective; it is a bit humbling as well as daunting.

I want to close by returning to the three profiles of exclusive, inclusive, and pluralist and their implications for evangelism, proselytizing, and conversion. I am increasingly convinced that the future of religion, and whether it will be a benign or a destructive force, has less to do with *what* we believe than with *how* we believe. Exclusive versions of faith may have the advantage of being firm, steady, sure, and certain, but they are risky. As Peter Berger has noted, if you believe in the supernatural inerrancy of your faith, then other faiths cannot be different; they have to be wrong. From being wrong to being in rebellion against the Truth is but a few steps, and from being in rebellion to being actively evil and therefore in need of eradication may not be the logical conclusion, but you can get there from here.

The inclusive model steps away from some of these problems, but still runs the risk of making believers of other faiths, as well as nonbelievers in any faith, actors in a theological narrative not of their choosing. To say that "Christianity is the best religion but allows that others could be saved" assumes that "salvation"—or at least "salvation" as understood in the Christian tradition as being saved from sin—is a goal shared by other religions. Even if we do some anthropological reduction of "salvation" to some bland functional commonality, are we speaking the same language as, for example, those of Eastern faiths for whom salvation is escape from the cycle of reincarnation?

The pluralist model, as the Rev. Weingartner notes, is in some ways so "American": "To each his own, as long as no one gets hurt." And the pluralist model, *if* defined as "Christianity is one valid religion among other more or less equally valid religions," does seem to reduce important issues of faith, and the corollary issues of ethics, behavior, and morality, to personal preference—or, as we sometimes say, the difference between the "Ten Commandments" and the "Ten Suggestions."

In closing, I want to ask if there is another possibility for a pluralist model. I say this as a Jew, with a tradition that, as Dr. Berger's paper demonstrates, has a long history of straddling the inclusive-pluralist line. But I wonder what evangelism, proselytism, and conversion might look like if the issues were framed from the human perspective rather than the divine perspective. Or, to put it in the terms I used to suggest to prospective converts to Judaism:

- How do you imagine it would be different relating to God through the symbols, holidays, and sacred stories of Judaism than it has been up until now relating to God through the symbols and holidays and sacred stories of Christianity?

- In what ways do you imagine it being different having as your master story the story of the Exodus instead of the story of the crucifixion and the resurrection?

I do not want to reduce religious faith to banalities and bromides. I think we likely share that concern. And I do not want to suggest that the faith-choices we make should be easily taken; I am fond of the warning to avoid "cheap grace."

But I am hopeful that when one faith tradition comes into relationship with another, that we can emulate what the Rev. Weingartner so eloquently described as an evangelism rooted in John 20:21, "As the Father has sent me, so I send you"—"[to be] invitational without being coercive, passionate without being manipulative, confident without being triumphalistic."

I am curious as to whether such a view of evangelism can be grafted onto a view that might yet be called pluralistic. And I look forward to our continuing to explore together the possibilities that God has placed before us out of the trust that God has placed in us.

Reflections on Conversion and Proselytizing in Judaism and Christianity

David Berger

Setting aside disputes regarding the State of Israel, there is no more sensitive subject in the universe of Jewish-Christian relations than conversionary aspirations on the part of Christians. The reasons for this appear obvious—and in large measure they are—but they are also marked by layers of complexity that we would do well to examine.

Contemporary discussions of this issue usually take for granted that Judaism in principle eschews efforts to proselytize others. Thus, a *locus classicus* in the Talmud in effect instructs Jews approached by a Gentile expressing an interest in conversion to suggest that the prospective convert urgently seek out a psychiatrist. Why, after all, would anyone in his or her right mind join a defeated and persecuted people? Only one who persists despite this effort at discouragement is eligible to pursue the goal of becoming a Jew.[1]

Nonetheless, some see this passage not as an expression of an anti-proselytizing principle but as the reaction of Jews who had lost the contest for pagan adherents and decided to make a virtue of their failure. The argument for the position that there were widespread Jewish efforts in the Greco-Roman world to attract converts rests upon the presence of "God-fearing" semi-proselytes throughout that world as well as explicit or near-explicit assertions in several texts. In this forum, the most relevant of those texts is the assertion in Matthew 23:15 that Pharisees compass land and sea to make one proselyte. While the question of ancient Jewish proselytizing remains a lively matter of dispute, it is worth noting the obvious. Whether or not one endorses the plural form "Judaisms" in vogue among some historians, it is evident that ancient Jewish attitudes toward a host of religious questions ranged across a large spectrum, so that indications of both proselytizing activity and opposition or indifference to such activity do not constitute a puzzling contradiction. Unless there are independent grounds to conclude that conflicting evidence about this issue testifies to historical development, such evidence can easily be read as a reflection of very different approaches to proselytizing that coexisted among Jews in the Hellenistic-Roman-rabbinic period.[2]

As Judaism moved into the Middle Ages, it is evident that an explicit rabbinic text would carry more weight than evidence from Matthew or Greco-Roman artifacts and literature. Jewish reluctance to proselytize was, of course, greatly reinforced by the attendant dangers of such efforts in both the Christian and the Muslim worlds. Setting aside the danger, the very fact that Jews were a small, relatively powerless minority rendered the idea that they could win over large numbers of converts unrealistic.

Beyond all this, there was, I think, a fascinating dialectic that played itself out in the Jewish psyche. To become a Jew is to join a people, not just a faith. The concept of Jewish chosenness, of the special sanctity of Israel as a collective, rendered the objective of a mass conversion to Judaism problematic. Even in the *eschaton,* all the nations may call upon God together in a clear voice (see Zephaniah 3:9), but they remain discrete nations. In Jewish eyes, those nations would presumably follow the Noahide code, binding in historical times as well as at the end of days, which defines God's expectations of non-Jews in a manner that keeps them separate from Israel. Since obedience to this code provides eternal felicity to its non-Jewish adherents, the drive to convert Gentiles to Judaism is diminished even further.

At the same time, it is far from clear that medieval Jews refrained from missionizing only or even primarily because they saw another route to salvation for Gentiles. Given the realities of the medieval Jewish condition, many Jews so resented their persecutors that they had no interest in their salvation; rather, they looked forward to their damnation. While Hitler maintains so unique a position in the history of Judeophobia that analogies can be dangerous and even offensive, it is nonetheless instructive to consider how Jews would have reacted in the last months of World War II to the prospect of a suddenly repentant Hitler who will enter the World to Come as a righteous man. Distasteful as this analogy is, it provides a graphic means of grasping the psychology of people who yearned for the destruction and damnation of their oppressors.[3]

Complicating the issue further is the relationship between Christianity and the requirements of the Noahide code. David Novak has written with considerable plausibility that a case can be made that Christianity is a quintessential fulfillment of that code since it not only establishes the obligatory moral framework but even meets the Maimonidean requirement that non-Jews observe the code out of belief that it is a product of divine revelation.[4] Nonetheless, this position conflicts with a theological point that was at the forefront of the medieval Jewish psyche, to wit, the status of worship directed at Jesus of Nazareth as a hypostasis of the triune God. Almost all medieval Jews saw this as a form of *avodah zarah,* or worship of an entity other than God, which prima facie violated one of the seven Noahide commandments. During the Paris Disputation of 1240, R. Yehiel of Paris displayed considerable unease when he was more or less forced to imply in response to a direct question that Christians could be saved through their own faith, and other medieval Jews unhesitatingly answered this question in the negative.[5]

In sum, then, Jews in the Christian world refrained from missionizing as a result of an extraordinarily complex constellation of theological, historical, and psychological considerations not always consistent with one another: The Jewish people should retain its uniqueness even in eschatological times; non-Jews have an avenue of salvation without joining that people (though that avenue is probably not Christianity); missionizing was dangerous; its chances of meeting with significant success were minuscule; and the persecutors of Israel should receive their just punishment for all that they had done.

Despite all this, the impulse to have Christians recognize the truth was not absent from the medieval Jewish psyche. Members of a minority regularly mocked for their religious error and periodically pressured to renounce it enjoyed a sense of validation and enormous satisfaction when adherents of the majority faith recognized their own error. While this is a point whose psychological validity is almost self-evident, here is a text from the *Nizzahon Vetus,* a late-thirteenth-century Northern European polemic that I edited several decades ago, that spells it out:

> With regard to their questioning us as to whether there are proselytes among us, they ask this question to their shame and to the shame of their faith. After all, one should not be surprised at the bad deeds of an evil Jew who becomes an apostate, because his motives are to enable himself to eat all that his heart desires, to give pleasure to his flesh with wine and fornication, to remove from himself the yoke of the kingdom of heaven so that he should fear nothing, to free himself from all the commandments, cleave to sin, and concern himself with worldly pleasures. But the situation is different with regard to proselytes who converted to Judaism and thus went of their own free will from freedom

to slavery, from light to darkness. If the proselyte is a man, then he knows that he must wound himself by removing his foreskin through circumcision, that he must exile himself from place to place, that he must deprive himself of worldly good and fear for his life from the external threat of being killed by the uncircumcised, and that he will lack many things that his heart desires; similarly, a woman proselyte also separates herself from all pleasures. And despite all this, they come to take refuge under the wing of the divine presence. It is evident that they would not do this unless they knew that their faith is without foundation and that it is all a lie, vanity, and emptiness. Consequently, you should be ashamed when you mention the matter of proselytes.[6]

In this environment, a classic Talmudic commentary cites a medieval French proselyte's interpretation of a rabbinic text declaring converts to be as damaging to Israel as a serious disease. The reason for this, says the proselyte, is that converts observe the Torah with such care that they put born Jews to shame.[7]

It is a matter of no small interest that in addressing the question of the permissibility of teaching Torah to non-Jews, Maimonides took a stringent position with respect to Muslims even though he saw them as exemplary monotheists and a more lenient one with respect to Christians even though he saw them as worshipers of *avodah zarah*. The reason he provides is that unlike Muslims, who consider the text of the Hebrew Bible unreliable, Christians accept the accuracy of that text and are therefore more susceptible to being persuaded of the true faith if they can be made to understand the correct meaning of the Bible. I am not prepared to say that Maimonides advocated a Jewish mission to Christians, but he clearly hoped that in sporadic, personal encounters, Jews might be able to demonstrate the superiority of their faith. Similarly, I am convinced that in the streets of medieval Christian Europe, some Jews challenged their Christian neighbors with arguments designed to prove the truth of Judaism, though here too these contacts do not add up to a Jewish mission or near-mission. The motive was primarily to reinforce Jewish morale, not to create a cadre of proselytes.[8] This motive also plays a role in moderating my earlier observation about the desire of some medieval Jews for the damnation and destruction of their oppressors. Such a desire conflicts with the hope for eschatological vindication, a hope that provides its full measure of psychological benefit only if the deniers of Judaism acknowledge their error at the end of days and proclaim, in the words of the High Holiday liturgy, "The Lord God of Israel is King, and his kingship rules over all."[9]

Jacob Katz argued that, by the sixteenth century, the assertiveness that marked medieval Jewish attitudes toward Christianity, particularly in Northern Europe, began to wane, and that this transformation affected attitudes toward converts and conversion. The Jewish community had turned inward and no longer sought to impress the Christian world with its ability to attract outsiders. But as Jews moved toward modernity, other considerations emerged. Significant authorities began to affirm that Christianity is not considered *avodah zarah* when practiced by non-Jews. Thus, the likelihood that Christians could attain salvation increased exponentially. For Moses Mendelssohn, religious toleration became an almost transcendent ideal, and he famously expressed dissatisfaction with Maimonides's requirement that the Noahide code confers salvation only upon those who accept it as revelation. R. Israel Lipschutz, an important nineteenth-century commentator on the Mishnah, asserted as an almost self-evident truth that God would not fail to provide heavenly reward to Johannes Reuchlin for his defense of Jewish books against those who would have destroyed them.[10]

If Christians can attain salvation as Christians, the motive for a Jewish mission is markedly diminished. In modern times, this is often taken for granted as *the* reason why Jews have refrained from proselytizing. In other words, Jewish opposition to mission is a function of a deeply held principle recognizing the salvific potential of other religions. As we have seen, the history of Jewish attitudes regarding this question is far more complicated, but there is an element of truth in this assertion even with respect to the premodern period. As my brother-in-law Allen Friedman has put it, medieval Christians and Muslims did not expect to meet anyone who was not a co-religionist in heaven; even Jews with a restrictive view of salvation expected to meet a few righteous Gentiles.

Thus far, I have addressed the views of Jews in a traditional society and their Orthodox successors in modern times. It goes without saying that almost all non-Orthodox Jews maintain that Christianity provides its adherents with the ability to find favor in the eyes of God, and those non-Orthodox Jews who believe in an afterlife affirm that good Christians have a portion in the World to Come. For such Jews, proselytizing is a symptom of an intolerant, even immoral, theology of exclusion.

Before attempting to evaluate this position, let me turn to Christian approaches to missionary activity directed at Jews, which is, of course, the primary target of this pejorative evaluation. It is hardly necessary to say that classical Christianity strove to spread the good news and that Jews were not excluded as objects of this effort. At the same time, a theology developed that granted Jews special, even unique, toleration both because they were seen as witnesses to the truth of Christianity and because Romans 11, however one reads it, speaks of their continued separate existence when the fullness of the nations arrives.[11] Thus, although it was clearly desirable for individual Jews to save themselves through conversion, systematic efforts to convert large numbers of Jews were rare before the thirteenth century. An article on Jewish conversion in thirteenth-century England in a recent issue of *Speculum* asserts that even at this relatively late date, Robert Grosseteste "view[ed] Jewish conversion as a consequence of the end of history rather than as a current possibility or even a desire."[12]

Though the vision of Jewish conversion at the end of days persisted, the thirteenth century saw the exponential growth of efforts to convert the Jews en masse. As time passed, some of these efforts developed an eschatological perspective, while others resulted from the desire to establish a uniformly Christian Europe. The earlier absence of conversionary programs does not bespeak a strong interest in the welfare of Jewish souls, and I see little indication that the primary motive of the new policy was a sudden concern for the fate of Jews who would otherwise be condemned to hellfire, though some missionaries undoubtedly took satisfaction in the benefit that they brought to the objects of their ministry. The treatment of new Christians in *this* world certainly left much to be desired. They were sometimes deprived of their property, the conditions in the halfway houses for converts were often lamentable, and other efforts to meet the needs of individuals removed from their families and support systems were sporadic and generally inadequate.

When converts were suspected of Judaizing in late-medieval and early-modern Iberia, they were, of course, subjected to terrible consequences. Here, we confront the logic of imposing one's faith on an unwilling other in its most acute form, since the torments inflicted by the Inquisition were imposed at least in part for the sake of the immortal souls of the unfortunate Judaizers. But the souls of unconverted Jews are presumably just as destined to damnation as those of insincere converts, so that as a matter of cold logic the policies of the Inquisition could just as well have been applied to the former. But they were not. The tradition of toleration, even in an age of expulsions and intense missionary pressures, maintained some modicum of its original standing.

And so we return to modern and contemporary times. The question of the propriety of a Christian mission directed at Jews depends first on the underlying theology of salvation maintained by the Christian group in question. Such theologies range across a broad spectrum:

- Jews, like all other non-Christians, are condemned to eternal hellfire. Non-Christians, including Jews, are at a distinct disadvantage in the struggle for salvation, but such salvation is not ruled out.[13]
- Jews, uniquely among adherents of non-Christian religions, can be saved no less readily than Christians can because they are already with the Father.
- Salvation is readily available to all good people irrespective of religion.

Even the last two positions do not in themselves rule out proselytizing since spreading the good news could be desirable or obligatory because of the inherent value of ultimate truth without reference to the eternal destiny of the non-Christian. Still, the first two positions, and especially the harsher of the two, greatly strengthen the argument for an active mission.

How then does a Jew, or at least this Jew, respond to such an argument? As long ago as 1983, I expressed strong opposition to Jewish efforts to instruct Christians about what to believe regarding their own religion, and I have repeated this position on numerous subsequent occasions. I confessed, however, that with respect to missionizing, "even Jews who hesitate most about intervention in the internal affairs of Christianity have some mixed feelings." I went on to say that "the Jewish mandate to protect Jews from conversion is no less a religious requirement than any Christian mandate to convert them, and, although my basic sympathies are with the 'non-interventionists,' in the case of aggressive missionizing aimed specifically at Jews, the overriding principle of *pikkuah nefesh,* or danger to life (including spiritual life), may well prevail."[14] In short, if I could persuade a Christian uncertain of his or her position regarding mission to the Jews that proper Christian belief should affirm the possibility of salvation for unconverted Jews, I would try to do this.

Nonetheless, I do not regard honest advocates of proselytizing who adhere to the harshest position regarding Jewish salvation as evil in any sense. Thus, I take the position that someone who has declared war on me and my people is nonetheless a fine person whom I can embrace as a friend in other contexts. There is, of course, an emotional tension in this position, and I ask myself whether an argument for Jewish exceptionalism can be formulated that does not impinge on Christian doctrine. I think it possible that this question can be answered in the affirmative. Christians in the modern world, including those with exclusivist views of salvation, definitively reject coercive methods, whether physical or economic, to enforce conformity to Christian belief and practice, and they do this not only because such methods would be ineffective but also because they abhor them in principle. This appears to mean that even saving another's soul does not outweigh all competing considerations. One who refrains from religious coercion recognizes that the apparently transcendent benefit does not outweigh the harm done to the coercer's moral personality, to that of his or her collective, or to civil society as a whole, not to speak of the immediate suffering of the presumed beneficiary.

In light of these considerations, we are now in a position to ask if there is any moral harm inflicted by noncoercive proselytizing. It can certainly damage, even poison, intergroup relations, and it renders respectful dialogue about religious matters next to impossible. These concerns apply to proselytizing directed at any group; the question is whether they are serious enough to set aside the salvific advantage of conversion to Christianity. At the very least, they may persuade Christians who believe that the other party's salvation is not at stake to eschew active missionizing.

In dealing with Jews, the moral objections to conversionary efforts increase exponentially. First, even in an open society, there is a tinge of pressure, if not genuine coercion, when members of a majority religion carry out sustained campaigns to convince the minority to abandon its faith. Eighteen years ago, the *New York Times* published a letter in which I objected to its accepting advertisements from Jews for Jesus containing biblical proof texts for Christian doctrines. Setting aside the well-known issue of the ethically objectionable misappropriation of Jewish symbols, the letter argued that publishing such religious polemic puts a Jewish respondent in an untenable position. Jews would either have to explain in a counter-ad why the verses in question cannot legitimately be understood christologically, which "would pollute the atmosphere of interfaith relations and create concrete dangers for the Jewish minority," or they would have to remain silent, thus accepting "a quasi-medieval position of being bombarded by public attacks on their faith without opportunity for candid response."[15]

Second, the history of Christian treatment of Jews is genuinely relevant to this moral calculus. The Jewish community reacts to missionary efforts by Christians through the prism of Crusades, Inquisition, blood libels, accusations of host desecration and well poisoning, depictions of Jews as instruments of the devil, and assorted massacres. This reaction is not merely understandable; it is thoroughly legitimate. The Jewish people managed to survive these religiously motivated efforts to destroy it, but contemporary efforts to wipe it out by kinder means are tainted by this history. Like it or not, the Christian missionary to the Jews is continuing the work of Count Emicho, Vincent Ferrer, Torquemada, and Chmielnicki. Jews for Jesus can proclaim as loudly and as often as they wish that these persecutors of Jews were not Christians, but there is no avoiding the fact that they acted and were perceived as acting in the name of Christianity. Even if proselytizing other groups is appropriate, proselytizing Jews is arguably not.

Let me end more softly by returning to my anti-interventionist mode. In a contemporary context, it is a matter of the first importance to recognize that belief in eschatological verification is very different from mission. I have made this point in several essays, but it bears repetition here. Participants in dialogue often affirm that even the assertion that your faith will be vindicated at the end of days constitutes morally objectionable triumphalism. I regard this position as itself morally objectionable. Both Jews and Christians are entitled to believe that their respective religions are true in a deep and uncompromising sense, and that this truth will become evident to all the world in the fullness of time.

1. *Bavli Yevamot* 47a.
2. For a book-length discussion of this issue arguing that Jews did not proselytize before the second century C.E., see Martin Goodman, *Mission and Conversion: Proselytizing in the Religious History of the Roman Empire* (Oxford, 1994).
3. Some forms of Christianity, at least today, take a position on forgiveness of enemies that can be quite jarring to Jews. During a break at an international meeting in Lower Manhattan between Catholic clergy, primarily cardinals, and Orthodox Jews arranged by the World Jewish Congress, the group walked to ground zero, where Cardinal Lustiger of France recited a spontaneous prayer. I was stunned when I heard the words, *"Pardonnez les assassins."* I cannot imagine a Jew who would share this sentiment, particularly in light of the fact that the 9/11 murderers left themselves no opportunity to repent. My discomfiture was enhanced later in the day when another cardinal spoke of how we can learn from a Jewish Holocaust survivor who converted to Catholicism and declared that she forgives those who tormented her in the camps.
4. "Mitsvah," in *Christianity in Jewish Terms,* ed. Tikva Frymer-Kensky, David Novak, Peter Ochs, David Fox Sandmel, and Michael Signer (Boulder, CO, 2000), p. 118.
5. See my discussion in "On the Image and Destiny of Gentiles in Ashkenazic Polemical Literature" (in Hebrew), in *Facing the Cross: The Persecutions of 1096 in History and Historiography,* ed. Yom Tov Assis et al. (Jerusalem, 2000), pp. 80–81.
6. *The Jewish-Christian Debate in the High Middle Ages: A Critical Edition of the Nizzahon Vetus with an Introduction, Translation, and Commentary* (Philadelphia, 1979; soft cover edition, Northvale, NJ, and London, 1996), #211, English section, pp. 206–207. I commented on this passage in "Jacob Katz on Jews and Christians in the Middle Ages," in *The Pride of Jacob: Essays on Jacob Katz and His Work,* ed. Jay M. Harris, (Cambridge, MA, 2002), pp. 52–54.
7. *Tosafot* to *Qiddushin* 70b, s.v. *qashim gerim.*
8. See the argument in my "Mission to the Jews and Jewish-Christian Contacts in the Polemical Literature of the High Middle Ages," *American Historical Review* 91 (1986): pp. 576–591.
9. For a discussion of the scholarly debate about these matters, see "On the Image and Destiny of Gentiles in Ashkenazic Polemical Literature," pp. 74–91. Several participants in that debate also pointed to a medieval hymn in the High Holiday liturgy that describes in recurrent, celebratory language how all the world's inhabitants will gather to worship the true God. For an English translation of this hymn, see, for example, *The Complete Artscroll Machzor: Rosh Hashanah* (New York, 1986), pp. 495, 497.
10. *Tiferet Yisrael* to *Avot* 3:14 (*Boaz* #1).
11. For a detailed analysis of Christian readings of this difficult chapter, see Jeremy Cohen, "The Mystery of Israel's Salvation: Romans 11:25–26 in Patristic and Medieval Exegesis," *Harvard Theological Review* 98 (2005): pp. 247–281.
12. Ruth Nisse, " 'Your Name Will No Longer Be Asenath': Apocrypha, Anti-martyrdom, and Jewish Conversion in Thirteenth-Century England," *Speculum* 81 (2006). pp. 738–739.
13. This is the position expressed in the controversial Catholic document *Dominus Iesus.* See my analysis in "*Dominus Iesus* and the Jews," *America* 185:7 (September 17, 2001): pp. 7–12, also available at bc.edu/research/cjl/meta-elements/texts/cjrelations/resources/articles/berger.htm. Reprinted in *Sic et Non: Encountering* Dominus Iesus, ed. Stephen J. Pope and Charles C. Hefling, (New York, 2002), pp. 39–46.
14. "Jewish-Christian Relations: A Jewish Perspective," *Journal of Ecumenical Studies* 20 (1983): pp. 17–18.
15. "Jews for Jesus Ad Poses Painful Choices," *New York Times,* January 9, 1988, p. 26.

Reflections on Conversion and Proselytizing: Response to David Berger

Leanne Van Dyk

David Berger's paper on conversion and proselytizing in Judaism and Christianity is important for a number of reasons, in my view. For one thing, it considers the issue from both directions—Jewish-to-Christian proselytizing and Christian-to-Jewish proselytizing. For the first, Berger notes a range of different approaches in the Hellenistic-Roman-medieval times to Jewish efforts at the conversion of others. Even though there was, as Berger says, "an extraordinarily complex constellation of theological, historical, and psychological considerations" that would repress Jewish missionizing of others, perhaps especially Christians, there was at least an apologetic impulse that emerged now and then.

Another reason I think David Berger's paper is important is it addresses clearly the issue of the salvific claims of both traditions and how those claims influence the issue of proselytizing. This is where I would like to focus my remarks, from the perspective of the Reformed and Presbyterian Christian tradition.

Let me remind you of the couple of sentences from Rabbi Berger's paper that summarize his historical survey: "Jewish opposition to mission is a function of a deeply held principle recognizing the salvific potential of other religions. As we have seen, the history of Jewish attitudes regarding this question is far more complicated, but there is an element of truth in this assertion even with respect to the premodern period" (p. 135).

The Christian tradition's perspective on the salvific potential of other religions is a big question indeed. We shall restrict our focus only to the salvific potential of Jews. The Presbyterian Church has engaged this question in some significant ways in several important papers in the last twenty years or so. The theological streams that were identified by Robert Weingartner this morning, including some basic theological shifts toward a more missional, Trinitarian, and incarnational theology, have opened up some new possibilities for discussion on this important question.

The 1987 document of the Presbyterian Church (U.S.A.), *A Theological Understanding of the Relationship between Christians and Jews* reflects some of these new possibilities. The document makes clear that supersessionism must be replaced by a biblical theology that emphasizes the faithful promises of God with the Jews as God's chosen people. This requires a process of repentance on the part of Christians, continuing self-awareness of Christian language and practices that have been experienced negatively by Jews, and ongoing conversation and listening. Furthermore, the doctrine of election, a doctrine of great importance to Reformed Christians, has significance with respect to Jews. To be sure, there are tensions in an understanding of this doctrine, because Christians understand election as fully revealed in Jesus Christ and Jews understand the continuity of election in ways connected to people, identity, and land. But, as the 1987 PCUSA document states, "we believe that God has bound us together in a unique relationship for the sake of God's love for the world."

The basic acknowledgment that God works in covenant faithfulness for the sake of God's love for the world in both traditions is a critically important step. Not all Christian people are ready and willing to take this step. But it can be supported from a number of vintage Reformed doctrines. From an affirmation of the sovereignty and incomprehensibility of God, the Reformed Christian humbly acknowledges that God's ways are far beyond our knowledge and God's ultimate purposes are within God's divine counsel. From an affirmation of the divine goodness of all things, Reformed Christians gratefully acknowledge that wherever there is goodness, wherever there is knowledge, wherever there is joy, kindness, compassion, art, music, cooperation, reconciliation, urban renewal, or any other good thing, there is God's divine presence. So, it is within the framework of a Reformed understanding of God that God may—and does—choose to work God's purposes for the world through Christians and through other peoples of the world.

So, if God works for good in a faithful and continuous way through Jews, Christians, and other peoples as well, in a Reformed Christian theological framework, there would seem to be no ban on the salvific possibility for those outside the Christian faith. Christians may modestly choose to take a

certain agnosticism with respect to the salvific possibility for non-Chr[i]
admitting that God's saving scope is not known. Although there
difficulties with some New Testament texts on this modest agnosticism,
does fit within the framework of key Reformed doctrines.

But this does not yet solve the problem. Can Christians, according to the inner logic and narrative of the Christian faith, proselytize Jews, who themselves are recipients of the electing grace of God? Or are Christians required by the inner logic of their faith to evangelize Jews? This is the more pressing question.

With respect to this question there seems to be some genuine polarities. Ultimately, I think caution and modesty are required. The polarities are these: On the one hand, the Reformed Christian acknowledges what we have just said—that we have a commitment to God's redemptive purposes in the world, including God's ongoing, faithful covenant with the Jews. This would seem to preclude overt proselytizing of Jews, surely an insult and an affront, especially considering the grim history of oppression and persecution. However, the Christian is called to live with what might be called the full Christian view of reality, the whole Christian story and perspective. That means, for Christians, that God's redemptive purposes in the world are revealed in Jesus Christ. So, although supersessionism must be corrected, it is theologically legitimate, on a Christian account, to perceive God's ongoing, faithful covenant with the Jews as fulfilled in Jesus Christ.

Here, clearly, is the difficult part. A Reformed and Presbyterian theological approach, as several key documents have articulated in recent years, can affirm God's divine and salvific intention with respect to the Jews. But deep within the Christian narrative and logic is the testimony to the risen Lord Jesus Christ, who calls us to believe, to witness, to proclaim, and to serve in his name. Christian faith is faith in God, the living God of Israel. But that God, for the Christian believer, is further revealed to be the Triune God: Father, Son, and Holy Spirit.

One way forward, for Christians, is to become more textured and historical. Because proselytizing has been—and still continues to be—such a painful and annihilating experience for Jewish communities, Christians can advance Christian-Jewish dialogue by learning to avoid negative language and practices, including proselytizing.

Instead, Christians can recognize that the unique Christian call to witness to the faith takes a variety of forms appropriate to the context. It is not appropriate, given the context, the history, the common election by the God of Israel, the continuing grave dangers in teachings and practices of contempt, for Christians to engage in outright proselytizing of Jews. But it is appropriate for Christians to give testimony to their faith in many ways other than verbal persuasion.

"Giving testimony to one's faith"—this is different from proselytizing. Verbal persuasion from Christians to Jews is not appropriate. But Christians live in the light of Jesus Christ. Expressing that life in relationally congruent ways takes discernment.

Although our brother in the Reformed faith John Calvin certainly did not have in mind this particular cluster of issues, the challenge of dialogue and mutually respectful relationship between Christians and Jews, he once said that the Christian sacraments, baptism and the Lord's Supper, are meant to serve our praise to God and to serve our testimony to the world. This means that Christians are to live as communities that embody in concrete ways our baptismal practices, as communities that embody in concrete ways our eucharistic practices. Such practices include forgiveness, hospitality, the commitment to peace and justice, reconciliation, love, and mercy. When Christians live their sacramental practices as praise to God and as testimony to the world, they are engaging in testimony in concretely visible ways that require relationship, texture, and context. Christians are living their faith, which is testimony, a requirement and call of their faith.

One of David Berger's closing remarks is that "both Jews and Christians are entitled to believe that their respective religions are true in a deep and uncompromising sense." Thus, when Christians engage in the testimony of life, relationships, sacramental practices writ large, they are engaging in one expression of their belief. But they are not proselytizing, which in the case of their Jewish neighbors is not appropriate within a broad Reformed vision of God's sovereignty and ultimate divine purposes. Thus, I agree with David Berger's statement in his paper, "Even if proselytizing other groups is appropriate, proselytizing Jews is arguably not."

Identity

Changes in American Jewish Identities since 1948: From Norms to Aesthetics

Steven M. Cohen

Jews Within

In the sixty years that have elapsed since the founding of the State of Israel, profound changes have taken place in Israel, in American Jews' relationship with Israel, and in American Jews' identities. With regard to the latter (which has bearing upon Israel and American Jews' ties to Israel), two major changes are among the most salient and influential. One is the enormous change in the integration of Jews into the larger American society. In contrast with just fifty years ago, today's Jews have far fewer Jewish spouses, friends, neighbors, and co-workers.

This increasing integration certainly reflects several positive developments, such as lower anti-Semitism, rising Jewish achievement, and greater acceptance of Jews by non-Jews. Not only do most young American Jews have loving relationships with non-Jews, but hundreds of thousands of non-Jews love Jews—a common circumstance now, and a fairly rare occurrence just a few decades ago. At the same time, this integration has brought some adverse consequences for Judaism and Jewishness, including diminished attachment to a sense of Jewish kinship, to Jewish community, to Israel, and to Jewish peoplehood. The link between numerous social ties to other Jews and numerous affective ties to collective Jewish things (including Israel), however, is clear and undeniable.

Aside from integration, the other major development in the lives of American Jews and Judaism is the rise of the Jewish Sovereign Self, as Arnold Eisen and I argued in *The Jew Within*.[1] As compared with the parents and predecessors in 1948, Jews today feel far more ready to assert whether, when, where, and how they will express their Jewish identities, shifting from normative constructions of being Jewish to aesthetic understandings. A normative approach assumes that being Jewishly involved is both good and right. Moreover, Jewish norms, although often in conflict, in effect declare that certain ways of being Jewish are better than other ways of being Jewish. Such norms can derive from God, parents, nostalgia, tradition, *halakha* (Jewish law), and/or belonging to the Jewish people. An aesthetic approach, in contrast, is less judgmental and directive. It sees being Jewish as a matter of beauty and culture, as a resource for meaning rather than as an ethical or moral imperative.

As late as the 1960s, engaged American Jews still maintained a consensus that being Jewish was a matter of obligations. One could violate the norms, but then one felt guilty about it. The world has changed and the Jewish world has changed. Fewer people today regard being Jewish as a matter of norms and obligations.[2]

The combination of increasing integration into American society on the one hand and decreasing emphasis on Judaism as a normative system on the other has had a powerful influence. The twin forces have led to substantial changes in what it means to be a Jew in America, as defined and experienced by the American Jewish public—what Charles Liebman referred to as the folk religion, as opposed to the elite religion, of American Jews.[3] These developments have produced changes in Orthodoxy, Conservatism, and Reform—the rubrics that continue to define a large number of American Jews, even in the postdenominational age in which we think we live.

The Major Denominational Labels

The major labels that American Jews use to define their ways of being Jewish remain Orthodox, Conservative, and Reform, albeit with other possibilities—such as Reconstructionist and Jewish Renewal—and there is growth in nondenominational and postdenominational tendencies, as well. Demographically, the JCC (Jewish community center) movement is, however, the largest institutionally based association in American Jewish life, with about a million Jewish members. It even outnumbers Reform Judaism, the largest denominational movement in American Judaism. But few observers think of the two hundred JCCs as constituting a movement within Judaism, notwithstanding an impressive organizational range and complexity that embraces early childhood education, day camps, youth groups, continentally based sports events, adult Jewish education, cultural events, communitywide organizing, and engagement with Israel.

The denominational nomenclature is so prevalent in the United States in large part because American society defines being Jewish as primarily a religious option: It's Protestant, Catholic, Jew—and now Muslim, Hindu, and so on—rather than Italian, Irish, Hispanic, Jewish.[4] In other regions of the Diaspora, where being Jewish is more overtly ethnic, denominational labels are far less compelling. It is worth reviewing each denominational camp.

Growing Larger and Sliding Right

In broad strokes, Orthodoxy has been demographically growing.[5] Its population, according to all standard sociological measures, scores highest in terms of Jewish commitment, education, activity, and social ties. On average, on a person-for-person basis, Orthodox Jews undertake more hours of Jewish education, perform more rituals, give more charity, have more Jewish friends, more often visit and move to Israel, more readily claim to be Jewishly committed, and on and on.

At the same time, Orthodoxy has gradually become more separatist and sectarian with respect to other Jews.[6] This "sliding to the right" is partly due to a triumphalist conviction that only Orthodoxy will survive the assimilatory influence of the larger society, and in part, a reaction to what Orthodoxy sees as failure and immorality in non-Orthodox versions of Judaism.

Deep within, most committed Orthodox Jews see other systems as violating Torah-true, authentic understandings as to what Jews should do and what they should believe. They thus have far more of a problem with Conservative or Reform rabbis than with Conservative or Reform Jews. This attitude expresses itself in many ways, such as the refusal of Orthodox rabbis to in any way lend legitimacy to non-Orthodox rabbis, even as many Orthodox bodies make a massive investment and commitment to reach and educate non-Orthodox Jews as individuals. Of the most traditional Orthodox figures many say, in effect, "To non-Orthodox denominations, nothing; to non-Orthodox Jews as individuals, everything."

Ethnic Decline and Conservative Shrinkage

The Conservative movement has traditionally reflected the underlying ethnicity of Jewish America.[7] Marshall Sklare referred to the Conservative synagogue as an "ethnic Church," drawing its strength from the ties of family, community, and peoplehood—or *ethnos*—that once widely characterized American Jews.[8] As Jewish ethnicity has weakened, with the decline of Jewish marriages, friendships, and neighborhoods,[9] so too has Conservative Judaism. In the 1950s and 1960s, it was the major affiliation of synagogue Jews, about two-thirds of whom belonged to Conservative congregations. Now it has declined to about one-third, and is rapidly shrinking demographically.

Yet Conservative Judaism sill occupies a critical place—ideologically, socially, and philosophically—between Orthodoxy and Reform. The movement offers a model of intensive Jewish living that is both modern and accessible to large numbers of American Jews. It boasts an institutional infrastructure that embraces congregations, day schools, camps, youth movements, Israel-based institutions, publications, and informal networks, to say nothing of its thousands of rabbis, cantors, educators, other professionals, and lay leaders. Those who care about a healthy American Jewry should worry about how to help the Conservative moment revive itself and become again a strong pillar of American Jewry.

Jews (and Others) Choosing Judaism

The Reform movement, for its part, has made a signal contribution to American Judaism by strongly advancing and developing the notion of "Judaism by choice."[10] In effect, its leaders have taught that for Judaism to be compelling and sustainable Jews must make their own choices, which are informed by teaching that is Judaically authentic and at the same time relevant to the contemporary, modern context.

This approach has attracted and sustained the involvement of hundreds of thousands of Jews, including many with minimal exposure to Jewish education and social networks. And, under the leadership of Rabbi Eric Yoffie, at the helm of the highly regarded Union for Reform Judaism, the movement has grown to nine hundred-plus congregations, many of which display an extraordinary level of energy and vibrancy. With four campuses in the U.S. and Israel, the Hebrew Union College–Jewish Institute of Religion, under the extraordinary leadership of Rabbi David Ellenson, has been training scores of rabbis, cantors, educators, and communal professionals annually for an expanding movement with ongoing demands for its ranks of professional leadership.

At the same time, perhaps half of the couples joining Reform temples have a partner who was not born Jewish, only a minority of whom have converted to Judaism. Because the Reform movement attracts these people, it has a population of congregants that, on average, is not highly educated in Jewish terms, at least when compared with their Orthodox or Conservative counterparts taken together.

Not coincidentally, the Reform movement, its synagogues, and its rabbis are often blamed for serving as the primary home for apparently "weak" Jews in their midst. In response, we can do a thought experiment and assume that the Reform movement decided to close shop. What would happen to all these Jews, particularly those who are intermarried, or had weak childhood education in Judaism, or both—as is often the case? Certainly, some would join Conservative synagogues, but probably the vast majority would not be attached to Jewish life. And, notwithstanding the large number of mixed-married and poorly educated Jews, over the years the movement's official policies have placed more emphasis on ritual practice, Jewish learning, Zionism, prayer, and Hebrew, trends embodied and exemplified by its newly published siddur, *Mishkan T'filah*.

Reform rabbis, educators, and lay leaders are thus engaging with and struggling to engage with their population, some of whom are among the most marginally involved in conventional Jewish life. This struggle is to their credit. Sometimes they succeed. On other occasions, they fail, as is manifest in the large number of congregants who leave their temples upon the bar/bat mitzvah of their youngest child; perhaps about half do so. Even more worrying, perhaps, are the large numbers of children raised in Reform Judaism who marry out, more by far than the other two major movements. But, with that said, Reform is now the largest Jewish denominational movement in the United States, holding steady in recent years, as the number of non-Jewish Reform congregants grows, while the number of Jewish Reform congregants (be they born-Jews or converts to Judaism) slowly declines over the long haul.

The Orthodox Struggle with *Clal Yisrael*

All three major religious movements are standing at a crossroads. One major struggle within Orthodoxy is over whether Orthodoxy will remain part of the real *Am Yisrael* (Jewish People) in America—not the Jews they may want, but the Jews we actually have. That struggle translates into the questions: Can one have common educational, intellectual, or communal relationships, not only with non-Orthodox Jews but also with non-Orthodox rabbis? How does one maintain dialogue and genuine collaboration with them?

For many Orthodox, the break with Jewish law as they understand it by Conservative, Reform, and other non-Orthodox movements is too high a barrier to overcome. The ordination of gay and lesbian rabbis is one issue. Also, the seeming acceptance of intermarriage and the incorporation of large numbers of non-Jews into Jewish congregations deeply trouble Orthodox rabbis of all persuasions.

The high rates of intermarriage, patrilineal descent, and what they regard as illegitimate conversions mean to many Orthodox parents that their children might unknowingly marry what to them are non-Jews, albeit those who were raised and educated in Reform or Conservative congregations. Significant numbers of Orthodox Jews insulate their children not only from the influences of the larger society, but also from intimate contact with non-Orthodox Jews.

Yet despite these tendencies, a number of notable efforts seek to promote more openness and engagement with all of Jewry. One finds an internal struggle at Yeshiva University over which way the institution will go under the leadership of Richard Joel as its president, either in the direction of greater sectarianism or greater engagement with all of Jewry.

The newly established Yeshivat Chovevei Torah, headed by Rabbi Avi Weiss, is producing rabbis committed to the unity of the Jewish people.

Conservative Turnaround?

The population of the Conservative movement is shrinking. Reflecting trends that date back to 1960 or so, there are probably twice as many Conservative senior citizens as there are Conservative children.

The newly emerging Conservative leadership—both the recently installed and the soon-to-be appointed—will be addressing the critical demographic challenges of shrinkage and aging. Any transition from great leaders of the older generation to younger persons of great talent raises hopes for change. With Arnold Eisen as the newly appointed chancellor of the Jewish Theological Seminary (JTS), there is a widespread expectation of revival in the movement, notwithstanding that JTS is just one important element in the Conservative institutional array.

Among major Conservative institutions, JTS is not alone in the transition to a new and younger leadership. In the three major professional leadership positions of the Conservative movement, the older generation is giving way to a new one. As with JTS, that will also happen within the next two years at the United Synagogue of Conservative Judaism and the Rabbinical Assembly. The three leaders who have steered these bodies over the past two decades deserve respect and admiration. One must hope that the transition will mean not only a change in personnel but also a thoroughgoing and appropriate shift in culture, language, and ethos that only a new generation can bring.

Thus, the emerging generation of prominent Conservative rabbis, congregational leaders, thinkers, and others will need to reconfigure the Conservative movement so that it regains the attachment of its erstwhile natural constituency. These are young-adult Jews who are socially progressive, religiously liberal and, at the same time, religiously and textually serious, and committed to high-quality spiritual experiences. In the recent past, the exodus of such individuals to Orthodoxy or to nonaffiliated communities has deprived many Conservative congregations of their highest-caliber potential leadership.

"Who Lost BJ?"

Over the years, the Conservative movement has been extraordinarily productive and has created important endeavors—many of which, however, are no longer associated with it. It is American Judaism's biggest exporter of homegrown talent, people, ideas, and institutions. Conservatism just cannot seem to hold on to some of its finest creations.

The Reconstructionist movement is but one example of this tendency, as is the havurah movement of the 1960s and 1970s.[11] The American Jewish University—the former University of Judaism—is no longer Conservative, while its rabbinical school is still formally Conservative. The Jewish Museum is affiliated with the JTS, yet hardly anybody knows this. The best-known synagogue in the United States is B'nai Yeshurun (BJ) on New York's Upper West Side, which was formerly Conservative but disaffiliated some years ago. Just as some conservative American politicians used to ask, "Who lost Red China?" there must be some Conservative Jewish leaders who ask (or should ask), "Who lost BJ?" This innovative congregation, with arguably the highest profile in North America, is one more formerly Conservative export.

So too are the many independent *minyanim* (prayer groups) that have been started by people trained in the Conservative movement.[12] These leaders were and are capable of being leaders in the Conservative movement, yet have decided—at least for now—to build their communities outside the formal boundaries of Conservatism.

One might thus conclude that Jewish intensification often means leaving Conservative Judaism. The questions then become: How does one create a space where these people will have a sense of belonging? How can they remain within the Conservative orbit even if they operate with no formal affiliation with the usual Conservative institutions?

The Intermarriage Challenge

The extent of intermarriage and intergroup friendship is truly significant. About two-thirds of older American Jews have mostly Jewish friends. In contrast, two-thirds of the under-thirty generation have mostly non-Jewish friends. Most young Jews today who have a partner—married or not— are either married or romantically involved with non-Jews. I can say with relative certitude that none of my grandparents ever dated a non-Jew, and I can say with equal certitude that the vast majority of Jews my children's ages have had intimate and loving relationships with non-Jews.

The Reform movement, in the forefront of efforts to engage intermarried Jews in congregational life, is tackling the question of how to keep the intermarried and their children attached to Judaism in an authentic way. This issue is particularly challenging as so many non-Jews with hardly any Jewish background come into Reform temples with their Jewish partners, many of whom themselves have weak Jewish backgrounds.

More and more, Reform temples consist of two contrasting sorts of congregants. One segment consists of growing numbers of well-groomed alumni of NFTY, religious schools, and URJ camps; the other comprises Jewish and non-Jewish congregants with minimal Jewish social and educational capital. The growth of both sorts of populations propels seemingly contradictory tendencies. For example, more alternative services have been springing up in Reform temples' chapels and basements. At the same, the larger sanctuaries on Shabbat mornings are filled with one-Shabbat-a-year worshippers celebrating bar and bat mitzvahs. And a good fraction of the bar/bat mitzvah families will soon leave the congregation (a troubling event, to say the least).

Both intermarried Jews and their non-Jewish spouses function as full members of Reform congregations and serve as temple board members and officers, albeit with some limitations on the leadership opportunities available to the non-Jewish partner. Their needs and values shape temple practices, policies, and personnel, underscoring the challenges posed by the presence of so many non-Jews and their intermarried spouses. For example, how does the rabbi clearly promote the conversion of non-Jewish spouses to Judaism without undermining the attempt to welcome mixed-married couples? Even more pointedly, how does one teach a confirmation class of adolescents that Jews should marry Jews when half the sixteen-year-olds are the children of Jewish and non-Jewish parents? While these dilemmas are most keenly felt in Reform temples, they emerge in Conservative and Reconstructionist congregations as well.[13]

Losing the Intermarriage Battle?

No matter how well Reform congregations handle the intermarried families they reach, American Judaism as a whole is failing to reverse the deleterious effects of intermarriage on the Jewish population as a whole. As HUC-JIR sociologist Bruce Phillips reports, of those raised by two Jewish parents, almost 98 percent were raised as Jewish by religion; of those raised by one Jewish parent and one non-Jewish parent, the figure drops to 39 percent; and of those raised by a "half-Jew" and a non-Jew, that is with one of four Jewish grandparents, just 4 percent are raised in the Jewish religion.[14] On a proportionate basis, the number of Orthodox Jewish children is almost twice the number of Orthodox middle-aged people, while the number of non-Orthodox children falls to almost half of non-Orthodox middle-aged people. Of people with at least one Jewish parent who are now elderly, over 90 percent identify as Jews; of young adults with at least one Jewish parent, less than half identify as Jews. Because of intermarriage, and all it represents and brings about, we are in a sort of Jewish population meltdown with grave consequences for the future of Conservative, Reform, and other Judaic movements outside of Orthodoxy.

Outreach and welcoming are certainly having an influence, bringing large numbers of intermarried Jews into our congregations, but the true challenge lies not with the intermarried Jews we see, or we know, or who are in our generally more committed families where, thankfully, many intermarried young people are making Jewish choices. The real problem lies with the intermarried we never see, the ones who live in areas of the country distant from congregations, the ones with only a single Jewish parent who begin their married lives with only a tentative tie to being Jewish. The two-generation outflow of such individuals—clearly visible in all our population studies—is truly sad and worrisome. Well over a million Americans today, perhaps two million, report they had a Jewish parent or grandparent, yet identify as Christian or as otherwise non-Jewish.

And, whatever their true number, the vast amount of recent intermarriage promises hundreds of thousands more in the coming years.

Multiple Modes of Jewish Engagement

All this should not ignore the many other ways outside of religious congregational life in which American Jews are Jewishly engaged. Many still live in such Jewish neighborhoods as New York's Upper West Side, Squirrel Hill (Pittsburgh), and Silver Spring (Maryland), even as more move to such radically different locales as Las Vegas and other sparsely settled Jewish environs in the Mountain and Pacific regions. Jews in areas of greater residential concentration, largely in the Northeast and Midwest, not only have more neighbors that are Jewish; they also report more Jewish spouses, more Jewish friends, and more Jewish institutional ties. Jews in the older areas of settlement often still have an ethnic style; many manifest Jewishness through domestic political concerns or with regard to Israel.

On another plane, the JCC movement, as I mentioned earlier, is widely overlooked as a locus of Jewish community-building, to say nothing of its great strides in informal Jewish education. Furthermore, American Jews have a rich cultural life in music, art, literature, scholarship, journalism, dance, museums of various kinds, and now on the Internet.

Indeed, there are hundreds of millions of pages on the Internet on Jewish matters. Obviously, none existed fifteen years ago. There is a documented increase in Jewish involvement in social-justice activism, of which Ruth Messinger and the American Jewish World Service (AJWS) is the most visible phenomenon. There are more Jewish cultural activities than ever, be they concerts, musical events, drama, art exhibitions, or Jewish literature magazines.[15] There is thus a plethora of Jewish life that is being led by people in their twenties and thirties outside the traditional network. And we cannot ignore the ongoing influence of more pervasive movements and what we may call Jewish sensibilities, be they nearly forty years of Jewish feminism,[16] or the more recently emerging Jewish spirituality movement with its shaping of prayer, healing, and pastoral clergy such as by Rabbi Rachel Cowan and others.

Particularly exciting is the work of many of the younger generation—Jews in their twenties and thirties—who are involved in self-initiated acts of Jewish communal creation.[17] The newly established independent *minyanim* and rabbi-led emergent spiritual communities is particularly impressive. About eighty of these have sprung up all over the United States, several of them outside the major Jewish centers. Some such communities—Hadar and IKAR come to mind—report upwards of three thousand people on their mailing lists, while other communities number as few as sixty or seventy participants (they avoid using such conventional words as *members* or *congregations* or *officers*).

Extended Singlehood

Today, reflecting a worldwide pattern, most non-Orthodox Jewish adults under the age of forty are not married. In the recent past, Jews used to marry five to seven years after leaving university. This now happens after ten to fifteen years, if at all. There are also somewhat higher divorce rates than at mid-century. All this means that among non-Orthodox Jews there is a large percentage of unmarried people, usually without children. In the past, childrearing has brought Jews to congregations and JCCs.

Since this younger generation is spending many more years unmarried and without children, the Jewish community must develop institutions they can use. Few will come to JCCs, synagogues, or federations as currently constructed. There, they would find mainly married people, most of them married to Jews, and often with young children of their own, or middle-aged and older empty-nesters.

Strengthening the Jewish Collective and Ties to Israel

The decline in commitment of many Jews to the Jewish people, Israel, and the Jewish community is deeply worrying. Fewer Jews see themselves as obligated to support the collective interests of the Jewish people, to feel attached to Israel, or even to relate personally to the very notion of the Jewish people at all.[18]

The interplay between intermarriage and declining ties with the Jewish collective can be seen in recently collected data among non-Orthodox American Jews that makes three powerful points:

1. However measured, younger Jews are much less attached to Israel than older Jews. (See graphs 1–5.)
2. The intermarried are far less attached to Israel than the in-married or single Jews. (See Graph 6.)
3. Younger intermarried Jews are even more alienated from Israel than their older counterparts. (See Graph 7.)

In fact, were it not for the statistical inclusion of the intermarried, overall rates of attachment to Israel among the non-Orthodox would be holding steady. This is not to say that intermarriage brings about alienation from Israel. It is to say that whatever brings about intermarriage, plus whatever effect intermarriage may have on its own, operates to depress attachment to Israel and, by extension, to the Jewish community and the Jewish people.

The interpersonal and intimate ties of Jews with non-Jews pose major questions as to how one can strengthen, preserve, or make meaningful the Jewish commitment to the collective, without seeming or being racist. How does one argue for and promote Jewish marriage and friendship in this world without appearing bigoted and insular? Causes such as Israel, building the Jewish community, or caring about Jews locally and all over the world demand, at least empirically, the establishment and nurturing of strong Jewish networks of friends and family. Yet, to many Jews, younger somewhat more than older, teaching to forge and pursue such in-group ties seems so un-postmodern and un-American.

Graph 1

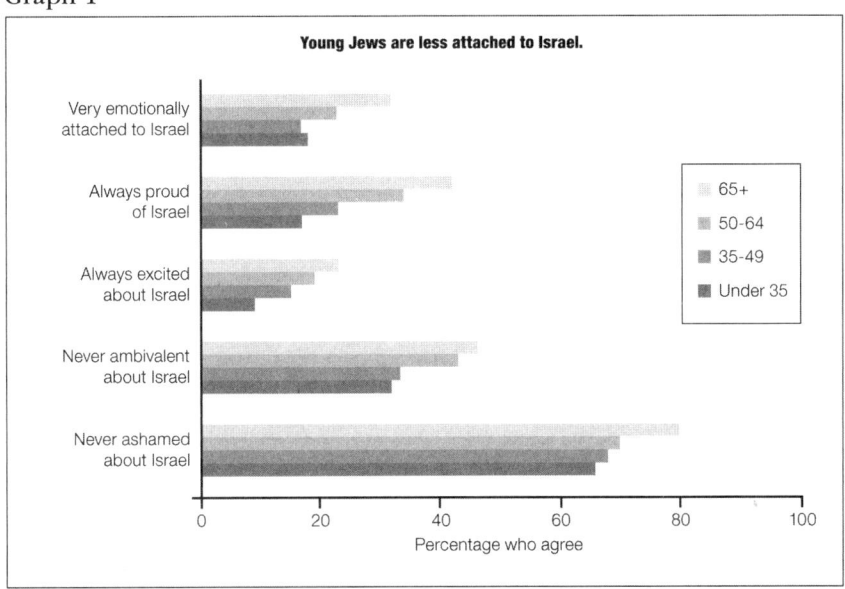

Graph 2

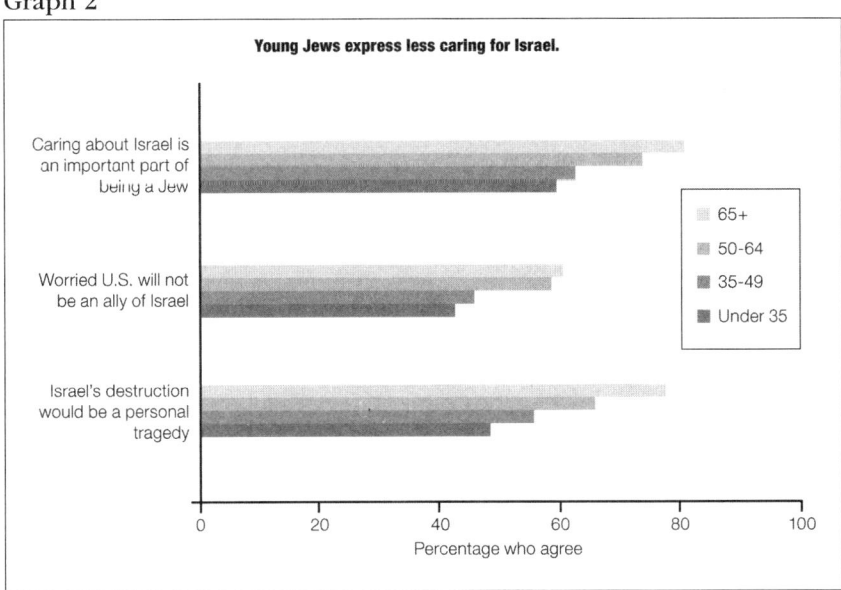

Graph 3

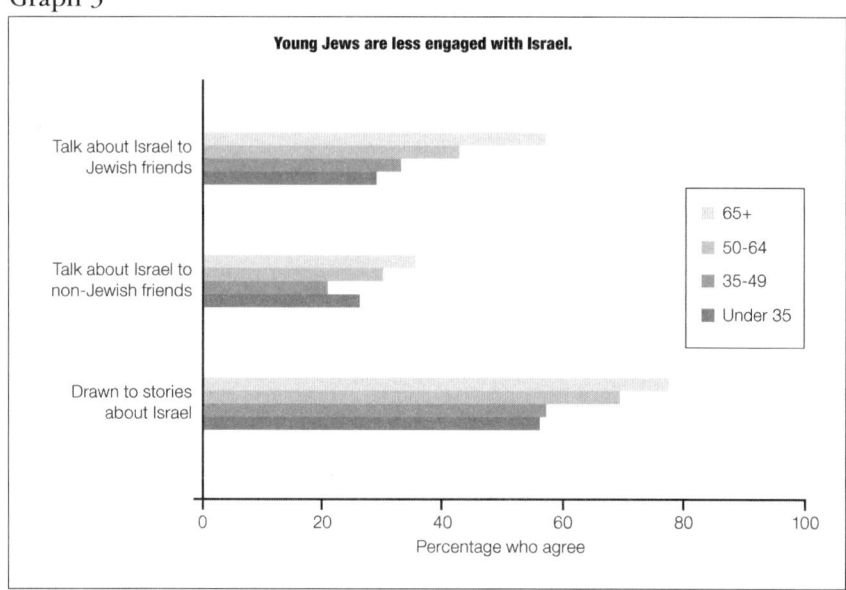

Graph 4

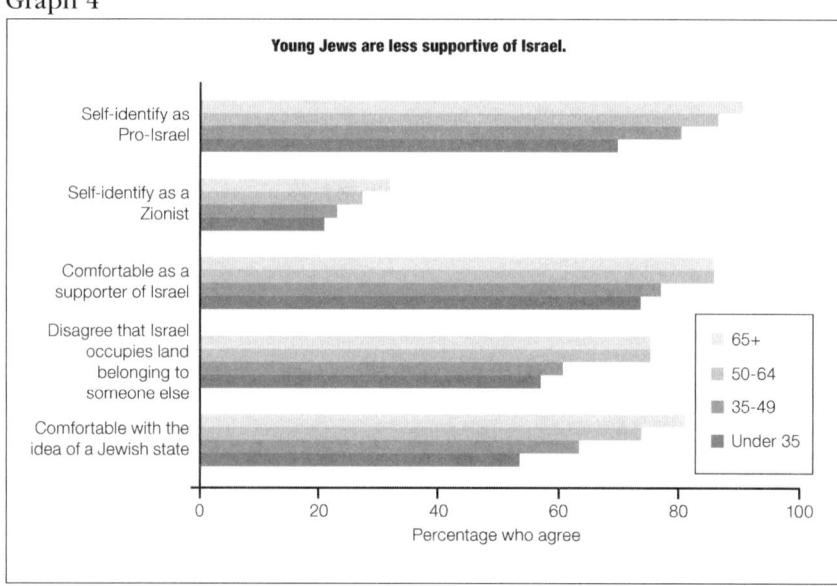

Graph 5

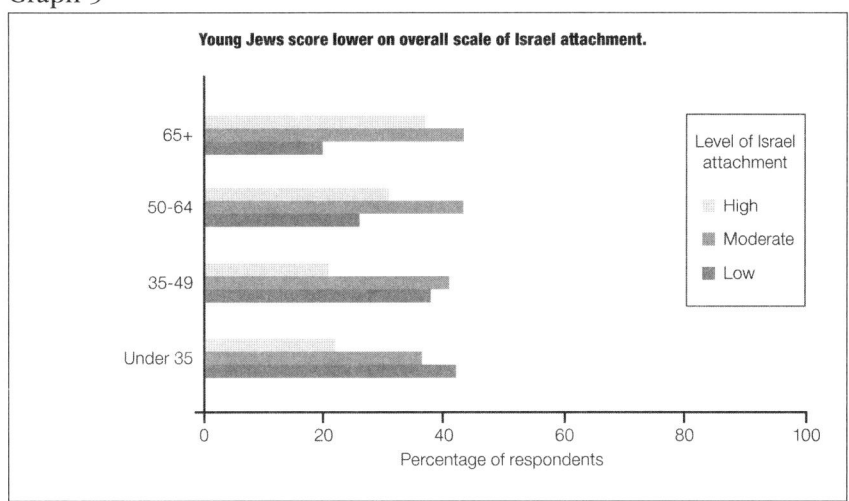

Graph 6

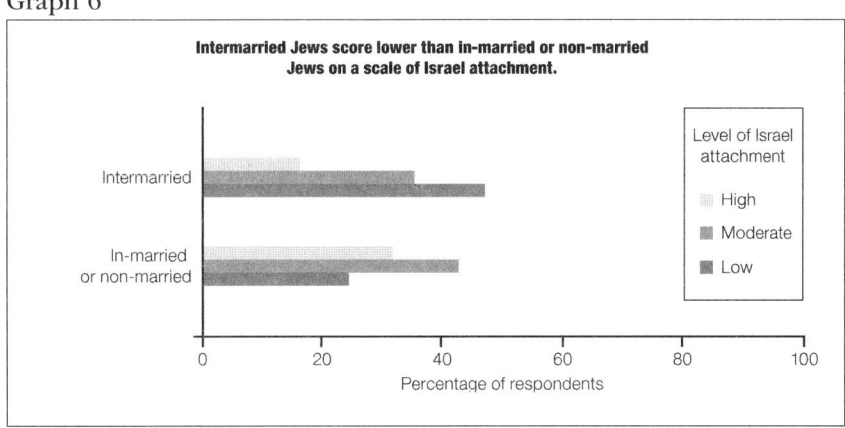

Graph 7

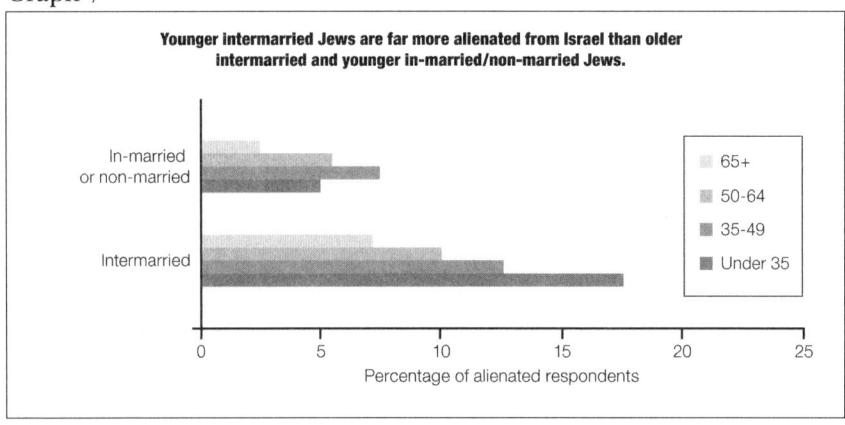

Taking Hold of Torah

If Judaism is a matter of norms, of right and wrong, one can teach one's children that Jewish involvement is right, and distancing from Jewish life is wrong. But if to be Jewish is a matter of aesthetics, then one can teach only that Jewish engagement is akin to the love of music and art. Such engagement can lend purpose and meaning and spiritual enrichment, but it is by no means a moral decision.

In fact, many Jews now see being Jewish the same way as loving music or art. It is a good thing to do, but for them it is not a matter of right or wrong. They have no sense that for a Jew to be Jewish is the right way to be, akin to one's patriotic duty as an American or as another nationality.

Such morally laden language and concepts, while Judaically authentic, are admittedly not the most immediately compelling way to reach indifferent contemporary Jews. We need to develop a third way of speaking, modeling, and teaching, one that combines the normative and aesthetic approaches, that appeals to Jews so that they will find it meaningful to be obligated, or to quote the title of Arnold Eisen's book, that they engage in *Taking Hold of Torah*.[19] We need both individual autonomy (taking hold) and a turn to Torah, in the broadest sense.

Rabbis and other leaders in all three movements and beyond are working on blending the Judaism of meaning with the Judaism of obligation. They are struggling to bridge the longstanding gap between the Judaic mission to which they are committed and the reality of the American Jewish marketplace in which they work. To the extent that they succeed, the future of American Jews and Judaism will be assured. Fortunately and unfortunately, the diversity of American Jews and the inevitability and rapidity of change makes the task of bridging Judaic mission and Jewish market an ongoing and never-finished challenge.

Excerpted and adapted from an article that appeared originally in *Changing Jewish Communities* 15 (March 2008). Available at jcpa.org/JCPA/Templates/ShowPage.asp?DBID=1&LNGID=1&TMID=111&FID=254&PID=0&IID=1747.

1. Steven M. Cohen and Arnold Eisen, *The Jew Within: Self, Family, and Community in America* (Bloomington: Indiana University Press, 2000).
2. Charles S. Liebman, *Deceptive Images: Toward a Redefinition of American Judaism* (New Brunswick: Transaction Books, 1988).
3. Charles S. Liebman, *The Ambivalent American Jew: Politics, Religion and Family in American Jewish Life* (Philadelphia: Jewish Publication Society, 1973).
4. Will Herberg, *Protestant, Catholic, Jew: An Essay in American Religious Sociology* (New York: Doubleday & Company, 1955).
5. Laurence Kotler-Berkowitz, et al, *The National Jewish Population Survey 2000–01: Strength, Challenge and Diversity in the American Jewish Population* (New York: United Jewish Communities, 2003).
6. Samuel C. Heilman, *Sliding to the Right: The Contest for the Future of American Jewish Orthodoxy* (Berkeley: University of California Press, 2006).
7. Nathan Glazer, *American Judaism,* 2nd edition (Chicago: University of Chicago Press, 1972).
8. Marshall Sklare, *Conservative Judaism: An American Religious Movement,* new augmented edition (New York: Schocken Books, 1972).
9. Steven M. Cohen, *Religious Stability, Ethnic Decline* (New York: Florence G. Heller/JCCA Research Center, 1998).
10. Michael Meyer, *Response to Modernity: A History of the Reform Movement in Judaism* (New York: Oxford University Press, 1988).
11. Riv-Ellen Prell, *Prayer and Community—The Havurah in American Judaism* (Detroit: Wayne State University Press, 1989).
12. Steven M. Cohen, J. Shawn Landres, Elie Kaunfer, and Michelle Shain, *Emergent Jewish Communities and Their Participants: Preliminary Findings from the 2007 National Spiritual Communities Study* (Los Angeles: The S3K Synagogue Studies Institute, 2007).
13. Sylvia Barack Fishman, *Double or Nothing? Jewish Families and Mixed Marriage* (Hanover, NH: University of New England Press, 2004).
14. Bruce Phillips, "American Judaism in the twenty-first century," in Dana Evan Kaplan, ed., *The Cambridge Companion to American Judaism* (Cambridge: Cambridge University Press, 2005), pp. 397–415.
15. Steven M. Cohen and Ari Y. Kelman, *Cultural Events & Jewish Identities: Young Adult Jews in New York* (New York: National Foundation for Jewish Culture, 2006).
16. Sylvia Barack Fishman, *A Breath of Life: Feminism in the American Jewish Community* (New York: The Free Press, 1993).
17. Steven M. Cohen and Ari Y. Kelman, *The Continuity of Discontinuity: How Young Jews Are Connecting, Creating, and Organizing Their Own Jewish Lives* (New York: Andrea & Charles Bronfman Philanthropies, 2007).
18. Steven M. Cohen and Ari Y. Kelman, *Beyond Distancing: Young Adult American Jews and Their Alienation from Israel* (New York: Andrea & Charles Bronfman Philanthropies, 2007). See also Steven M. Cohen and Jack Wertheimer, "Whatever Happened to the Jewish People," *Commentary* 121, no. 6 (June 2006): pp. 33–37. Also available at commentarymagazine.com/viewArticle.cfm/Whatever-Happened-to-the-Jewish-People-10079.
19. Arnold M. Eisen, *Taking Hold of Torah* (Bloomington, IN: Indiana University Press, 1997).

Presbyterian Disestablishment

Joseph D. Small

Presbyterians appear prominently in lists of America's "mainline" Protestant churches. Mainline churches are the denominations that developed from the sixteenth-century Protestant Reformation and arrived early in North America: English Puritans and other independents in New England, Dutch Reformed in New York and New Jersey, Anglicans in Virginia, Scotch-Irish Presbyterians in Pennsylvania and the Carolinas. These groups became the Congregationalists, Presbyterians, Reformed, Episcopalians, and (later) Methodists. They dominated the religious, civic, and cultural life of the United States for 350 years.

Presbyterian, Episcopal, and Congregational churches were the historically elite mainline churches. They were influential out of proportion to their numbers, over-represented among presidents, members of Congress, Supreme Court justices, and judges. Together with the Dutch Reformed, Presbyterians and Episcopalians were prominent in industry and finance. American education was deeply influenced by Presbyterian Calvinist values. (An old, old joke: A Catholic asks a Presbyterian, "Why don't you have parochial schools?" The Presbyterian replies, "We do. We call them public schools.")

But now, the mainline churches are in decline—in numbers, but, more significantly, in eminence and influence. Sociologists and cultural commentators refer to them as "sideline," "old-line," and "offline" churches. The marginalization of the historic mainline churches helps shape contemporary Presbyterian identity.

Disestablishment

Social historians identify three distinct disestablishments of the Church in North America: *legal disestablishment* in the eighteenth century, *civic disestablishment* in the nineteenth century, and *cultural disestablishment* in the twentieth century. It is the cultural disestablishment of the Church that has been especially painful and bewildering to the mainline.

Legal Disestablishment

Some of the original British colonies embraced state-sanctioned and state-supported churches. Puritans in Massachusetts and Anglicans in Virginia, along with others, institutionalized the ecclesiastical affiliations of the majority. Protests against state churches occurred from the outset, however, and legal disestablishment was well under way in the colonies by the time of the revolution. Independence from English rule was accompanied by independence from religious hegemony as "separation of Church and state" was embedded in the new republic's Bill of Rights: "Congress shall make no law respecting an establishment of religion or prohibiting the free exercise thereof, or abridging the freedom of speech, or of the press." The wall of separation between Church and state began as a low fence, yet it has become progressively higher and thicker, leading some contemporary commentators to complain that the state's neutrality has been replaced by antagonism to religion.

Civic Disestablishment

Legal disestablishment did not abolish the standing of the churches in American society, however. It left intact the social and civic dominance of the mainline—Congregational, Presbyterian, and Episcopalian churches—together with the Reformed and Methodists. But this preeminence was soon to weaken as waves of immigration throughout the nineteenth century brought other religious groups to the United States. German and Scandinavian Lutherans were joined by Irish, Italian, and Eastern European Catholics, and Jews from throughout Europe.

The proliferation of churches was broadened by the emergence of American-born denominations such as the Disciples of Christ and numerous free and holiness churches, as well as the Mormons and other non-Christian groups. All of this led to the *civic disestablishment* of all churches, but especially of the old mainline. Since no church or family of churches could claim a majority, none could be granted civic dominance; all churches were immersed in the new reality of Christian pluralism.

Protestants worked to keep Catholics on the Christian periphery and Jews on the religious periphery. However, both Catholics and Jews became increasingly prominent in the nation's political, economic, and cultural life, and increasingly integral to the religious landscape. The nineteenth-century civic disestablishment of the churches left in its wake a pervasive American religiosity that was later celebrated by Will Herberg as *Protestant, Catholic, Jew.*

Legal disestablishment took place early in the nation's history, at a time when state churches remained the norm in Europe. Civic disestablishment then broke the residual hegemony of the founding churches. Through all of this, however, a generalized cultural establishment of the churches endured. The United States remained a "Christian nation." Conceptual, social, and cultural establishment endured long after legal and civic establishments were only memories; Christianity and Americanism were merged in a unified national religiosity.

Christianity helped to shape American optimism and pragmatism while America's version of modernity helped to shape the churches. This symbiotic relationship strengthened the nation and rewarded the churches. Christianity was the favored *cultus* of the *polis*. Canadian theologian Douglas John Hall identifies this cultural establishment as "part and parcel of our whole inherited 'system of meaning,' a system intermingling Judeo-Christian, Enlightenment, Romantic-idealist, and more recently nationalistic elements."[1]

Cultural Disestablishment

The World War II decades following were tumultuous times. Virulent anticommunism, the civil rights movement, Vietnam, the struggle for women's rights, the sexual revolution, Watergate, and more led to a diffusion of the prevailing national purpose. The blurring of national vision hastened the culture's departure from the moral articulators of that vision— the churches. During the second half of the twentieth century, the churches became effectively distanced from the dominant culture. By the end of the century, the old mainline churches were marginalized, previously marginal evangelical churches were reluctant and ineffective social players, and religion generally was relegated to private life. The era 1960–2000 saw the rapidly accelerating *cultural disestablishment* of the churches.

The growing distance between North American culture and the Church, and especially the old mainline churches, may be quantified in numerous ways. Mainline Protestant churches have experienced precipitous declines in membership, while the Catholic Church's stream of religious vocations has dried to a trickle. The large network of church-related colleges and universities has been weakened as schools distance themselves from denominational identification. News coverage of religion constricts while entertainment media have replaced stock treatment of religious themes and characters with dismissive characterizations of Christianity and fascination with the occult.

More telling than the sum of specific indicators, however, is the dramatic shift in public attitudes toward Christianity and its churches. Simply put, Christianity is no longer conspicuous in American consciousness and its churches are no longer integral to American culture. The reasons for the cultural disestablishment of the Church are complex, the product of multiple forces over long periods. Nevertheless, the reality of cultural disestablishment is conspicuous in the contemporary North American religious landscape: Christianity is but one of the many religious communities that have found a home here, and it is no longer accorded special status in American culture. The Church is only one of a profusion of religious options ranging from enduring traditions such as Islam, Buddhism, and Hinduism to New Age spiritualities. Increasingly, Americans see themselves as spiritual, but not religious.

The disestablishment of the Church in North America differs from the process of secularization in Europe, where religion itself shrivels as more and more people believe less and less. Ingolf Dalferth gives voice to the feeling of many in Europe:

> Both inside and outside the various Churches, the ever more pervasive mood is that of living in an age of epilogue, of fading memories, of a futile clinging to yesterday. God, many believe, has had his time, and here at the end of the second millennium that time seems to have run out. . . . The influence of the Churches is unmistakably diminishing, and the objections of Christians increasingly fade away unheard. One no longer expects much of Christians, at least not regarding anything determinative for today.[2]

Americans, however, remain a religious people who profess faith in God, are confident of God's providential care, and anticipate special divine interventions in their lives. Polls consistently show that over 90 percent of Americans believe in "god," and that over 80 percent consider themselves "christian." But American religiosity is theologically diffuse and not necessarily connected to a *community* of faith, a particular church. Religion is privatized, and the churches remain relevant to American religiosity only to the extent that they provide spiritual goods and services that enhance personal well-being.

The profusion of religious options, coupled with American privatism that relegates religious faith to the realm of personal choice, has made it difficult for American Christianity to understand its new context theologically. It is uncertain about how to understand the great world religions, puzzled by the emergence of nontraditional spiritualities, and ambivalent about once-

certain theological affirmations. Cultural indifference to Christian re
bewilders the churches. The churchlessness of more and more pe
including the Church's own children, confounds the old mainline.

While the latest disestablishment affects all Christian denominations, its influence on the old mainline churches is dramatic. Evangelical, holiness, and pentecostal churches were never legally or civically established. Ethnically cohesive bodies such as the various Lutheran churches were not fully engaged in the civic life of the society. Catholics and Jews, victims of the prejudice and discrimination of Protestant America, always had to swim against the cultural stream. Since these groups always understood themselves as living in various degrees of tension with American society, the culture's movement away from the churches came as only a mild surprise. In stark contrast, the mainline churches were particularly ill prepared for their failure to maintain a central place in national life.

The Presbyterian Predicament

The long and complex process of disestablishment has reduced the Presbyterian Church's stature, relegating it to the cultural periphery and forcing it to vie for the attention of an increasingly indifferent society. The denomination was ill prepared, ecclesially and theologically, for the loss of its central place in national, institutional, family, and personal life. Unable to comprehend the magnitude of its cultural disestablishment, the Church has evidenced an odd combination of denial, melancholy, nostalgia, and optimism. Once wedded to the culture, and then abandoned by it, the PCUSA is always tempted to avoid evident reality by imagining the possibilities of restoration, relying on technique to bring about a renewal of Presbyterian influence. The Church seeks ways to become noticed and attractive again—by appealing to demographic cohorts, providing a wide range of personal services, promoting its mission, or attempting to reassert psychological and social influence.

The biblical formulation for the relationship between the Christian community and the culture is embedded in Presbyterian consciousness: We are to be in the world, but not of it. Thus, Paul implores Christians, "Do not be conformed to this world, but be transformed by the renewing of your minds" (Romans 12:2), while also counseling against separatism from "the immoral of this world, or the greedy and robbers, or idolaters, since you would then need to go out of the world" (1 Corinthians 5:10). *In,* but not *of*—on the one hand, no flight from the realities of the world in which we live; on the other hand, no conformity to the way things are. But, of course, it is not so simple. What does it mean to engage the world without becoming captive to it? Jürgen Moltmann goes so far as to speak of a double crisis: the *crisis of relevance* and the *crisis of identity.*

The more theology and the Church attempt to become relevant to the problems of the present day, the more deeply they are drawn into the crisis of their own Christian identity. The more they attempt to assert their identity in traditional dogmas, rights and moral notions, the more unbelievable and irrelevant they become. This double crisis can be more accurately described as the *identity-involvement dilemma*.[3]

The crisis, the identity-involvement dilemma, goes far beyond matters of cultural style and social mores. The dilemma resides in the deepest contours of faith and faithfulness, and emerges in various forms in different cultural contexts. The most significant reality in the way contemporary Presbyterian grapple with the dilemma is the ongoing cultural disestablishment of the Church. The cultural disestablishment of mainline Protestantism in general, and Presbyterianism in particular, provides the puzzling context for contemporary Presbyterian identity. Should Presbyterians strive to be relevant and run the risk of becoming indistinguishable from liberal bourgeois culture? Or should Presbyterians seek to become resident aliens in the culture and run the risk of losing touch with the realities of American life? The alternatives are not quite that stark, of course, which only leads to the real dilemma going unnoticed and thus unaddressed.

The Church's difficulty in responding to the new realities of cultural disestablishment and pervasive pluralism has been exacerbated by internal theological disarray. Not surprisingly, the pluralism of American society is evident in the pluralism within American churches. The traditional assumption that a core of Christian faith was shared throughout the Presbyterian Church has been challenged by the emergence of feminist thought, the rise of the religious right, stronger theological and social voices of racial and ethnic communities, ethical warfare over a range of sexuality issues, and confusion over the relationship between science and Christian faith. These and other realities contribute to a loss of routine confidence in traditional authorities and weaken commitment to traditional truths.

The Mall of America

North American society resembles a sprawling shopping mall. Specialty boutiques are scattered randomly throughout the mall, catering to diverse tastes, offering new possibilities, and encouraging impulse purchases. The churches are confined to small religious shops located in one wing of the mall, competing with one another for a dwindling market share. As people wander through society's shopping mall, they are free to choose whether to enter any of the religious boutiques and what, if anything, they will buy. This segmentation and privatization of American society should not be contrasted with a mythic golden past when America was a unified society and churches were important parts of the whole. Yet it is clear that North American culture has changed, and that life today is different from life in previous generations.

Sociologist Peter Berger describes our situation as the loss of "a quality of *intactness*." He goes on to say, "the ground on which we are standing has been profoundly shaken, and most of us feel it in our bones."[4]

What is true of North American culture is also true *within* the Church. The contemporary Presbyterian Church is no longer a community of shared certainty in commonly acknowledged truths and common patterns of living. The Church has never been a unified community of unanimous perspective, of course. A casual reading of the New Testament letters is sufficient to confirm that the Church has been characterized by diversity from the beginning. Yet the New Testament letters assume that unity in the faith is a central aim of Christian community, and that diversity itself is an element of unity, not an alternative to it. That assumption does not go unquestioned among contemporary American Presbyterians.

In a pluralistic world, Presbyterians desire a Church that is inclusive of the world's rich diversity. Celebration of diversity goes beyond appreciation for the natural, God-given variety of race, ethnicity, gender, and personal gifts, however. We also make room in the Church for a wide variety of preferences, opinions, convictions, and beliefs. Many people within the Church simply assume that theological and moral truths are different for different Christians. Since a wide variety of beliefs emerges from a wide range of personal and communal experience, even *Christian* beliefs are thought to be diverse. "God alone is Lord of the conscience,"[5] Presbyterians say, taking that to mean that all beliefs should be respected—even encouraged—in the Church and that no attempt should be made to impose one "version" of the truth. The Church lives within the culture, and so it is not surprising that the culture's acceptance of multiple truths is found within the Church.

In the Presbyterian Church (U.S.A.), as in all of mainline Protestantism, confessional identity and denominational loyalty are being replaced by conservative and liberal identities that seem to have deeper roots in secular culture than in the apostolic tradition. At the same time, Presbyterian loyalties are becoming more local, more focused on the single congregation, and less attached to any wider Christian family. While some celebrate the reemergence of the congregation as the locus of Church, the danger for Presbyterians is that fragmentation without broader confessional identity produces a denomination and its congregations without sufficient density of distinctive "faith and life" for either denomination or congregation to be meaningful propositions.

Enduring Features of Presbyterian Identity

Disestablishment and postmodern diffusion are not the sum of Presbyterian identity; they are only the context within which Presbyterian identity is shaped. A maxim of the Church's Reformed tradition is *ecclesia reformata semper reformanda secundum verbum Dei*—"the Church reformed, always to be reformed according to the word of God." This conviction places

Presbyterians in a tradition of continuous engagement with Scripture, not as a historical exercise but as a resource for contemporary expression of Christian faith and life. At its best, the Presbyterian Church has dealt with Moltmann's identity-involvement dilemma by bringing the biblical witness to God's relationship with the world into encounter with the world's current realities. At its best, the Presbyterian Church has not retreated into doctrinal positions, rigidly defending and asserting them. Nor has it dissolved its theological and moral convictions in a sea of cultural interests, needs, and wishes. Instead, it has sought to articulate its faith and faithfulness within the realities of its cultural context.

Presbyterian attentiveness to both identity and involvement can be seen in the tradition of Reformed churches' commitment to confess their faith anew in each place and time. The formulation of confessional statements *in loco* and *in tempore* is understood as part of the mandate of proclamation entrusted to the Church. Each church in each time is responsible to confess and proclaim the faith. When it uses creeds and confessions from other places and times, it does not simply recite historic formulations. It appropriates those creeds and confessions as contemporary articulations of the gospel. The preface to the Presbyterian Church (U.S.A.)'s Confession of 1967 puts the matter succinctly. It begins with the conviction: "The church confesses its faith when it bears a present witness to God's grace in Jesus Christ. In every age, the church has expressed its witness in words and deeds as the need of the time required."[6]

This confession-making characteristic of Reformed churches distinguishes the Presbyterian Church (U.S.A.) from churches that grant defining authority to a particular creedal era, churches that hold to one formative confession of faith, churches that reside in a continuous development of doctrine, and noncreedal churches. The Presbyterian Church (U.S.A.) acknowledges eleven historic creeds, confessions, and catechisms in its constitutional *Book of Confessions* as contemporary declarations "to its members and to the world" of "who and what it is, what it believes, and what it resolves to do."[7] Reformed confessions are always subordinate and accountable to Scripture, however. The Westminster Confession of Faith (1647), the most widely embraced confession among Presbyterian churches worldwide, acknowledges that "all synods or councils . . . may err, and many have erred; therefore they are not to be made the rule of faith or practice, but to be used as a help in both."[8] Creeds, confessions, and catechisms are vital, but Scripture is the "unique and authoritative witness" to God's Way in the world, "the witness without parallel."[9] The PCUSA's *Book of Confessions*, containing affirmations of faith from the fourth century to the twentieth, expresses both the confidence and modesty of Presbyterian theology. The Church expresses its faith openly, yet with the knowledge that it is being reformed continuously, not by its own insights or efforts alone, but also through the insights of the Church in different times and disparate cultures.

No one time and place is determinative, and each time and place is best understood in relationship to other times and places.

The preeminence of Scripture, accompanied by foundational Reformed convictions about Christian faith and life, provides the Presbyterian Church (U.S.A.) with distinct angles of vision on Christian faith in relationship to contemporary American culture. These perspectives remain at the heart of Presbyterian ethos. They must be re-appropriated in every generation, however. The current challenge before the PCUSA is to claim its heritage as the way to avoid falling on one side or the other of Moltmann's dilemma.

The heart of Presbyterian convictions about Christian faith and faithfulness can be understood through reference to the apostolic benediction: "The grace of the Lord Jesus Christ, the love of God, and the communion of the Holy Spirit be with all of you" (2 Corinthians 13:13). The defining characteristics of grace, sovereign love, and communion are contemporary challenges as well as inheritances from the past. What has been true of the Presbyterian Church is not assured in the present or guaranteed in the future.

Grace of Christ

Within Presbyterian faith and life, grace is at the center of all that is known and experienced of God. The distance between God and humankind is bridged by God in Christ, setting people free from anxiety about the adequacy of their lives and the depth of their belief. Neither faith nor works can restore communion between God and humans; neither is a precondition of God's love in Christ. Instead, both faith and works are expressions of gratitude for the gracious benevolence of God, shown fully in Jesus Christ. The priority of grace is articulated as God's free election of a community for both salvation and service. Presbyterians understand election in terms of covenant, God's gracious promise and act of saving care for his people. The covenant of grace is sealed in baptism, nourished in the Lord's Supper, and lived out in vocation.

The well-loved first question of the sixteenth-century *Heidelberg Catechism* expresses Presbyterian confidence in God's grace:

> Q. What is your only comfort, in life and in death?
> A. That I belong—body and soul, in life and in death—not to myself but to my faithful Savior, Jesus Christ . . . .[10]

Secure in the unmerited grace of election, Presbyterians are liberated for thankful response to God's unconditional love in lives of obedient service. Reformed theologian Karl Barth says that, "Grace and gratitude belong together like heaven and earth. Grace evokes gratitude like the voice of an echo. Gratitude follows grace like thunder lightning. . . . We are speaking of the grace of God who is God for man, and of the gratitude of man as his response to this grace. . . . The two belong together, so that only gratitude can correspond to grace, and this correspondence cannot fail.[11] Human gratitude is expressed in more than thoughts and feelings, for as we are liberated for thankful response to God's unrestricted love, we are also freed for gracious relationships with other people. As men and women who know the grace of the Lord Jesus Christ, we no longer need to make calculations about the worth, power, or ability of other people as a precondition for our love. We, too, can live grace-filled lives as we, too, love all people freely and unreservedly.

Traditional Presbyterian convictions concerning God's grace cut against the grain of contemporary American culture (even much contemporary American Christianity). American culture is preoccupied with *self*-potential, *self*-reliance, *self*-motivation, *self*-help, *self*-actualization, and *self*-fulfillment. The Presbyterian perspective that we are dependent on God, not on ourselves, is a powerful witness in the midst of the culture's free-market tendency toward forms of social Darwinism that prize success and blame disadvantaged people for their own hardship. The grace of Christ does not reward the beautiful, rich, and famous, dismissing those who fall short of society's image of success; neither should Christ's people. Yet Presbyterians are always susceptible to cultural metrics of competition and production, placing value on market-defined accomplishment. The Presbyterian Church's ministers and members must deepen their knowledge of and commitment to the grace of the Lord Jesus Christ, a foundational element of our heritage, for fear that the PCUSA become swallowed up in the cultural wave of celebrating achievement.

Sovereign Love of God

Presbyterians have always affirmed that the creator of heaven and earth is powerfully present in the world, sustaining and governing all things in the accomplishment of God's holy purpose. At its best, Reformed theology has paired the sovereignty of God with God's gracious love, and the holiness of God with God's providential care. The Confession of 1967 captures this admirably, when it declares, "the power of God's love in Christ to transform the world discloses that the Redeemer is the Lord and Creator who made all things to serve the purpose of his love."[12] Reformed theology never sentimentalizes God's love, however; it knows that the Lord is God, not human, the Holy One in our midst (see Hosea 11:9). Thus, the *Scots Confession* begins by acknowledging "one God alone, to whom alone we must cleave, whom alone we must serve, whom only we must worship, and in whom alone we put our trust."[13]

Reformed emphasis on the sovereignty of God leads to an acute awareness of the dangers of idolatry. Idolatry signals that the people of God place trust in any human construction—ecclesial, political, cultural, or personal—rather than in the God to whom we belong, body and soul, in life and in death. Awareness of idolatry's lures leads to characteristic Presbyterian practices, ranging from simplicity of worship and faithful stewardship to resisting the comprehensive claims of political and cultural systems. While "separation of Church and state" is axiomatic of American political life, this does not mean that Christian faith and life are spiritually sequestered. Divisions between the "religious" and the "secular" are illusory; God is not concerned with only so-called spiritual matters, while remaining indifferent to social patterns of racial bigotry, class inequity, abuses of political power, global warming, and market-driven consumerism. The Confession of 1967 declares:

> God's redeeming work in Jesus Christ embraces the whole of human life: social and cultural, economic and political, scientific and technological, individual and corporate. . . . It is the will of God that the divine purpose for human life shall be fulfilled under the rule of Christ and all evil be banished from creation.[14]

Our culture places faith in the essential goodness of the American people and the basic rightness of American approaches to the world. The Presbyterian conviction that it is God, not we, who is in control of the world is always in danger of falling prey to cultural forces that seek to shape us. The Theological Declaration of Barmen, addressed to the situation of Germany in the early 1930s, is received by the PCUSA as an affirmation that remains relevant to our time and place: "We reject the false doctrine, as though the Church were permitted to abandon the form of its message and order to its own pleasure or to changes in prevailing ideological and political convictions."[15] Yet Presbyterians are not invulnerable to the lures of the market and the attractions of social ideologies. We Presbyterians, so recently at the center of American civic, cultural, and political convictions, must deepen our knowledge of and commitment to the sovereign love of God, a foundational element of our heritage, lest the PCUSA become captive to gods that are not God.

Communion of the Holy Spirit

Presbyterians have always insisted that faith originates and is lived out in a community called, formed, equipped, and maintained by the Holy Spirit. The Spirit calls the Church to be one, holy, catholic, and apostolic—a distinctive community of obedience and service. The Church is to be a sign in and for the world of the new reality that God has inaugurated in Jesus Christ. The Church's response to its calling is always ambiguous, of course, but Presbyterians are confident that the Holy Spirit continues to lead the community into the truth of the gospel. Utter realism about the Church and confidence in the Spirit's guidance lead toward Church structures that engage the whole people of God. Ordinary people are chosen by the community to serve as ministers, elders, and deacons with the conviction that through them God distributes spiritual gifts to the Church. Presbyterian concern that everything be done decently and in order reflects a resolve to shape ecclesial life in ways that keep the Church open to the Spirit's leading and for faithful witness in the world.

The Presbyterian Church adheres to a particular pattern of ecclesial governance because it understands that Church order and ordered ministries are indispensable elements in ensuring the Church's fidelity to the Word. Presbyterian polity embodies two key elements that give shape to the Church's communal nature. First, clericalism is resisted. The Church's pattern of ministry breaks down the distinction between clergy and laity by instituting two "lay" ecclesial ministries—deacon and elder. Elders and deacons, like ministers, are ordained to their office. Second, the Church's various ministries are corporate, not only within each order of ministry, but among the orders. No person can exercise an ordered ministry independently, and no order of ministry can function apart from its essential relationship to other orders.

This communal character of Presbyterian orders of ministry is evident in their exercise within corporate assemblies. Ministers and elders serve together on sessions, presbyteries, and general assemblies. In assemblies beyond the congregation, ministers and elders are usually represented in equal numbers. In congregations, shared presbyterial responsibilities include providing for the proclamation of the word, administering the sacraments, instructing the faithful in sound doctrine, and structuring discipline that ensures free space for Word and Sacrament to take root in the life of the Church and its members. Ordered ministries are structured expressions of the ministry of the whole people of God.

The communal character of Presbyterian Church life stands in contrast to prevailing organizational patterns in American society. It is also out of step with many high liturgical churches and many megachurches that draw sharp distinctions between clergy and laity, or between leaders and members. Even so, the Presbyterian Church (U.S.A.) regularly places undue confidence in its own structures, transforming gatherings of the faithful into efficient organizations, and relational communities into bureaucratic institutions. We Presbyterians must deepen our knowledge of and commitment to the communion of the Holy Spirit, a foundational element of our heritage, in order to resist the pressures toward turning ministers into congregational CEOs, elders into members of the board of directors, deacons into service providers, and members into customers of the Church's business.

Engagement with God's Mission in the World

In response to the grace of Christ, the love of God, and the communion of the Holy Spirit, Presbyterians seek to live gratefully by following God's movement into the world. The Confession of 1967 declares:

In each time and place, there are particular problems and crises through which God calls the Church to act. The Church, guided by the Spirit, humbled by its own complicity and instructed by all attainable knowledge, seeks to discern the will of God and learn how to obey in these concrete situations.[16]

The Presbyterian Church, and the Reformed tradition generally, understands that God has made and called good our being *in* the world. Human departures from God's Way have bent creation out of shape; God's people are called to strive for *shalom* once again.

The Presbyterian Church once regarded itself as the nation's moral guide, instructing others about their responsibilities. Disestablishment can serve as the Church's liberation from civic and cultural pretension, freeing it for faithful service of God and neighbors. Yet this does not come naturally or easily. The disestablishment of the Church and the reality of a religiously plural world place Presbyterians in unfamiliar territory. Can the Church be fully immersed in the world without becoming indistinguishable from the world? Can the Church claim anew its faith and faithfulness without becoming remote from the world? Presbyterian congregations, presbyteries, and national agencies live out daily the identity-involvement dilemma.

1. Douglas John Hall, *An Awkward Church* (Louisville: Office of Theology and Worship Occasional Paper No. 5, 1993), p. 8.
2. Ingolf U. Dalferth, "Time for God's Presence," in Miroslav Volf, et al., eds., *The Future of Theology: Essays in Honor of Jürgen Moltmann* (Grand Rapids: Eerdmans, 1996), p. 127ff.
3. Jürgen Moltmann, *The Crucified God* (New York: Harper & Row, 1973), p. 7.
4. Peter Berger, *Facing Up to Modernity* (New York: Basic Books, 1977), p. 183.
5. Presbyterian Church (U.S.A.), *Book of Order* (Louisville: Office of the General Assembly, 2009), G-1.0301a.
6. Presbyterian Church (U.S.A.), *Book of Confessions* (Louisville: Office of the General Assembly, 2002), 9.01–9.02, p. 253.
7. *Book of Order*, G-2.0100a.
8. *Book of Confessions*, 6.175, p. 158.
9. *Book of Confessions*, 9.27, p. 257.
10. *Book of Confessions*, 4.001, p. 29.
11. Barth, *Church Dogmatics*, IV.1, p. 41.
12. *Book of Confessions*, 9.15, p. 255.
13. *Book of Confessions*, 3.01, p. 11.
14. *Book of Confessions*, 9.53, p. 262.
15. *Book of Confessions*, 8.18, p. 249.
16. *Book of Confessions*, 9.43, p. 259.

CONTRIBUTORS

David Berger is Ruth and I. Lewis Gordon Professor of Jewish History and dean of the Bernard Revel Graduate School of Jewish Studies, Yeshiva University.

Steven Cohen is research professor of Jewish social policy, Hebrew Union College-Jewish Institute of Religion.

Reuven Hammer is head of the Rabbinical Court of the Rabbinical Assembly of Israel.

Stephen R. Haynes is associate professor of religious studies, Rhodes College.

Richard Hirsh is the executive director of the Reconstructionist Rabbinical Association and teaches at the Reconstructionist Rabbinical College.

Vernon Kurtz is rabbi of North Suburban Synagogue Beth El in Highland Park, Illinois.

Eugene March is Arnold Black Rhodes Professor of Old Testament Emeritus, Louisville Presbyterian Theological Seminary.

Daniel Polish is rabbi of Congregation Shir Chadash, Poughkeepsie, New York.

Gilbert S. Rosenthal is director of the National Council of Synagogues.

David F. Sandmel is Crown Ryan Professor of Jewish Studies, Catholic Theological Union.

Joseph D. Small is director of the Office of Theology and Worship, Presbyterian Church (U.S.A.).

Leanne Van Dyk is professor of Reformed theology and dean and vice president of academic affairs, Western Theological Seminary.

Rebecca Weaver is John Q. Dickinson Professor of Church History, Union Presbyterian Seminary.

Robert Weingartner is executive director of The Outreach Foundation of the Presbyterian Church (U.S.A.).

Anna Case-Winters is professor of theology, McCormick Theological Seminary.